Critical Conscious Language Bilingua...

This book features case studies that address dual language bilingual education (DLBE) programs, which offer content instruction in two languages to help youth develop fluent bilingualism/biliteracy, high academic achievement, and sociocultural competence. While increasingly popular, the DLBE model is a framework that comes with unique hurdles and challenges.

Applying a pioneering critical consciousness approach, the volume provides readers with narratives, awareness, and tools to support culturally and linguistically diverse students and their families. Organized around four major areas—policy, leadership, family and community engagement, teaching and teacher learning—the volume's case studies bring together stories from policymakers, educational leaders, family and community members, and teachers. The case studies spotlight examples in which power imbalances have been identified and shifted through critically conscious actions and offer insight into how to ensure all DLBE programs are nurturing, empowering, multilingual environments for all students, particularly racialized, immigrant, and transnational students. Accessible and varied, the case studies address important topics such as anti-Black racism, digital access, disability, school-district relations, working with undocumented families, and more. Each chapter includes a case narrative, teaching notes, discussion questions, and/or teaching activities to support stakeholders who wish to develop and enact equity in their DLBE policies, classrooms, and professional development.

A key resource for supporting student needs and transformative inquiry in the classroom, this book is ideal for graduate students, professors, leaders, educators, and other stakeholders in bilingual and language education.

Lisa M. Dorner is Associate Professor of Educational Leadership and Policy Analysis at the University of Missouri, Columbia, USA.

Deborah Palmer is Professor of Equity, Bilingualism, and Biliteracy in the School of Education at the University of Colorado, Boulder, USA.

Claudia G. Cervantes-Soon is Associate Professor of Bilingual Education at Arizona State University, USA.

Dan Heiman is Assistant Professor of Bilingual/Biliteracy Education in the Department of Teacher Education at the University of Texas at El Paso, USA.

Emily R. Crawford is Associate Professor of Educational Leadership and Policy Analysis at the University of Missouri, USA.

Critical Consciousness in Dual Language Bilingual Education

Case Studies on Policy and Practice

Edited by Lisa M. Dorner, Deborah Palmer, Claudia G. Cervantes-Soon, Dan Heiman, and Emily R. Crawford

NEW YORK AND LONDON

Cover image: Martha Samaniego

First published 2023
by Routledge
605 Third Avenue, New York, NY 10158

and by Routledge
4 Park Square, Milton Park, Abingdon, Oxon, OX14 4RN

Routledge is an imprint of the Taylor & Francis Group, an informa business

ISBN: 978-1-032-14697-3 (hbk)
ISBN: 978-1-032-12793-4 (pbk)
ISBN: 978-1-003-24059-4 (ebk)

DOI: 10.4324/9781003240594

Typeset in Bembo
by Apex CoVantage, LLC

This book is dedicated to all of the children who are developing bilingualism in school; may the book inspire your adults and communities to find new ways to ensure your educational experiences are just and humanizing.

Contents

Foreword xi
Acknowledgments xiv

Introduction: Why This Book and Why Now 1

SECTION I
Policy and Critical Consciousness 19

1 ***¡Ya basta!* Changing Paradigms, Policies, and Practices for English Learners** 21
ELENA IZQUIERDO

2 ***Revolisyon an ap Kontinye*: Honoring Haitian Creole Through a Dual Language Program in Boston Public Schools** 30
AYANNA COOPER

3 **"We Can Change the Academic Trajectory of Our Children in a Snap": Developing a High-School Dual Language Program for Spanish-Speaking Students with No Feeder Program** 39
ESMERALDA ALDAY, OLIVIA HERNÁNDEZ, AND KATHRYN I. HENDERSON

4 **Centering Immigrant Voices and Experiences in a Dual Language Bilingual School: Teachers as Critical Pedagogues and Policymakers** 47
DINA LÓPEZ AND TATYANA KLEYN

5 **"Shifting Lenses Instead of Always Grinding Forward": Using Ethnography to Challenge Raciolinguistic Ideologies in Dual Language Education** 55
KARLA VENEGAS, NELSON FLORES, AND JENNIFER PHUONG

6 **Using Critical Policy Analysis in Collaborative Professional Learning Communities to Enhance Dual Language Bilingual Educators' Critical Consciousness** 67
VERÓNICA E. VALDEZ, M. GARRETT DELAVAN, AND JUAN A. FREIRE

SECTION II
Leadership and Critical Consciousness 75

7 **The Convergence of Critical Consciousness and Culturally Sustaining Leadership Practices in Dual Language Bilingual Education** 77
SANDRA LEU BONANNO

8 **The Power of *Plática*: Expanding Dual Language Bilingual Education at the District Level with a Bilingual Redesign Committee** 85
OLIVIA HERNÁNDEZ AND KATHRYN I. HENDERSON

9 **Dual Language, Dual Purposes: A Community in Conflict** 95
DAVID DEMATTHEWS AND LEYLA OLANO

10 **Black and Bilingual: Challenges in Decentering Whiteness in Dual Language Bilingual Education** 104
RHONDA J. BROUSSARD, FAITH R. KARES, NICOLE CARIDAD RALSTON, AND MARIA PATRIZIA SANTOS

11 **Vietnamese Dual Language Immersion: Commodifying an Uncommodified Language and Culture** 112
MICHAEL BACON AND VÂN TRUONG

12 *De La Lucha a La Victoria*: The Journey to Save a Dual Language Bilingual Education Teacher Preparation Program 121
CRISTINA ALFARO

SECTION III
Families, Communities, and Critical Consciousness 129

13 Fostering Critical Consciousness with Immigrant Families: The Story of a Chinese Immigrant Mother in a Mandarin-English Dual Language Program 131
WENYANG SUN

14 Cultivating Critical Consciousness with Mothers of Bilingual Students 139
MARÍA DE LOS ÁNGELES OSORIO DE LA ROSA AND JODY SLAVICK

15 When Life Gives You Lemons: Critically Conscious Family Engagement in a Virtual Dual Language Kindergarten Class During a Pandemic 149
YALDA M. KAVEH AND CORY BUCKBAND

16 Contextualizing Parent Activism in One of Milwaukee's Bilingual Public Schools 158
LUIS "TONY" BÁEZ AND ANDREW H. HURIE

17 Relational Pedagogies and the Building of a Social Architecture of Authentic *Cariño* in the Teaching of Healing Practices at Academia Cuauhtli 168
CHRISTOPHER MILK BONILLA AND ANGELA VALENZUELA

SECTION IV
Teaching, Teacher Learning, and Critical Consciousness 177

18 Black Liberation in Bilingual Education: A Case for Black Freedom Dreaming 179
BRITTANY L. FRIESON AND VIVIAN E. PRESIADO

19 ***Intentando Incluir a Todes*: A First Grade Team's Gender-Inclusive Pedagogies** 187
CAITLÍN DOUGHERTY, DEBORAH PALMER, STACIE ALDANA, AND MARY GILREATH

20 **English-only as a Magic Pill? Dispelling the Myths About Disability and Dual Language Bilingual Education** 196
STEVE DANIEL PRZYMUS

21 **Professional Development Through Critical Conversation and *Testimonio* at Simón Bolívar Elementary** 205
CAROLINE HESSE, JILLIAN LA SERNA, AND EMILY ZOELLER

22 **Bridging Testimonio Pedagogy with Dual Language Bilingual Education in a K/1 Classroom: One Teacher's Journey to Critical Consciousness Through a Master's Course** 213
JUAN A. FREIRE AND JUDITH FLORES CARMONA

23 **A Sense of Belonging: Biliteracy Instruction That Loves and Centers Latinx Emergent Bilingual Students and Their Families** 222
CARMELA VALDEZ AND ROSALYN HARVEY-TORRES

24 **Growing Critical Bilingual Literacies: Counter-narratives and Social Justice in Bilingual Education** 230
LUZ YADIRA HERRERA AND CARLA ESPAÑA

25 **Building on Emotion: Experiencing, Confronting, and Reflecting on Patterns of Language Use in a TWI DL Classroom** 238
BRENDA SANTIAGO GONZÁLEZ AND RACHEL SNYDER BHANSARI

Contributors Biographies 246
Index 257

Foreword

Challenging Hegemonic Discourse

Concientización y Acción (Critical Consciousness and Action)
Belinda Bustos Flores

This book calls for us to activate our critical consciousness to challenge hegemonic discourse through action: historicizing communities and ourselves; critical listening; embracing discomfort; interrogating power; and affirming identity, *acompañamiento* (solidarity), and translanguaging. In this foreword, I have anchored these actions in *dichos* (popular proverbs) that have guided my personal and professional life as a bilingual teacher, counselor, professor, and associate dean.

Historicizing: *Dime con Quién Andas y Te Diré Quien Eres* (Birds of a Feather Flock Together)

To make our struggles visible and deconstruct the past, we have to recognize the historical underpinnings of bilingual education. The Bilingual Education Act (BEA) was an attempt to address the educational inequities for non-English-dominant children; however, the intent was to ensure English acquisition, not bilingualism.

The BEA did have positive ripple effects; Title VII funds supported bilingual preparation and implementation. I was fortunate to be a Title VII trainee, and as a teacher, I worked in a school in which maintenance bilingual program demonstration projects were federally funded. As empirical evidence demonstrated the positive impact of bilingual education, support grew among educators and the community, and the demand for bilingual education increased and was affirmed in the courts, e.g., Lau Remedies.

Critical Listening: *La Sabiduría Viene de Escuchar* (Wisdom Comes from Listening)

As bilingual/dual language proponents, we must challenge ourselves, build on what we have learned, and engage in critical listening to counter hegemonic norms and gain *sabiduría* (wisdom). We must acknowledge that dual language bilingual education (DLBE) has been popularized as a means to appease critics. As we have been forewarned, this approach has led to the privileging of English speakers, rather than serving minoritized learners.

In various chapters, we see evidence of educators engaging in critical listening with marginalized communities in the creation of DLBE research-based programs to support their students' cultural, historical, and linguistic growth. Using democratic principles and shared governance, these practitioners are implementing DLBE with fidelity. As an associate dean, I have worked with a district to strengthen their DLBE program based on community needs. We formed a university–school district partnership to create DLBE community lab schools to ensure oversight by the university and the use of research-based practices, and to curtail a leader from simply eradicating a DLBE program.

Embracing Discomfort: *Al Mal Tiempo, Buena Cara* (Every Cloud Has a Silver Lining)

While researchers have demonstrated the effectiveness of strong DLBE models, there continues to be an onslaught of threats. We see evidence of educators embracing this discomfort when others have attempted to dismantle DLBE programs. We have witnessed how the gentrification of communities can lead to tension and unequal power distribution. As leaders we have to grapple with opposition, while developing strategies to counter tensions.

We cannot remain silent when external pressure arises; there are times when we must use our positionality to create the needed change. As a young scholar, I remember being told not to push the "bilingual education agenda" and to research teachers in general, if I expected to succeed in academia. I could not abide by this advice or allow the silencing of my voice. Upon being tenured and promoted, and as department chair, I restructured the vision and mission, hired committed faculty, and engaged the faculty in development opportunities to amplify their critical consciousness and practices.

Interrogating Power: *Hay Que Perturbar el Poder* (Power Should Be Shaken Up)

Bilingual education is considered a threat—much like critical race theory is today—to the Americanization of the populace. I recall how Reagans policies impacted Title VII funding for potential bilingual educators, including myself. Further, Ron Unz led English-only efforts to eradicate bilingual education in Arizona, California, and Massachusetts. As a bilingual educator, I witnessed that English-only policies along with accountability pressures based on state exams often dissuaded school districts from offering additive bilingual education.

During a school district meeting, I was informed that Spanish would not be used in bilingual classrooms. I countered with DLBE research and theory. The district representative's response was that "research and theory were being set aside" to ensure students' success. I retorted, "Well, we have an obligation to prepare our candidates as bilingual educators. So, our decision will be to no longer place our candidates in your district." The superintendent replaced this representative. Rather than being beholden to hegemonic discourse that serves to undermine our critical work, *hay que perturbar el poder.*

Affirming Identity, *Acompañamiento*, and Translanguaging: *La Persona Bilingüe y Bicultural Vale por Dos* (A Bilingual and Bicultural Person is Worth Double)

I see these actions as intersecting and evident in various chapters. The importance of awakening and affirming identity is a thread that has been present in my research and practices. Due to hegemonic discourse, subjugated individuals need opportunities to *despertar el ser* (self-awakening) and disrupt deficit thinking about their language and culture. Too often heritage bilinguals are shamed for their translanguaging practices, when these community linguistic practices are valued ways of being and thinking. Forming solidarity with the *comunidad* to center their needs is critical and we can learn much. *Colegas* (colleagues) and I implemented a family biliteracy program for young children at a dual language school. We derived our topics from the families, and in turn had great participation. For example, an activity of how making tortillas was a scientific process included the local *panadera* (baker) to share the process of making *pan dulce* (traditional Mexican sweet bread). We formed strong bonds with the families, who were more than willing to help us and proud that they had contributed to our research. I have been fortunate as an educator to have the *apoyo* of the *comunidad* (support of the community), which brings to mind another *dicho*, "*El pueblo unido jamás será vencido*" ("The people united will never be defeated"). When faced with obstacles, *acuérdense* (remember), "*Juntos podemos alcanzar nuestras metas*": together, we shall overcome. Hence, I invite you to read and learn from the critical case studies presented in this book *porque saber es poder y la lucha sigue* (because knowledge is power and the fight continues).

Belinda Bustos Flores
The University of Texas at San Antonio
San Antonio, Texas, USA

Acknowledgments

This book was written as the COVID-19 pandemic ebbed and flowed. This means that each editor, chapter author, and peer reviewer contributed to this volume while also facing new challenges and balancing new responsibilities at both home and work. We know that your dedication to this project reflects the generosity, spirit, and demand for equity you bring to your bi/multilingual communities—and beyond. You are simply an inspiration! Special thanks is due to our authors, as well as the other reviewers listed here, who each provided essential feedback in a blind peer review process, drawing upon experiences in various multilingual contexts and schools: Chris Belcher, Edwin Bonney, María Cioé Peña, Arlene Galve Salgado, Suzanne García-Mateus, Michael Guerrero, Sarah Hairston, Jeong-Mi Moon, Idalia Nuñez, Sophia Piral Lee, Jana Sawyer, Ivonne Solano, Mandy Stewart, Brendan Thiry, Zhongfeng Tian, and Todd Whitaker. We also thank our Routledge editor, Karen Adler, for shepherding this work into existence; graduate student editors, Cory Buckband and Sophia Piral Lee, for so effectively and happily supporting our final efforts to compile the book; and the author of our foreword, Belinda Bustos Flores, for so quickly and beautifully reflecting on this volume. Finally, our sincere gratitude to all of the students, family members, teachers, and educational leaders who strive every day to enact critical consciousness in our schools: you are the *raison d'être* for the stories included here . . . *muchísimas gracias*, *mèsi*, *cảm ơn*, 谢谢, *Ahéhee'*, thank you!

Introduction

Why This Book and Why Now

#StandWithUkraine #AsylumRights #BlackLivesMatter #Transgender-DayOfVisibility #StopAsianHate

We write this introductory chapter amid challenges that feel insurmountable: millions of people from Ukraine, Ethiopia, and Yemen fleeing their homes due to unprovoked and civil wars; countless Central Americans pleading for asylum in the United States; and an on-going pandemic disproportionately killing people of color. Black, Brown, LGTBQ+, and other marginalized communities continue to experience violence and inequity across our educational, legal, and civil institutions time and time again.

But there is hope and love in the world too. People are welcoming refugees into their homes, youth are committing their lives to activism against racism, and new organizations are working to fairly distribute life-saving medical care. We know how to fight back against oppression. But it takes opening our hearts and minds, developing our consciousness of inequities, and figuring out how to take action. This is the heart of this book, specific to dual language bilingual education (DLBE). We strive to find answers to this question: how can we ensure equity in DLBE spaces?

Dual language bilingual programs aim to develop bilingualism, biliteracy, and sociocultural competence while meeting grade-level academic standards (Howard et al., 2018). There are at least four DLBE program models, which are traditionally defined by the student groups they imagine serving (see Definition of Terms). One of these groups is transnational and racialized language learners who are, more often than not, otherwise marginalized in US schools. Well-implemented DLBE programs, with their roots in the historical and political fight for civil and educational rights for children who speak languages other than English, have been shown to be demonstrably effective for this group (e.g., Steele et al., 2017; Umansky & Reardon, 2014).

Unfortunately, not all programs are well implemented, and they exist in spaces with colonial and racist histories, as pointed out by Guadalupe Valdés's (1997) cautionary note decades ago. Even when DLBE programs are designed specifically for racialized and transnational language learners, research has documented persistent challenges to equity (Cervantes-Soon et al., 2017). For example, studies have found a lack of access for

DOI: 10.4324/9781003240594-1

marginalized students; a bias toward monolingual and "standard" ways of using language; inadequate teacher and/or leadership preparation; unwelcoming family/community engagement; and conflicting policies—all of which tend to favor the English language and English-dominant students, regardless of a program's best intentions (Dorner, 2016). In short, Guadalupe Valdés's cautions (1997) still ring true today.

Given these circumstances, we believe *now* is the time to showcase what we can do—and in fact, what stakeholders have already done—to confront these challenges.

In this volume, we have collected stories from policymakers, educational leaders, family and community members, teachers, and students who have identified, named, and then shifted DLBE power imbalances through their critically conscious actions. We present their work as *case narratives*, and we include *teaching notes*, *discussion questions*, and *teaching activities* to support educators and family/community members who want to develop and enact equity in their DLBE spaces.

There is no better time for such work. We live in an ever-changing, transnational world where migration is often the result of dispossession, violence, poverty, and injustice, and where youth and families are forced to start new lives uprooted from their communities of origin. For them, multilingualism has deep significance, because the possibility to sustain their languages and develop new ones is a fundamental human right for surviving and thriving. Over 25% of US school children live in immigrant families. Bilingual programs are also growing exponentially, with over 3,600 documented in the US as of 2021 (American Councils Research Center, 2021). Let's build upon our colleagues' successes through critical consciousness.

Constructing, Rather Than Deconstructing, Through Critical Consciousness

We, the editors of this volume, developed this book project after years of working as bilingual educators and scholars and after conducting a review of research documenting inequities in one particular form of DLBE, two-way immersion (TWI). We concluded that critical consciousness should be the new, fourth goal of such programs (Cervantes-Soon et al., 2017). Here, we extend this argument to all DLBE:

> Critical consciousness involves the process of overcoming pervasive myths through an understanding of the role of power in the formation of oppressive conditions (Freire, 2007). [DLBE] teachers, students, and parents can take part and take action only to the extent that they problematize the history, culture, and societal configurations that brought them together. [DLBE] children, parents, teachers, and school leaders must work toward critical consciousness in order for the programs'

> integrated groups to result in cross-cultural understanding and greater equality; each stakeholder must interrogate [their] own position, privilege, and power. By reframing [DLBE] spaces as problem-posing (Freire, 2007), we can raise critical consciousness around the discourses, macro-level inequalities, and power relations that shape [DLBE] practice, pedagogy, and policies.
>
> (Cervantes-Soon et al., 2017, p. 419)

Central to developing such consciousness is cyclical *praxis*. Our goal is not to simply deconstruct, but to reconstruct—to call out inequality and then work to rebuild more just systems—and to do so continuously over time. In turn, we have theorized how DLBE stakeholders can develop critical consciousness through four actions (Palmer et al., 2019): (1) historicizing our communities and ourselves, (2) critical listening, (3) embracing discomfort, and (4) interrogating power. In our most recent work, we have identified additional practices that are the result of critical consciousness at work and that also contribute to its ongoing development: (5) affirming identities, (6) *acompañamiento*, and (7) translanguaging (Heiman et al., forthcoming).

- *Historicizing communities and ourselves* means deconstructing mainstream explanations of the past, foregrounding communities' local histories and ways of knowing, situating ourselves within our own socio-historical paths, and uncovering previously invisibilized narratives of struggle. This also means to examine the colonial legacies that frame the constructs, discourses, policies, tools, standards, and materials that we use daily in our work.
- *Critical listening* considers ways of engaging students, educators, and families with one another for meaningful and transformative connection through developing curiosity and attention, sharing, caring, reciprocity, and responsivity. Critical listening means amplifying silenced voices and taking them seriously to shape our programs.
- *Embracing discomfort* entails practicing how to experience and learn from the inevitable unsettled feelings that emerge from recognizing, reflecting on, and acting against the ways in which one's privilege, sense of entitlement, or silence reify and reproduce social injustice.
- *Interrogating power* is about calling out oppression and working to push those in power to take note of injustice and to transform systems. It also involves interrogating our own power and privilege and our role in perpetuating or disrupting inequities.
- *Affirming identities* means making sure everything about a school centers and affirms the histories and cultures of those who might otherwise be marginalized by structures of power: the curriculum, policies, instructional practices, and ways of being in schools should reflect and honor students and their communities.

- *Acompañamiento*, an idea identified by Sepúlveda (2011), calls up solidarity; it literally means *keeping company* or *accompaniment*. It means ensuring there are spaces and opportunities for co-conspirators (often those with more power in society) to be present with those who have been marginalized, to become bodies standing alongside each other as they take critically conscious actions.
- *Translanguaging* for critical consciousness means embracing the bilingual and vernacular languaging practices of bi/multilingual communities and radically centering these practices (rather than monolingual "standard" or "academic" language practices) in school (Sánchez & García, 2022).

Perhaps most importantly, we have moved from conceiving of critical consciousness as another pillar or goal to advocating for it as the very foundation of DLBE (Heiman et al., forthcoming).

How to Use This Book (Review of Chapters)

This book includes examples of critical consciousness in action at four levels of stakeholders: (1) policy, (2) leadership, (3) families and communities, and (4) teaching and teacher learning. In most of these case examples, authors use pseudonyms, although some decided to use actual names for places or individuals. And while some case examples are based on actual events, others are amalgams of the authors' experiences. In addition, although language equity is a theme throughout the book, many chapters address more than just language equity or linguistically marginalized students and families. Our authors explore, for example, issues of anti-Black racism (Chapters 10 and 18), digital access (Chapter 15), Indigenous knowledges (Chapter 17), gender identity (Chapter 19), disability (Chapter 20), and other intersections that are as much a part of the dynamics of DLBE programs as they are in any educational space. Work toward justice in DLBE schools must account for the various intersectional identities of those who inhabit them.

As we introduce each chapter here, readers may begin to notice that the development of consciousness and stakeholders' related actions fall on a continuum. Some chapters portray the beginning steps of this work, while in other contexts, stakeholders have already taken action and begun to experience results, for instance, through new policy or practice. We invite readers to engage with each chapter as inspiration and aspiration, not as regulation; there is no one defined "recipe" for this work (Flores et al., 2021; Pacheco & Chávez-Moreno, 2021; Bartolomé, 1994). Context matters, and so we encourage educators to consider what fits their contexts and how they might adapt the ideas therein for their own situations. Besides describing each chapter in the sections that follow, we also provide Table 0.1 as a summary of each chapter's geographic context, DLBE program type, and grade level of students.

Policy

In this section, we take a broad view of policy, understanding it as a social and cultural process that happens over time. That is, policy is not merely a legislative act or statement by a school district; it is a set of actions taken by multiple stakeholders, including teachers (Menken & García, 2010) and families (Dorner, 2012), who are all shaped by their particular contexts (Levinson et al., 2009). Enacting policy includes allocating resources, inventing procedures, exchanging ideas, and reorganizing relationships (Ball et al., 2012); these "enactments" can occur within classrooms, schools, districts, and larger government offices.

Three of the chapters present case studies of systemic policy change enacted at the district or school level. We start with Chapter 1, by Elena Izquierdo, who shares the story of a district on the Texas border that significantly redesigned its education for designated English learners after uncovering gross impropriety and unethical behavior by leaders across the system. This case introduces us to Deputy Superintendent Matilde, who led her district through critical conversations and historicizing to develop dual language bilingual education as *the model* for all their English learners.

The next two chapters examine significant policy changes at the school level. Chapter 2 by Ayanna Cooper presents the development of Toussaint L'Ouverture Academy, a Haitian-Creole/English two-way immersion program housed within an elementary school in Boston. Named for the leader of the Haitian revolution—heralded as the only successful revolt of enslaved peoples in history—Cooper's case examines how educators and community members together revolutionized education for their children, and have fought to keep the revolution going. As the program expanded year by year, interrogating power, critical listening, and historicizing were each essential to confronting policy challenges, from curriculum development to teacher preparation, and developing a program centered on linguistic social justice.

Meanwhile, the case narrative in Chapter 3 by Esmeralda Alday, Olivia Hernández, and Kathryn I. Henderson tells the story of one Texas school district that implemented a unique dual language program at the high school level, despite not having a DL feeder program. Feeling there was no time to waste, the development and enactment of critical consciousness allowed educators here to "fundamentally change the academic trajectories of students" who had been marginalized over time, never having had any access to academic content or instruction in their home language until this major policy shift.

The remaining three chapters in this section present policy enactment within DLBE schools and programs, specifically how groups of educators came together to analyze or transform policies through their critical consciousness. In Chapter 4, Dina López and Tatyana Kleyn take us to a dual language bilingual school in New York City, where all students learn in both Spanish and English. Here, the authors present a case study in which the teacher is centered as the critically conscious policymaker who responds to a parent who resists her classroom storybook reading about a family that includes one parent who is undocumented. This case demonstrates how together teachers and school leaders can take a "firm stance" in policy, creating a climate and mission statements that support teachers' work as critical pedagogues and policymakers and underscore the role of schools to prepare students "to critically engage with privilege and inequity."

In Chapter 5, we see another kind of partnership for critical consciousness. Karla Venegas, Nelson Flores, and Jennifer Phuong present how school leaders in a hyper-segregated and long-standing Latinx neighborhood in Philadelphia came together with researchers to critically interrogate their policies and practices. Specifically, they considered how they were labeling students in deficit-oriented and confusing ways, all of which obscured "the joy and genius of our linguistically diverse children." Through analyses of ethnographic data from the research team, the school- and university-based educators together activated critical listening and engaged with discomfort as they sought to understand and figure out how to change the way their school viewed students who were simultaneously labeled as "English learners" and "English-dominant."

Finally, in Chapter 6, Verónica E. Valdez, M. Garrett Delavan, and Juan A. Freire present another case of educators coming together to interrogate policy and practice. This chapter, which is set in a two-way strand program in Utah, tells the story of Andrea and Kim, who started a professional learning community and led their colleagues to critique DLBE state policies, in order to transform them. They discussed student recruitment and enrollment, promotional materials and media, required teacher credentials, and language separation policies. After their critically conscious work together, the educators not only felt empowered to think more deeply about DLBE equity for youth designated as English learners, but they also made material changes for them.

Taken together, the cases in this first section provide inspiration and direction for educational stakeholders across the policy system; they are stakeholders that can, as Chapter 3 points out, change the trajectories of racialized and transnational language learners. The next section focuses specifically on educational leaders and their work at critical consciousness in DLBE.

Leadership

School leaders make an indelible impact on the schools, districts, and communities where they serve. Regardless of whether they enact a servant or transformational leadership-based style, and regardless of their place in an organizational hierarchy, leaders are front and center in creating school environments that raise the critical consciousness of *all* stakeholders around social justice issues (Rodriguez & Crawford, 2022; Theoharis, 2007). The specific focus of this section is how K–12 district and school leaders handle and overcome—sometimes creatively—the various obstacles to build and support DLBE programs. Together, these chapters provide powerful lessons and strategies leaders have used to facilitate DLBE programs that challenge and push against Eurocentric and English-dominant forms of schooling.

Chapter 7 by Sandra Leu Bonnano is situated in a Spanish-English elementary school that serves a majority Latinx population and also a mix of students who identify as white, Black, Asian, and Pacific Islander. This case portrays a bilingual principal, Amy Howards, who identifies as a white ally and who strives to honor Latinx community members' cultural values and practices, but whose teachers resist shifting the school from a monolingual model of practice to being fully bilingual. Howards's challenge is moving her school from professing a commitment to social justice to embodying it; this includes self-reflection, interpersonal work on school norms, and institutionalizing a focus on valuing the agency, knowledges, and lived experiences of school community members. Leu Bonnano supplements the case study with a critical consciousness framework that leaders can use to help catalyze and sustain linguistic and cultural diversity.

Chapter 8 by Olivia Hernández and Kathryn I. Henderson shifts readers from the building level to a district-wide view of the process of DLBE expansion. This case, situated in an urban Texas district led by author Hernández, demonstrates the importance of leaders' willingness to engage in critical listening and discomfort in the planning process. District leaders aimed to redesign their programs from a transitional bilingual education model, which moves students toward English-only instruction, to a fully DLBE model. They formed a bilingual redesign committee to facilitate the process, build communal support for the expansion, and ensure program sustainability through *collaborative decision-making*. Critical to the committee's success was group engagement in *pláticas* (dialogues), in which multifaceted, reflective conversations incorporated listening, inquiry, storytelling, and creation.

Next, Chapters 9, 10, and 11 present examples of educational leaders' using critical consciousness to work through and overcome conflict. Chapter 9 by David DeMatthews and Leyla Olana takes place in the southwestern US in an urban, predominantly Latinx and Black community undergoing gentrification, along with simultaneous school consolidation and the development of new DLBE programs. An elementary school principal, Principal Reveles, must navigate the complex socioeconomic and racial dynamics inside and outside the school and cultivate trust with teachers and families. To enhance collective input on his school's DLBE program, Reveles creates a bilingual leadership team that brings together diverse family members; bilingual, general, and special education teachers; a district administrator; and a leader in the parent-teacher association. Paramount to the leadership team's success is Reveles's setting core goals for the new DLBE program to prioritize linguistically marginalized students, be research-based, and incorporate team members' diverse knowledges and perspectives of the school's past, present, and future.

Meanwhile, Chapter 10 by Rhonda J. Broussard, Faith R. Kares, Nicole Caridad Ralston, and Maria Patrizia Santos explicitly interrogates how leaders can prioritize centering Black students in DLBE programs. They stress the urgent need for anti-racist policies and practices that encourage efforts to hire, promote, and retain Black leaders. Central to their case is Victor, a Black principal and the only leader of color in an open-enrollment, French-language charter school with a majority Black population on the Gulf Coast. He strives to activate critical consciousness to move "fixed mindsets" with his DLBE colleagues but struggles: white supremacy culture has become ingrained in both white and Black American teachers who stigmatize Black English and whose identities and experiences do not match those of the school's students. Despite soliciting and providing feedback and prioritizing an anti-racist environment, the hoped-for changes prove elusive. Without additional support and critically conscious partners, Victor leaves the principalship. This powerful narrative underscores the imperative for districts to have critically conscious policies and practices that recruit, retain, and promote Black leaders. It also points to how all educational stakeholders must engage in critical consciousness efforts if equity is to be realized.

Chapter 11 by Michael Bacon and Van Truong, both acting principals, is set in the Pacific Northwest. This case interrogates how and why certain languages (e.g., Spanish, Mandarin) are coveted and commodified by white families at the expense of less commonly taught languages like Vietnamese, which better represents the community and community needs in the district. In this case, school principals and district leaders together recognize that Vietnamese emerging bilingual students are the second largest language group in the district, but they resist implementing a two-way immersion program with their cultural, academic, and linguistic needs in mind. Instead, they rationalize that not enough white and non-Vietnamese families would join such a program. The district commits to racial equity work and a new racially just education policy over time. This coincides with Vietnamese community leaders, including a Vietnamese American leader who steps into an ESL director position, advocating for their community's needs and representation in DLBE programs. Like Chapter 10, this case study exemplifies how diverse leaders who mirror and defend their communities are necessary at senior leadership levels and also how communities can organize to successfully advocate for DLBE programs that reflect their languages and culture.

Finally, Chapter 12 by Cristina Alfaro is the bookend for this section. It is unique and essential, since Alfaro provides a first-hand account of lessons learned over the course of three decades as a champion for bilingual education. Her inspirational account also provides insight into what it takes to engage in an ongoing struggle for justice and reclamation of language rights. She traces the roots of her *lucha* (fight) to save a dual language/English learner teacher preparation program as a university-level department chair.

When she is a young student, a white teacher punishes her for breaking a rule to not speak any other language in the classroom other than English, but ultimately, this catalyzes her efforts to critique unjust language policies and engage in work where bilingualism and biliteracy are viewed as assets. Alfaro highlights how discovering one's voice, ideological consciousness, and ideological clarity are key traits for all DLBE leaders, since they impact beliefs and pedagogical practices toward linguistically diverse students and families.

Families and Communities

The chapters in the families and communities section present a diverse range of parent, family, and community experiences and engagement with critical consciousness in DLBE. As individual cases, they span geographical, ethnolinguistic, and historical contexts to provide a picture of resilient communities whose heritage languages have been minoritized and devalued. Each individual case offers insight into the complex processes involved in the development of critical consciousness, illustrating the ways in which the journey begins as an internal interrogation of structures of inequity and how they progress and grow as individuals share their perspectives with others and engage in various actions for change. For example, Chapter 13 by Wenyang Sun centers on a Chinese immigrant mother in the southeastern US whose children are enrolled in a Mandarin/English DLBE program and who begins to recognize that the ways in which the program is framed not only prioritizes the needs and interests of white English-speaking children, but also perpetuates the construction of Asian families as model minorities and deepens divides between them and other families of color. In addition, this mother questions taken-for-granted assumptions, such as the notion that the 80:20 model is more beneficial to language-minoritized children. Through the narrative, doors of opportunity to foster critical consciousness are evident, revealing the need to create spaces for collective and dialectical interrogations, when parents like Aimei can not only share concerns and interrogate power together, but also can strategize collectively to make their voices heard and engage in transformative action.

Chapter 14, by María de los Ángeles Osorio and Jody Slavick, comes from the central western US. This case shares and contrasts the experiences of two mothers who built and acted upon their critical consciousness when community members, including a caring, experienced teacher and a "community education specialist," were deeply involved in their journeys of critical consciousness. This chapter illustrates some of the possibilities when parents, educators, and other community members begin to collaborate to raise each other's consciousness and engage in advocacy work to challenge restrictive language education policies that are aligned with English-only state assessment requirements. However, this chapter also demonstrates that, even when engaging with others, the journey of critical consciousness is not a straight and linear path. Instead, there are challenges throughout the way that produce discomfort and sometimes even disappointment. Yet every experience can contribute to greater growth and deeper understanding of what it means to enact critical consciousness and the kind of collective work and dispositions that are necessary to engage with the tensions that emerge.

An example of such dispositions is illustrated by Yalda M. Kaveh and Cory Buckband's Chapter 15, who switch the focus to a teacher who engages in humanizing pedagogies resulting from critically conscious family engagement in the remote instruction forced by the COVID-19 lockdown. Rather than constructing the home experiences of minoritized children as substandard and deficient, or the pause from the regular school context as a pathway to learning loss, Gloria, the teacher, recognizes what children are learning at home with their families, and centers parents' knowledge and wisdom of whatever they need to do with the children during such unprecedented times as essential and valuable. This example reveals that critically conscious family engagement can have many facets, with one being a direct influence on the day-to-day classroom experiences, curriculum, assessment, and pedagogy. Moreover, critically conscious family engagement can help us re-evaluate the vision and purposes of schooling. This case is especially significant in that we see the potential of virtual DLBE classrooms in early childhood contexts, an underexplored nexus in DLBE. This nexus is especially urgent due to harmful discourses focused on learning loss and quick returns to "normalcy" in post-COVID-lockdown situations (de Royston & Vossoughi, 2021), which must be interrogated.

The next two chapters offer empowering illustrations of what is possible when critically conscious families, community members, and educators engage in transformative action. Chapter 16 by Luis "Tony" Báez and Andrew H. Hurie connects the historical trajectory of bilingual education in Milwaukee, Wisconsin, to contemporary struggles for community involvement and participation. At a Spanish-English DLBE school called Escuela Bilingüe Foster, parent committee members have been instrumental in securing the ability to determine its own language allocation model, meeting with district board members and advocating for particular interpretations of data. These members also design and deliver one lesson to students per quarter, maintaining connections to the students and families whom they serve and represent. The parent-community engagement, collective action, and advocacy allowed parents to bring about positive change for their school as a whole.

Extending beyond the confines of school-sanctioned spaces, curriculum, and pedagogies, Chapter 17 by Chris Milk and Angela Valenzuela describes a case of educators, families, community members, and activists constructively developing a curriculum unit around *curanderas* (women healers) and *plantas medicinales* (medicinal plants) at their Saturday Spanish-language day school, Academia Cuahutli. This curriculum is full of Spanish and Indigenous linguistic and epistemological connectivity, which challenges deficit ideologies that typically portray the schools' families as lacking intelligence and knowledge. Most notably, educators co-designed this curriculum with families about indigenous medicine and plant knowledge and encouraged family members to share any previous experiences with their children. Central to Academia Cuahutli is a "social architecture of authentic cariño" between students, families, and educators, which values and fosters subaltern and ancestral family knowledges. In this way, Academia Cuahutli becomes an agentic and decolonizing space for DLBE students, teachers, and families, where they can delink from the coloniality of knowledge and power and the pursuit of modernity that continuously aim to shape DLBE programs.

In sum, each case highlights the importance of community expertise, knowledge, and resilience for families and educators in DLBE programs who are driven to more equitably engage with each other as co-equals and collaborators. The cases also shed light on the evolving aspect of critical consciousness, from an internal questioning to collective and strategic transformative action, and finally to authentic communal love and creative and autonomous agency with the power to decolonize relationships, learning, language, and knowledge. Such themes are continued in our final section on teaching and teacher learning.

Teaching and Teacher Learning

The chapters in the teaching and teacher learning section, like the previous sections, span a broad range of contexts and experiences. Taken together, they illustrate how the overlapping actions of critical consciousness can be embodied in schools through classroom practice and teacher learning. Understanding learning, whether by students or by teachers, as co-constructed in interaction within sociocultural and historical contexts (Stillman & Anderson, 2017), we have organized the cases in this section to more thoroughly examine what kinds of interactions can robustly support learners to develop critical consciousness as they navigate complex contexts and histories.

The first two chapters provide an intersectional lens that actively aims to interrogate binaries, to critically listen to current problems in DLBE spaces, and to accompany Black and LGBTQ+ students. Chapter 18, by Brittany L. Frieson and Vivian E. Presiado, is a logical entry point to this section. Their dreaming of DLBE contexts that center the linguistic and cultural practices and epistemologies of Black students challenges the field to historicize how this centering of Black students has not been a priority in DLBE (Sung & Allen-Handy, 2019). Their case narrative pushes us to acknowledge that too often in DLBE spaces there is a Latinx/White binary that omits and silences Black identities and voices. This points to the necessity of ensuring that Black lives indeed matter in DLBE and its curriculum (Frieson, 2021; Martínez et al., 2022). The curricular dreaming that Frieson and Presiado propose in this case illuminates the praxis-cycle of critical consciousness: through engaging with discomfort and critical listening we can take curricular and pedagogical action that affirm Black student identities and interrogate dominative ways of being and knowing.

Meanwhile, Caitie Dougherty, Deborah Palmer, Stacie Aldana, and Mary Gilreath in Chapter 19 also interrogate traditional binaries, in this case, highlighting the complexities of engaging with the intersection of gender identity, language ideologies, and inclusive language practices. The arrival of a transgender first grader in a two-way DLBE program in Colorado, who asks the class to use "they/them pronouns" for them, spurrs a team of DLBE teachers (authors Stacie and Mary) to interrogate ideologies of linguistic purism and to lean into discomfort as they (re)invent their classroom norms and pedagogies for radical inclusion. The chapter explores the importance of *acompañamiento* not just for racialized bilingual students but for all students imbued with intersectional identities, histories, and lived realities who inhabit DLBE spaces.

The next two cases offer insight into the ways that professionals—including teachers, leaders, and instructional coaches—interact in DLBE schools to learn together and to engage in the actions of critical consciousness for enhancing classroom practices. In Chapter 19, Steve Daniel Przymus shares the story of a team of teachers supporting each other to interrogate and move to change the ways we view and ultimately teach our bilingual students who have been identified with disabilities. The chapter describes a bilingual formative assessment tool called "content-based story retells" that allows teachers to listen critically for students' bilingual languaging and better understand students' full linguistic repertoires, regardless of their disability labels. Like Przymus, Caroline Hesse, Jillian La Serna, and Emily Zoeller also explore the potential for professional learning when teachers engage critically with one another. In Chapter 20, they describe what happens when a school radically rethinks the way they use their professional development time, opening teachers up to critical listening to one another's *testimonios* (Delgado Bernal et al., 2012) and moving to action based on what they learn.

The final four chapters in the teaching and teacher learning section demonstrate the need to interrogate white-stream conceptualizations of academic achievement, bilingualism/biliteracy, and intercultural competence, the three traditional goals of DLBE (Howard et al., 2018). The interrogation of DLBE's three goals in these chapters overlaps with other actions of critical consciousness and is deeply immersed in current sociopolitical contexts that directly impact racially and linguistically minoritized students: virtual learning spaces due to COVID-19 (Cioè-Peña, 2022; Ladson-Billings, 2021), deeply polarized/anti-immigrant political climates, two-way contexts prone to gentrification processes (Delavan et al., 2021), and teacher education spaces that are generative sites for critical consciousness work (Caldas, 2017; Espinoza et al., 2021).

In Chapter 22, Juan A. Freire and Judith Flores Carmona highlight the *testimonio* pedagogy in Señora García's DLBE classroom that allows her to accompany her students and their lived experiences of immigration alongside Gloria Anzaldua's *Friends from the Other Side/Amigos del Otro Lado*, a *tema* and *texto* (see Herrera & España, Chapter 24) that relates to their identities.

Carmela Valdez and Rosalyn Harvey-Torres also interrogate the sociopolitical reality of Carmela's Texas first-grade classroom during the Trump presidency. In their case, Chapter 23, children are given the opportunity to push back against the erasure they and their families are experiencing through a bilingual writer's workshop. Valdez's interrogation of the traditional writer's workshop in favor of a transgressive, translanguaging space for young bilingual children leads to a praxis-cycle that centers the voices and realities of her students. Luz Yadira Herrera and Carla España's chapter (24) offer a framework they describe as *textos*, *temas*, and translanguaging to support teachers who wish to engage in the work of critical consciousness through literacy instruction in their elementary classrooms. They share the story of Crystal, a third-grade dual language bilingual teacher in California, as she engages students with challenging critical questions and encourages them to connect with their histories through rich children's literature that draws upon their full linguistic repertoire; this narrative is a beautiful portrait of exemplary pedagogy in a dual language classroom.

Chapter 25, the final chapter in the volume, explores the role of emotions in dual language bilingual teaching, particularly in the two-way context. Brenda Santiago González and Rachel Snyder Bhansari offer insight into the emotional praxis-work that Brenda undertakes as she identifies and struggles to respond to the entrenched discourse patterns of her privileged white English-speaking fourth graders in her two-way DLBE classroom. A first-generation college graduate and a Latina teacher, Brenda draws on her powerful emotions to engage her students in critical conversations, and subsequently to interrogate her own reactions to the program's mandate to separate English and Spanish in her instruction. Like all of the teachers highlighted in the chapters in this section, Brenda demonstrates that the process of developing and enacting critical consciousness in DLBE schools and classrooms is complicated, messy, and always emerging.

Definitions of Terms

Given the breadth of perspectives and contexts represented in this volume—across states, linguistic communities, schools, and programs, each with their own history and rationale—readers will find a variety of terms used by our authors. Authors also use particular terminology for political reasons. For example, some of us have chosen to capitalize racial categories such as Black and Brown, but not white, taking inspiration from Kimberlé Crenshaw (1991), and Maite Sánchez and Ofelia García (2022). The most common program terms are defined here. As we define these terms, however, and consider the various words authors use to describe the people in their communities, we encourage readers and writers to consider the following: (1) Terms and their definitions are always limiting, never perfectly accurate, and always changing (Kibler & Valdés, 2016). (2) Terms used to reference a group of people may not be the terms individuals themselves would use. (3) Each term comes with a particular history, power, and politics that we should question and consider. For instance, we prefer "dual language *bilingual education*" as opposed to "dual language immersion" to call attention to the history of "bilingual education" as a civil right accomplished for speakers of languages other than English (Dorner & Cervantes-Soon, 2020). (4) Acronyms can dehumanize and disconnect individuals from their contexts, so although we do use them in this volume, we also encourage spelling out and using full words when referring to groups of people (e.g., saying "emerging bilinguals" rather than "EBs").

Program Terms

Dual language bilingual education (DLBE): Educational programs that teach children through and with two or more languages, with the express purpose of developing bilingualism, biliteracy, grade-level academic achievement, and sociocultural competence. We assert that in order to serve students from racialized and language-minoritized backgrounds, DLBE must be infused with critical consciousness (as described earlier). Some contexts refer to DLBE as "dual language immersion" (DLI), or as one of the more specific program types, further defined by their imagined student population.

Heritage/indigenous language revitalization: Educational programs designed to support students to learn and develop their families'/communities' minoritized immigrant or indigenous languages. Sometimes these programs occur in outside-school contexts; other times they are part of school programming. Heritage and indigenous language programs work to maintain and revitalize minoritized languages and cultures in US society and to resist the colonizing influences of English.

One-way developmental bilingual education: DLBE program designed for students who enter school as speakers of a minoritized language (e.g., Spanish in the US), either as their dominant/mother tongue or as a heritage/bilingual language in their repertoire.

One-way foreign language immersion: DLBE program designed for students who do not have any background in the program's target language, most often children from monolingual English-speaking households in the US context.

Two-way immersion: DLBE program designed to integrate majority language speakers (e.g., English-dominant students in the US) and heritage/mother tongue speakers of the program's other language (e.g., Spanish speakers in the US). Students learn together, with the goal of developing each other's languages through balanced instruction in each program language over time.

References

American Councils Research Center. (2021). *2021 canvass of dual language and immersion (DLI) programs in U.S. public schools.* www.americancouncils.org/sites/default/files/documents/pages/2021-10/Canvass%20DLI%20-%20October%202021-2_ac.pdf

Ball, S. J., Maguire, M., & Braun, A. (2012). *How schools do policy: Policy enactments in secondary schools*. Routledge.

Bartolomé, L. (1994). Beyond the methods fettish: Toward a humanizing pedagogy. *Harvard Educational Review, 64*(2), 173–194.

Caldas, B. (2017). Shifting discourses in teacher education: Performing the advocate bilingual teacher. *Arts Education Policy Review, 118*(4), 190–201.

Cervantes-Soon, C. G., Dorner, L. M., Palmer, D., Heiman, D., Schwerdtfeger, R., & Choi, J. (2017). Combating inequalities in two-way language immersion programs: Toward critical consciousness in bilingual education spaces. *Review of Research in Education, 41*(1), 403–427. https://doi.org/10.3102/0091732X17690120

Cioè-Peña, M. (2022). Computers secured, connection still needed: Understanding how COVID-19-related remote schooling impacted Spanish-speaking mothers of emergent bilinguals with dis/abilities. *Journal of Latinos and Education*. https://doi.org/10.1080/15348431.2022.2051036

Crenshaw, K. (1991). Mapping the margins: Intersectionality, identity politics, and violence against women of color. *Stanford Law Review, 43*(6), 1241–1299. https://doi.org/10.2307/1229039

de Royston, M. D., & Vossoughi, S. (2021, January 18). Fixating on pandemic "learning loss" undermines the need to transform education. *Truthout*. https://truthout.org/articles/fixating-on-pandemic-learning-loss-undermines-the-need-to-transform-education/

Delavan, G. M., Freire, J. A., & Menken, K. (2021). Editorial introduction: A historical overview of the expanding critique(s) of the gentrification of dual language bilingual education. *Language Policy, 20*(3), 299–321. https://doi.org/10.1007/s10993-021-09597-x

Delgado Bernal, D., Burciaga, R., & Flores Carmona, J. (2012). Chicana/Latina testimonios: Mapping the methodological, pedagogical, and political. *Equity & Excellence in Education, 45*(3), 363–372. https://doi.org/10.1080/10665684.2012.698149

Dorner, L. M. (2012). The life course and sense-making: Immigrant families' journeys toward understanding educational policies and choosing bilingual programs. *American Educational Research Journal, 49*(3), 461–486.

Dorner, L. M. (2016). *The outstanding opportunities, but persistent challenges, of dual language education*. Cambio Center E-brief. Cambio Center, University of Missouri.

Dorner, L. M., & Cervantes-Soon, C. (2020). Equity for students learning English in dual language bilingual education: Persistent challenges and promising practices. *TESOL Quarterly 54*(3), 535–547. https://doi.org/10.1002/tesq.599

Espinoza, K., Nuñez, I., & Degollado, E. D. (2021). "This is what my kids see every day": Bilingual pre-service teachers embracing funds of knowledge through border thinking pedagogy. *Journal of Language, Identity, and Education, 20*(1), 4–17. https://doi.org/10.1080/15348458.2021.1864204

Flores, N., Tseng, A., & Subtirelu, N. (2021). *Bilingualism for all: Raciolinguistic perspectives on dual language education in the United States*. Multilingual Matters.

Frieson, B. L. (2021). Remixin' and flowin' in centros: Exploring the biliteracy practices of Black language speakers in an elementary two-way immersion bilingual program. *Race Ethnicity and Education*, 1–21. https://doi.org/10.1080/13613324.2021.1890568

Heiman, D., Cervantes-Soon, C., Dorner, L., & Palmer, D. (forthcoming). Creating a transformative foundation for dual language bilingual education: Critical consciousness at the core. In J. Freire, E. de Jong, & C Alfaro (Eds.), *Handbook of dual language bilingual education*. Routledge.

Howard, E., Lindholm-Leary, K., Rogers, D., Olague, N., Medina, J., Kennedy, B., Sugarman, J., & Christian, D. (2018). *Guiding principles for dual language education* (3rd ed.). Center for Applied Linguistics.

Kibler, A. K., & Valdés, G. (2016). Conceptualizing language learners: Socioinstitutional mechanisms and their consequences. *The Modern Language Journal, 100*(S1), 96–116. https://doi.org/https://doi.org/10.1111/modl.12310

Ladson-Billings, G. (2021). I'm here for the hard re-set: Post pandemic pedagogy to preserve our culture. *Equity & Excellence in Education, 54*(1), 68–78. https://doi.org/10.1080/10665684.2020.1863883

Levinson, B. A. U., Sutton, M., & Winstead, T. (2009). Education policy as a practice of power: Theoretical tools, ethnographic methods, democratic options. *Educational Policy, 23*(6), 767–795. https://doi.org/10.1177/0895904808320676

Martínez, R. A., Martínez, D. C., & Morales, P. Z. (2022). Black lives matter versus *Castañeda v. Pickard*: A utopian vision of who counts as bilingual (and who matters in bilingual education). *Language Policy*. https://doi.org/10.1007/s10993-021-09610-3

Menken, K., & García, O. (Eds.). (2010). *Negotiating language policies in schools: Educators as policy makers*. Routledge.

Pacheco, M., & Chávez-Moreno, L. (2021). Bilingual education for self-determination: Recentering Chicana/o/x and Latina/o/x student voices. *Bilingual Research Journal, 44*(4), 522–528. https://doi.org/10.1080/15235882.2022.2052203

Palmer, D., Cervantes-Soon, C. G., Dorner, L. M., & Heiman, D. (2019). Bilingualism, biliteracy, biculturalism and critical consciousness for all: Proposing a fourth fundamental goal for two-way dual language education. *Theory into Practice, 58*(2), 121–133. https://doi.org/https://doi.org/10.1080/00405841.2019.1569376

Rodriguez, S., & Crawford, E. R. (2022). School-based personnel for undocumented students through collective leadership in urban schools. *Journal of Research on Leadership Education*. https://doi.org/10.1177/19427751221081887

Sánchez, M., & García, O. (2022). *Transformative translanguaging espacios: Latinx students and their teachers rompiendo fronteras sin miedo*. Multilingual Matters.

Sepúlveda, E. (2011). Toward a pedagogy of acompañamiento: Mexican migrant youth writing from the underside of modernity. *Harvard Educational Review, 81*(3), 550–573.

Steele, J. L., Slater, R., Zamarro, G., Miller, T., Li, J., Burkhauser, S., & Bacon, M. (2017). Effects of dual-language immersion programs on student achievement. *American Educational Research Journal, 54*(1), 282S–306S. https://doi.org/10.3102/0002831216634463

Stillman, J., & Anderson, L. (2017). *Teaching for equity in complex times: Negotiating standards in a high-performing bilingual school*. Teachers College Press.

Sung, K. K., & Allen-Handy, A. (2019). Contradicting origins and racializing legacy of the 1968 Bilingual education act: Urban schooling, anti-blackness, and Oakland's 1996 black English language education resolution. *University of Maryland Law Journal of Race, Religion, Gender, and Class, 19*(1), 44–80.

Theoharis, G. (2007). Social justice educational leaders and resistance: Toward a theory of social justice leadership. *Educational Administration Quarterly, 43*(2), 221–258. https://doi.org/10.1177/0013161X06293717

Umansky, I. M., & Reardon, S. F. (2014). Reclassification patterns among Latino English learner students in bilingual, dual immersion, and English immersion classrooms. *American Educational Research Journal, 51*(5), 879–912. https://doi.org/10.3102/0002831214545110

Valdés, G. (1997). Dual-language immersion programs: A cautionary note concerning the education of language-minority students. *Harvard Educational Review, 67*(3), 391–429.

Table 0.1 Summary of Each Chapter's Context

Chapter		*Title*	*Geographic Context*	*DLBE Program Type and Languages*	*Grade Levels*
Policy	1	*¡Ya basta!* Changing paradigms, policies, and practices for English learners	Texas	One-way developmental, Spanish	District-wide K–12
	2	*Revolisyon an ap Kontinye*: Honoring Haitian Creole through a dual language program in Boston Public Schools	Massachusetts	Two-way, Haitian Creole and English – strand within a school	Elementary PK–5
	3	"We can change the academic trajectory of our children in a snap": Developing a high-school dual language program for Spanish-speaking students with no feeder program	Texas	One-way developmental, Spanish – strand within a school	High School 9–12
	4	Centering immigrant voices and experiences in a dual language bilingual school: Teachers as critical pedagogues and policymakers	New York	Two-way, Spanish and English – whole school	Elementary PK–5
	5	"Shifting lenses instead of always grinding forward": Using ethnography to challenge raciolinguistic ideologies in dual language education	Pennsylvania	"1.5-way," Spanish and English – whole school	Elementary & Middle K–8
	6	Using critical policy analysis in collaborative professional learning communities to enhance dual language bilingual educators' critical consciousness	Utah	Two-way, Spanish and English – strand within a school	Elementary K–6
Leadership	7	The convergence of critical consciousness and culturally sustaining leadership practices in dual language bilingual education	Colorado	Two-way, Spanish and English – strand within a school	Elementary K–6
	8	The power of *plática*: Expanding dual language bilingual education at the district level with a bilingual redesign committee	Texas	Transitional to two-way – Spanish and English	District-wide K–12
	9	Dual language, dual purposes: A community in conflict	Texas	Two-way, French, Spanish, English, and Chinese – whole school	Elementary
	10	Black and bilingual: Challenges in decentering Whiteness in dual language bilingual education	Gulf Coast	One-way immersion, French	Charter school
	11	Vietnamese dual language immersion: Commodifying an uncommodified language and culture	Oregon	Two-way, Vietnamese and English	District-wide K–12
	12	*De la lucha a la victoria*: The journey to save a dual language bilingual education teacher program	California	University dual language bilingual teacher preparation	Higher Education

(*Continued*)

Table 0.1 (Continued)

Chapter		*Title*	*Geographic Context*	*DLBE Program Type and Languages*	*Grade Levels*
Families and Communities	13	Fostering critical consciousness with immigrant families: The story of a Chinese immigrant mother in a Mandarin-English dual language program	North Carolina		K–5
	14	Cultivating critical consciousness with mothers of bilingual students	Colorado	One-way immersion, Spanish and English	Elementary K–5
	15	When life gives you lemons: Critically conscious family engagement in a virtual dual language kindergarten class during a pandemic	Arizona		K
	16	Contextualizing parent activism in one of Milwaukee's bilingual public schools	Wisconsin		K–5
	17	Relational pedagogies and the building of a social architecture of authentic *cariño* in the teaching of healing practices at Academia Cuauhtli	Texas	Heritage language/culture revitalization; Spanish, English, and Nahuatl	Elementary 3rd–5th grades
Teaching and Teacher Learning	18	Black liberation in bilingual education: A case for Black freedom dreaming	Illinois	Two-way, Spanish and English w/ attention to Black language	Elementary K–5
	19	*Intentando incluir a todes*: A first-grade team's gender-inclusive pedagogies	Colorado	Two-way, Spanish and English – whole school	Elementary 1st grade
	20	English-only as a magic pill? Dispelling the myths about disability and dual language bilingual education	Texas	One-way developmental, Spanish and English – whole school	Elementary
	21	Professional development through critical conversation and *testimonio* at Simón Bolívar Elementary	Wisconsin	Two-way, Spanish and English – whole school	Elementary
	22	Bridging *testimonio* pedagogy with dual language bilingual education in a K/1 classroom: One teacher's journey to critical consciousness through a Master's course	Southwest US	One-way developmental, Spanish and English	Elementary K/1st
	23	A sense of belonging: Biliteracy instruction that loves and centers Latinx emergent bilingual students and their families	Texas	Two-way, Spanish and English – whole school	Elementary 1st grade
	24	Growing critical bilingual literacies: Counter-narratives and social justice in bilingual education	California	One-way developmental, Spanish and English—whole school	Elementary 3rd grade
	25	Building on emotion: Experiencing, confronting, and reflecting on patterns of language use in a TWI DL classroom	Washington	Two-way, Spanish & English – strand within a school	Elementary 4th grade

Section I

Policy and Critical Consciousness

1 *¡Ya basta!* Changing Paradigms, Policies, and Practices for English Learners

Elena Izquierdo

Context

> I still remember not sleeping well the night before the first day of school, getting up before the rest of the family, and taking a long time getting ready for school. As I walked into the classroom, my excitement was quickly dampened as I selected a desk and was about to sit down, when the teacher said, "No, you don't get a desk. Go to the back of the room and sit at the table with the other students who don't speak English."
>
> (Deputy Matilde, personal communication, 2014)

Matilde was born in the US but raised in a border town in Mexico. She began school at six years of age and was placed in *pre-first* in a US school right across the border from where she lived. She vividly remembers getting ready for her first day of school and being so excited. She was wearing new clothes, had her school supplies, and had huge expectations for what was to come ahead. However, very quickly she began to feel small, dumb, and not worthy of being in the classroom. Beginning school as a six-year-old in *pre-first*, a classification made up by the teacher for those who did not speak English, Matilde was older than most of her classmates after that. Deputy Matilde shared feeling self-conscious of being a year older than her friends and not catching up to age-appropriate classmates. Matilde's mother was astute enough to secure a long-term tutor for her to learn to read and write in Spanish. This changed her educational trajectory, and by fifth grade she was an avid reader in both languages. Everything at school was written and spoken in English. She was expected to translate for newcomers as she reached the upper grades but was cautioned not to "chit chat" in Spanish. She suffered humiliation and punishment when caught speaking Spanish during recess. "Receiving swats and standing in the hall outside the principal's office gave me a lot of time to think about becoming a teacher who would do things differently for other students." As she stood by the principal's office, Matilde imagined being a principal of her own school and would

DOI: 10.4324/9781003240594-3

play scenarios of how she would "get after" teachers who would not teach, engage, or include all students in their class. She shared:

> The feeling of hopelessness and failure that I experienced in *pre-first* was something I never wanted for any of my students to feel as long as I was responsible for them as their teacher, their principal, or their principal's supervisor. Little did I know as an elementary school student that all those visits to the principal's office would serve as fertile ground for my career.
>
> (Deputy Matilde, personal communication, 2014)

After a long journey, Matilde became a Deputy Superintendent in Palomas Independent School District (ISD), located on the border of Mexico and the US, serving over 60,000 students: 80% Hispanic, 12% White, 70% economically disadvantaged, and 25% ELs. The superintendent and administration before her time had been part of a large-scale impropriety in gaming the system by using district data to keep low-performing students out of tested grade levels by improperly promoting or holding back students, preventing students from enrollment, or forcing students to drop out. These students were known as *los desaparecidos*, the disappeared. The objective was for scores to look better. After all was revealed, the superintendent was arrested and sent to jail, and many district leaders who were involved lost their education licenses, as well. As stories rebounded throughout the district and community, the state took over the district and named a new superintendent who immediately recruited Matilde, the new Deputy Superintendent responsible for all academics and school leadership. The new administration began to look for the "disappeared." However, the few who were found expressed that they did not want to return to school because they did not belong or did not learn anything. One student, Sofia, had been thrown out of her home by her father. He blamed her for being "kicked out" of school, not knowing what the "previous leaders" in the district were doing to them. Sofia cried as she shared that her dream was to graduate and have her own pizza place. But now she could not finish school, and she was pregnant. *Los desaparecidos'* lives had been hijacked. Deputy Matilde knew she was the right person for this position.

Case Narrative

The new leadership in Palomas ISD had to deal with a community who had lost trust in the district where ELs had been systematically oppressed. Deputy Matilde found deficit perspectives within some of her teachers, principals, and central office administrators who viewed ELs as liabilities. Her priority was to immediately and openly address the injustices done to ELs by acknowledging the damage and focusing on actions to transform the educational experiences of her students with the commitment to not losing any more, *not one more!*

Leading Through Critical Consciousness

Deputy Matilde's personal experiences growing up as an EL reminded her how it felt to be humiliated and marginalized; however, her position and the context in the district gave her the purpose and urgency, the what and the why, to transform EL schooling in Palomas ISD. The Deputy's positional authority facilitated the process to some extent; however, the work was messy since it demanded disrupting entrenched marginalizing conditions and questioning ideologies. For years bilingual education at Palomas ISD had been a transitional model with a varied and inconsistent program design, and with the goal of English at the expense of students' education. Some expressed that ELs had to learn English first, while others thought it was advantageous to know both languages. But it was more than just language. Deputy Matilde was familiar with the research pointing to strong educational outcomes for ELs in dual language bilingual education (Steele et al., 2017); the academic failure in subtractive and substandard programs (Valenzuela, 2010); and the power of additive education in continued cognitive development of a student's primary language (Baker & Wright, 2017). She also understood the urgency of addressing *las injusticias* (the injustices) that *los desaparecidos* had experienced. Deputy Matilde believed the shift to DLBE meant a transformation in deficit mindsets and low expectations for ELs: they can't speak English, so they are low achievers? Deputy Matilde also understood that to lead transformative change, other stakeholders needed to be included as active participants in a collective process to learn together about the historical practices and barriers to EL education in the district and be more informed and positioned to understand and analyze the issue at hand. Deputy Matilde identified district educators, bilingual directors from other districts, parents, and community and university members to be a part of the Dual Language Task Force (DLTF). They then began difficult, but crucial conversations with critical consciousness at the core, the what and the why.

Deputy Matilde's first meeting started with context, *los desaparecidos*, and although one could feel the discomfort in the room, she acknowledged the inequities and questioned the reasoning and actions which created it. Deputy Matilde's objectives were to listen critically to parents, educators, and the community; collectively create a historical account of the district's schooling of ELs; and confront the deeply rooted inequities in policies and practices with action. She first established the context, urgency, and purpose for the DLTF. Over time, she built critical consciousness and the DLTF developed a plan of action, which included a recommendation to change district policy to DLBE, a timeline of district-wide program implementation identified with associated program design and costs, and a plan for parental and community support.

Although the process was collective, it was quite messy because there were conflicting ideologies about what ELs needed and how we should teach them, and even "should we?" The conversations were uncomfortable as the assumed power of the district was questioned; however, in the process, the district's story and its history of EL education and its inequities were revealed. Transparent critical conversations now focused on all the inequities these students had historically experienced at every level.

Even as the DLTF historicized language education, critically listened, and embraced discomfort, the need to establish common ground on the research, goals, and benefits of DLBE was equally key because it was the response to fight the educational inequities experienced by their ELs. By understanding the benefits of DLBE for children, the DLTF's collective work through the transformation would be easier—not easy, but easier. The DLTF committed to meeting every Wednesday from 5–8 pm for two months. The ISD made all requested documents and staff available to the DLTF as they were provided information and presentations, and as they reviewed and disaggregated all data regarding EL schooling, Pre-K–12 grades.

Outside these weekly meetings, they interviewed numerous bilingual/ English language development teachers, principals, parents, and students on

Table 1.1 Action Planning

Dates	*Topics*	*Persons Responsible*
January 8–29 Wednesdays Four meetings (three hours each)	• Initial meeting introductions and role of DLTF • Setting the context: *los desaparecidos* and the district's story • Individual perspectives and/or reactions to the context • Revisit role of DLTF • ISD Bilingual Program presentation • DLBE Program presentation • EL demographic data presentation • DLTF request for district data: attendance; academic progress; language proficiency growth; secondary schedules; retention; number of graduates and dropouts; parent communications; and parent denials of bilingual services • Review of all data and presentations	Deputy Matilde Deputy Matilde Individual members of the DLTF Deputy Matilde ISD Staff DLBE Expert ISD presentation ISD DLTF
February 5–26 Wednesdays Four meetings (three hours each)	Developed report, recommendations, and a five-year district-wide plan of action to replace transitional with DLBE, to begin with kindergarten the first year; add a new grade each year; roll out, timeline with feeder patterns; potential cost for staff; materials; professional development	DLTF

educating ELs through dual language bilingual education. The DLTF were exposed to the conflicting ideologies throughout the district. This validated the need to guide the district into DLBE and raise the expectations for all. Then, they wrote their report.

The DLTF's report was built upon two tenets of equitable EL education reform to ensure the effectiveness and sustainability of DLBE: (1) the value of ongoing EL longitudinal data collection and analysis; and (2) the importance of disaggregating data to inform curriculum and instruction for ELs. The DLTF was ready to make its presentation at the school board meeting.

The room was at capacity with teachers, parents, students, and other community members. Many stated their support of DLBE during the public comments section of the meeting. The DLTF was very deliberate in crafting equity-driven language presented in their findings and made their recommendations. The district would achieve the following: (1) Replace transitional education with 50/50 simultaneous biliteracy DLBE for all ELs districtwide to begin the new school year (in 6 months), starting in kindergarten and adding a new grade level every subsequent year; it was a budget neutral move since the first year began with kindergarten and these bilingual classrooms were already staffed with certified bilingual teachers. (2) Rename the Department of English Language Acquisition to reflect the ISD's commitment to quality DLBE, high academic achievement, fluency, and literacy in both Spanish and English, and a paradigm shift that would now value a student's home language and cultural assets. (3) Develop a robust plan to engage EL parents and the wider community in DLBE awareness, engagement, and training; and recruit parents from both language groups. (4) Address the education of the EL students who would not benefit from DLBE since it would begin only in kindergarten the first year, and develop a district-wide curriculum articulation and accountability plan to strengthen the structures and alignment of curriculum in 1st–12th for all ELs. The report included feeder patterns and required funding for resources such as instructional materials, professional development, and assessments. Presented as a moral and ethical recommendation, primary language support would be structured, strategic, and systematic across all grade levels and feeder patterns; the ISD had to develop a consistent EL district message based on expectations and progress, and provide required whole-school professional development in understanding the diverse needs of EL. The board unanimously approved the recommendations and acknowledged the work of the DLTF. It felt like a celebration while everyone in the room was applauding and sharing their excitement. The task force was to continue meeting each month to review the progress being made. Now the real work had to begin.

¡Manos a la Obra! *Let's Get to Work!*

For Deputy Matilde the more complicated side of *messy* was about to begin. The deputy was now to engage with those who were associated with the system responsible for subjecting *los desaparecidos* to inequities, and as such, the discomfort level grew even more intense. She initiated three separate series of meetings specific to principals, district administrators, or teachers. Like the DLTF process, the first meetings focused on building critical consciousness and consequently all three district groups developed and acknowledged the historical context, contended with discomfort, discussed the board approved DLBE plan, and were provided a brief overview of DLBE research, goals, and benefits. As part of the process the deputy always asked for feedback, stepped back, and intentionally allowed for lively venting, and what she called "the coming out of ideologies."

Deputy Matilde initiated monthly principal institutes that would meet at the model school for DLBE—for principals only. This provided a space for principals to speak freely, to ask questions, to learn, to listen to one another, and to observe DLBE classrooms. She understood the critical role of principals in leading the school staff and community in supporting DLBE (Menken, 2017). At the end of the day, most of the principals expressed their support and willingness to start. After all, they already had the bilingual teachers and were merely changing the program model from an early exit to a DLBE model, or so they thought. This was a misconception throughout the district that was eventually clarified. Research continues to reveal that shifting from a transitional model of bilingual education to DLBE requires more than a bilingual certification (Henderson & Palmer, 2020; Izquierdo, 2021). Similar sessions for districtwide central office administrators from all departments were also held at the model school for opportunities to visit DLBE classrooms. Ultimately, they realized their role in districtwide DLBE. Not one person or one department would do it alone! Finally, "bilingual teacher after-school round-tables" were strategically organized at identified campuses across the district for all bilingual teachers.

Even though these were three distinct district groups (district administration, principals, and teachers), the process was similar: provide context and purpose and contend with discomfort through critical conversations as they shared their perspectives and provided feedback. All three groups shared similar concerns for the new direction to DLBE: professional development on DLBE; instructional resources in Spanish since the previous administration asked them to dispose of all Spanish materials; and teacher academic Spanish proficiency although they were bilingual-certified teachers. Most principals were willing to work, but some were passive resistors who never publicly challenged the new direction but did not support it. Most teachers were nervous but very excited; others did not see the reason to shift to DLBE. There were various and conflicting perspectives and ideologies, from *dual language and bilingualism is for all children and promotes equity*, to *dual language is good for most children, but not those who struggle in their native language*. However, one question that always came out was, "Why this year?" When asked why they had to implement DLBE so quickly that year, Deputy Matilde's response would return to context, "Not one more! *¡Ya basta!*"

Teaching Notes

This case study highlights a story of a courageous Latina who was once an English learner herself, and who, much later in life, led a districtwide transformation for educating historically marginalized ELs, *los desaparecidos*, and shifted the district policy for bilingual education from a transitional to dual language mindset. She challenged the status quo by building critical consciousness through providing context, revealing the story of her district's policies and practices in its EL schooling; acknowledging the injustices; and collectively with a Dual Language Task Force developing a plan of action to eradicate past practices and equitably serve the English learners in the district. Changing from a transitional to a dual language model requires a very significant shift in beliefs and ideologies, both complex and complicated because educators must question their own language ideology—this is not easy (Henderson & Palmer, 2020).

DLBE is more than a program. It is a comprehensive school reform that values families and communities. Social justice is foundational to equity-driven DLBE since it validates the student's language, culture, and identity and promotes access to high-quality instruction in both languages (DeMatthews & Izquierdo, 2019). DLBE is recognized as an approach to transforming schools because of its foundational assets-based perspective on linguistic diversity, inclusivity, and rigorous and culturally-sustaining curriculum that has advanced the education of ELs as evident in longitudinal studies (Steele et al., 2017).

Leadership for Critically Conscious Policy Development

Matilde's focus on critical consciousness stems from personal deeply rooted feelings of humiliation and marginalization in school because of her language and lack of English proficiency. As a district leader she was determined and positioned to change this narrative and take collective action to redress inequities through critical consciousness and oblige the district to understand the what and the why of this policy-driven leadership. Critical consciousness allowed for the action needed to achieve the shift to equitable policy. Research continues to emphasize the importance of leadership in DLBE (DeMatthews & Izquierdo, 2017; Menken, 2017) committed to the goals of DLBE which are not entirely focused on the achievement gap, but other critical factors. In this case study, Deputy Matilde demonstrated many of the principles foundational to leadership in DLBE. She included the entire district in its role in the DLBE rollout. She facilitated professional development at every level: teachers, parents, principals, and district administrators. She recognized the critical role of the principal in leading DLBE and committed to creating safe spaces for their professional growth. She included the DLTF at every phase of implementation and provided updates along the way. Most importantly, however, to shift to districtwide

DLBE, policy structures embedded in critical consciousness were essential in driving the action needed for equitable education. "Not one more! ¡*Ya basta!*"

Teaching Activities

1. **What does the research say and where did you see action that supports the research?** Define each of the terms that follow and use Deputy Matilde's case to identify events that are examples of these elements of critical consciousness (Palmer et al., 2019).
2. Discuss the relationships among DLBE, equity, social justice, and critical consciousness in policy development.

Table 1.2 Elements of Critical Consciousness

	Elements of Critical Consciousness	*Definition*	*Case Event*
1.	**Historicizing**		
2.	**Critical Listening**		
3.	**Interrogating Power**		
4.	**Contending with discomfort**		

References

Baker, C., & Wright, W. E. (2017). *Foundations of bilingual education and bilingualism* (6th ed.). Multilingual Matters.

DeMatthews, D. E., & Izquierdo, E. (2017). The importance of principals supporting dual language education: A social justice leadership framework. *Journal of Latinos and Education, published online*, 1–18. http://dx.doi.org/10.1080/15348431.2017.1282365

DeMatthews, D. E., & Izquierdo, E. (Eds.). (2019). *Dual language education: Teaching and leading through two languages*. Springer.

Henderson, K. I., & Palmer, D. K. (2020). *Dual language bilingual education: Teacher cases and perspectives on large-scale implementation*. Multilingual Matters. https://doi.org/10.21832/9781788928106

Izquierdo, E. (2021). The shift to equity [Review of the book *Dual Language Bilingual Education: Teacher Cases and Perspectives on Large-Scale Implementation* by K. I. Henderson & D. K. Palmer.] *International Journal of Bilingual Education and Bilingualism, Published Online*. https://doi.org/10.1080/13670050.2021.1924114

Menken, K. (2017). *Leadership in dual language bilingual education*. [White Paper]. Center for Applied Linguistics. www.cal.org/ndlf/pdfs/publications/NDLF-White-Paper-October-2017.pdf

Palmer, D., Cervantes-Soon, C. G., Dorner, L. M., & Heiman, D. (2019). Bilingualism, biliteracy, biculturalism and critical consciousness for all: Proposing a fourth fundamental goal for two-way dual language education. *Theory into Practice*, *58*(2), 121–133. https://doi.org/https://doi.org/10.1080/00405841.2019.1569376

Steele, J. L., Slater, R., Zamarro, G., Miller, T., Li, J., Burkhauser, S., & Bacon, M. (2017). Effects of dual-language immersion programs on student achievement. *American Educational Research Journal, 54*(1), 282–306. https://doi.org/10.3102/0002831216634463

Valenzuela, A. (2010). *Subtractive schooling: US-Mexican youth and the politics of caring.* SUNY Press.

2 *Revolisyon an ap Kontinye*

Honoring Haitian Creole Through a Dual Language Program in Boston Public Schools

Ayanna Cooper

Context

This chapter presents a case narrative to show how various stakeholders were critically conscious in their commitment to the development and implementation of an English/Haitian Creole dual language program. Stakeholders worked collectively across various social, political, and communal spaces to establish what they wanted for their children: a dual language program that would serve Black students of Haitian descent. This program provides an example of how, despite challenges with having the program approved, finding licensed teachers, and having a high-quality curriculum, dual language learning environments can be created for students when stakeholders are invested in the communities they serve.

The US Census Bureau reported that Haitians, those who were born in Haiti or who identify as Haitian, made up 3.7% of Boston's population from 2013–2017 (Walsh, 2020). While only 4.2% of K–12 English learners (ELs) are Black, the majority of foreign-born Black ELs are from Haiti (US Department of Education, 2019), and Haitian Creole is the sixth most common language of K–12 ELs in the United States (US Department of Education, 2019).

Despite these numbers in relation to Haitian Creole-speaking ELs, public school dual language programs serving this population specifically were nonexistent prior to 2017. For ELs, however, access to content and language development is a civil rights issue. The US Department of Education in partnership with the Department of Civil Rights and the Department of Justice (2015) provide program model guidance for state education agencies; the Dear Colleague letter states the following:

> Language assistance services or programs for EL students must be educationally sound in theory and effective in practice; however, the civil rights laws do not require any particular program or method of instruction for EL students. Students in EL programs must receive appropriate language assistance services until they are proficient in English and can

DOI: 10.4324/9781003240594-4

> participate meaningfully in the district's educational programs without language assistance services.
>
> (p. 12)

Of the many options to educate ELs, one model chosen by school districts in Massachusetts is the dual language program. This case study is situated in Boston Public Schools (BPS), which was the nation's first public school system and is home to the Mattahunt Elementary School's Toussaint L'Ouverture Academy (TLA)—the nation's first early-learning English/Haitian Creole dual language program, founded in 2017. The school is in Mattapan, a neighborhood in Boston that is home to a large Haitian immigrant population, and it is named after Toussaint L'Ouverture (1743–1803), an enslaved Haitian turned revolutionary who successfully led a revolt resulting in Haiti's independence from France. According to state-provided demographic categories, the Mattahunt Elementary School's current population includes about 400 students in grades Pre-K–5: 67% African American (32% Haitian), 27% Hispanic, 4% White, and 3% multiracial students (non-Hispanic); additionally, 66% are considered economically disadvantaged. Approximately 29% of the student population are identified as students with disabilities, and 40% as ELs. Haitian Creole and Spanish are the most common languages spoken by the students designated as ELs at Mattahunt.

The TLA employs a two-way immersion model, a form of dual language instruction, defined by the Massachusetts Department of Elementary and Secondary Education (2021) as having "approximately an equal number of students who are monolingual or dominant in English at the time of enrollment and students who are monolingual or dominant in the partner language at the time of enrollment." As of 2022, TLA was serving about 80 students in grades K–3, with plans to add one grade per year until fifth grade. TLA's program is unique for two reasons. (1) The program offers dual language to students who would otherwise have only one language program option (sheltered English immersion, which focuses on integrating content and language instruction in the target language), and (2) TLA partners English with a less commonly taught language, Haitian Creole.

Prior to the founding of TLA, Boston's Haitian community was growing. It became apparent to the community members that the need to maintain and educate the next generation of Haitian Americans citizens was imperative, revolutionary in nature, in order to preserve Haitian language and culture in a public-school setting. Together, they sought a solution. The following case narrative explains this story of TLA's revolutionary and critically conscious development.

Case Narrative

In the early 1980s, the Haitian community in Boston increased. A pioneer and founder of the Haitian Parent Association, Irlande Plancher, along with Haitian community members and school district personnel, began to champion the idea of a dual language English/Haitian Creole program. Part of preserving Haitian language culture for these community members meant having their children's home language taught and validated at school. Unfortunately, disagreements around pedagogical approaches and whether the dual language program should be English partnered with French or Haitian Creole stalled efforts. Some community members strongly favored French as the partner language while others insisted on Haitian Creole, Haiti's mother tongue, rather than French, the language of Haiti's colonizer. Community members held meetings debating the importance of which language should partner English. Some felt French should have been the partner language because it was more formal and prestigious than Haitian Creole. Others felt Haitian Creole was the language of all Haitians, not just those who were educated. For example, if students were taught English and French but their grandparents only spoke Haitian Creole, they would not be able to effectively communicate with their relatives. Ultimately it was agreed upon to teach the students English and Haitian Creole. This was a first for Boston public schools since at the time, the only dual language programs offered were English/Spanish serving predominantly Latinx students.

In addition to the issue of which language was to be taught, there were a number of other challenges discussed as the program was designed. One such challenge was finding the proper school to house such a program. It was important to situate the program in an area of Boston where there was a significant number of Haitian Creole-speaking families. The Mattahunt School, which was the ideal site, initially faced being closed due to several factors. Ultimately, the school was restructured, rebranded, and reopened to include the English/Haitian Creole dual language program. After three different superintendent changes across two decades of advocating and planning by dedicated community members, educators, politicians, and other stakeholders, everyone involved was overjoyed when the TLA classroom opened its doors to the first class of students during the fall of 2017. Subsequently, educators across the Boston school district employed and further developed critical consciousness as they developed TLA's policies and practices in their implementation of the program.

Developing Curricula

One of the first challenges was for TLA educators to choose and create instructional materials for the program. During its first year, the school was awarded a $30,000 grant from EdVestors to research early literacy practices in Haiti. School leaders and a small group of community members traveled to Haiti to visit schools and talk with Haitian educators.

Among other activities they visited the Matènwa, a school located on the island of la Gonâve, off the coast of Haiti, with limited access to electricity and running water. The Mattahunt team observed the Matènwa's dedication to education despite its limited resources, which affirmed their own commitment to teaching Mattahunt students Haitian Creole. They also met with a number of educators, Ministry of Education personnel, curriculum writers, tour guides, and local residents, and they further developed and witnessed critical consciousness in the commitment to developing literate citizens. As a result of that expedition, TLA's team made recommendations for continued professional learning including creating a bank of English/ Haitian Creole educational materials.

Even after TLA started creating authentic curricula, it still faced challenges. From a linguistic equity perspective, the district's Office of English Learners has had to stand boldly to advocate for funds to support the creation of materials for what they call low-incidence language programs, like TLA's. The bureaucracy associated with finding high-quality vendors to write curricula, and getting budgets approved and funds released in a timely manner have remained issues. Ms. Daphne Germain, the interim assistant superintendent for the BPS Office of English Learners, said, "Becoming an anti-racist organization, which BPS has committed to, requires dealing with anti-immigrant ignorance and biases around what is an 'acceptable' language from other people groups" (personal communication, June 3, 2021). This meant addressing the fact that there was no commercial Haitian Creole "standards-based foundational literacy curriculum" with complementary scope and sequence and assessments, so they would have to gain approval to create their own.

In turn, the teachers and consultants put in countless hours creating and "trans-adapting" the Mattahunt language arts curriculum into Haitian Creole. Curriculum writer Lionel Hogu described the trans-adapting process as making the curriculum relevant and authentic to Haitian culture. Trans-adapting is important for authenticity of language acquisition. For teachers, this meant not only teaching the curriculum units and administering assessments but creating them as well (see Figure 2.1). The teachers had not previously been trained to trans-adapt curricula and assessment but did so intuitively. They understood the importance of not teaching Haitian Creole in a vacuum. In addition, by working closely with the Haitian Language and Culture Center, the teachers were able to teach language arts and assess students in both languages.

Ensuring Professional Learning

Mattahunt school leaders have also had to remain steadfast in their approach to supporting TLA teachers' professional learning. One teacher affirmed that just being able to speak Haitian Creole was not enough to teach it to someone else. TLA teachers are highly credentialed, multilingual, and experienced professionals see Table 2.1). The Office of Educator Licensure in Massachusetts requires licensed educators to have a Sheltered English Immersion Endorsement. This endorsement is an effort to prepare general

Figure 2.1 TLA Teacher-Created Alphabet Poster

education teachers for ELs in content classes. It differs from an English as a Second Language (ESL) or a Bilingual Language Endorsement (noted in Table 2.1 as Dual Language Endorsement). In order to maintain their educator licenses, teachers have had to engage in 30 hours of professional development per year.

Unfortunately, TLA teachers' choices for professional learning focused on Haitian Creole foundational literacy, offered by BPS or externally, have been limited. This has meant that they have had to take the "DIY" (do it yourself) approach to professional learning. For example, a teacher at TLA completed a course at Boston College focused on literacy and ELs. Because the course did not specifically address foundational literacy in Haitian Creole, she had to make the connections herself between developing literacy in two languages and the necessary pedagogical approaches specifically for Haitian Creole.

Connecting with Culture and Community

Another important element of the TLA program related to critical consciousness has been its steadfast commitment to assuring the students know their roots and culture. In May of 2021, TLA students and staff participated

Table 2.1 Teacher Credentials

Name (Pseudonym)	*Language(s)*	*Credentials/Licensure*
Yvette *K–1*	English/Haitian Creole French	BS Finance and Insurance MEd Elementary Education SEI Endorsement Dual Language Endorsement
Patricia *K–2*	English/Haitian Creole	BA Communications MEd Early Education SEI Endorsement ESL License
Rose Marie *1st*	English/Haitian Creole	BS Education MEd Elementary Education Reading License SEI Endorsement Dual Language Endorsement
Jeanne *2nd*	English/Haitian Creole	BA Education MEd Special Education ESL License
Sheryl *3rd*	English/Haitian Creole	BS Health Education MEd Elementary Education ESL License

in BPS's annual Haitian Heritage Month Celebration. The students' artwork; dancing; science, technology, engineering, and math (STEM) projects; and bilingualism were featured. In addition, parents gave testimonials about why they enrolled their children in the program and how it has been beneficial. Historically, linguistic pride has not always been acknowledged and celebrated this way in Haitian culture. Rev. Dieufort J. Fleurissaint reflected about his secondary education in Haiti: "We were punished as students if we spoke Haitian Creole in our classes in High School. There was a stigma that existed, if you spoke Haitian Creole, you were uneducated" (personal communication, June 3, 2021). For him, seeing the students being instructed in both English and Haitian Creole at TLA has been "like a miracle." It was revolutionary for him to witness students having learning experiences opposite of those he had.

Teaching Notes

TLA serves as a model for others seeking to establish native-language instruction and English to the communities they serve. By elevating the Haitian Creole language and culture, and providing students with the opportunity to learn English and Haitian Creole in an environment that values their home language and culture, TLA has embodied linguistic social justice. The leadership team, led by Principal Walter Henderson and Assistant Principal Joelle Gamere, have been dedicated to assuring the TLA is academically rigorous and teaches and assesses language arts in both English and Haitian Creole. The academy's student achievement data supports their approach to teaching content and developing two languages simultaneously. To date, students from the pre-K Haitian Creole dual language program have outperformed their monolingual peers in letter recognition in English and Haitian Creole; native Haitian Creole speakers in the dual language program have acquired English at a faster rate than those in the sheltered English immersion program (personal communication, June 3, 2021). Also, the social-emotional wellness and confidence of the students in TLA are perceived as healthy and strong because of the consistent validation of Haitian language and culture (personal communication, June 3, 2021). By engaging in critical, sometimes uncomfortable, dialog, educators and families were able to agree that native language preservation, bilingualism, and biliteracy were important twenty-first-century skills they wanted for their children. After community members spearheaded efforts, school district personnel partnered with them and committed to all that would be involved with establishing and maintaining the dual language program. This school is now educating our nation's next generation of biliterate, bilingual, and bicultural citizens, opening up a world of academic and economic opportunities for them.

More research is needed about Black ELs in K–12 settings (Cooper, 2020) and especially how we can implement equitable dual language education for them. Their experiences in school, backgrounds, and plans for college and careers are noticeably absent from the field of teaching English to speakers of other languages (TESOL) and bilingual education (Flores et al., 2021). Though some initiatives with a focus on ELs serve as a form of linguistic equity, because they do not include Black ELs in those initiatives, they also serve as another form of exclusion, linguicism, and racism. In order to ensure dual language programs are accessible to communities of color, Wall et al. (2019), in their study on dual language programs, affirmed the need for (1) more attention to equity, (2) engagement in authentic dialog, and (3) reexamination of who the decision-makers are.

As noted in previous research, "Two way dual language (TWDL) bilingual programs are inherently complex and full of possibilities" (Palmer et al., 2019, p. 9). The complexity and synergy are evident in the experiences of those involved with establishing and maintaining TLA. When planning for dual language programs, a number of factors must be taken into consideration. Once logistical measures are in place (e.g., program location and required approvals granted), other considerations must be closely examined, such as qualified staff members; high-quality, standards-based curriculum and assessments; and required professional learning. Even several years after opening and after researching literacy instruction in Haiti, the TLA team still faced some significant challenges—namely, limited literacy resources in Haitian Creole. Without the key components (i.e., having a sufficient number of highly qualified staff members, a dual language curriculum, and resources and assessments in both languages), efforts to implement more dual language programs, especially in urban school communities, will fall short.

The TLA approach demonstrates the need for a collective effort, a committed community, and political allies. The school leaders and staff have demonstrated true persistence through the upheavals of leadership changes, budgetary constraints, and limited resources. The parents are committed to and want dual language for their children, even if they may not know the intricate details involved with "making it happen."

Conclusion

The stories, experiences, and outcomes for TLA students, their families, and stakeholders are not complete. Their quest to create a space for the development and growth of bilingual and bicultural citizens is a work in progress. From a community perspective, the dual language program should be expanded citywide to more schools to provide more students access to Haitian Creole, regardless of where they reside in the city. The dual language program should also extend from a primary model to include secondary grades. This requires continued dialogue across the system, with families, and activation of critical consciousness, as happened in this case.

When asked how they will know they have accomplished the goals they set out by establishing TLA, community member Lionel Hogu stated, "When the students graduate with the seal of biliteracy, that is how we'll know" (personal communication, June 3, 2021). TLA educators, students, and their families are an example of a cultural and linguistic revolution, having the audacity necessary to educate young Black, bilingual, bicultural, and biliterate students.

Teaching Activities

1. What *ti revolisyon* (revolution) will you start in an effort to advocate for linguistic equity? Write a paragraph.
2. Consider how you would plan a heritage month for your dual-language students. What activities would you include? What community and linguistic resources would you draw on? Write out your plan.

Discussion Questions

1. How do you define linguistic equity? How can the definition be transformed into action?
2. How are language and literacy aligned to the civil rights of students?
3. What opportunities are there to cultivate a shared vision for bilingualism and biliteracy through a dual language approach?

4. What existing policies, related to language education, are in place in Massachusetts that would support and affirm efforts for increased bilingualism and biliteracy?
5. How are Black students, native English speakers, and ELs, both US- and foreign-born, positioned—or not—to have access to dual language programs in your context?

References

Cooper, A. (2020). Justice for all: Realities and possibilities of Black English learners in K—12 schools. *Teachers College Record, 122*(13).

Flores, N., Subtirelu, N., & Tseng, A. (Eds.). (2021). *Bilingualism for all? Raciolinguistic perspectives on dual language education* (pp. 88–110). Multilingual Matters.

Massachusetts Department of Elementary and Secondary Education. (2021, August). *Dual language education programs*. www.doe.mass.edu/ele/programs/dle.html

Palmer, D., Cervantes-Soon, C., Dorner, L., & Heiman, D. (2019). Bilingualism, biliteracy, biculturalism, and critical consciousness for all: Proposing a fourth fundamental goal for two-way dual language education. *Theory Into Practice, 58*(2), 121–133. https://doi.org/10.1080/00405841.2019.1569376

U.S. Department of Education. (2019, October). *Top ten languages spoken by English learners (ELs) in the United States*. https://ncela.ed.gov/files/fast_facts/olea-top-languages-fact-sheet-20191021–508.pdf

U.S. Department of Justice & U.S. Department of Education. (2015). *Dear colleague letter: English learner students and limited English proficient parents*. https://www2.ed.gov/about/offices/list/ocr/letters/colleague-el-201501.pdf

Wall, D. J., Greer, E., & Palmer, D. K. (2019). Exploring institutional processes in a district-wide dual language program: Who is it for? Who is left out? *Journal of Latinos and Education, 21*(1)1–16. https://doi.org/10.1080/15348431.2019.1613996

Walsh, M. (2020). *A prosperous Boston for all: Haitians*. www.bostonplans.org/getattachment/c1a82525-5c19-45d5-8601-ccd51c99e154

3 "We Can Change the Academic Trajectory of Our Children in a Snap"

Developing a High-School Dual Language Program for Spanish-Speaking Students with No Feeder Program

Esmeralda Alday, Olivia Hernández, and Kathryn I. Henderson

Context

> We can change the academic trajectory of our children in a snap. The answer was right here under our nose. We've had these ESL [English as a second language] classes in our secondary schools forever. We have segregated them for a meaningful education with the intent to teach them English so they then would go into their mainstream classes and be successful. We have too much data showing that this will not work. We can teach them in secondary school in their home language and they will outperform their peers.
>
> (Assistant superintendent of Dual Language, ESL, & Migrant Education)

The secondary dual language (DL) program at Brackenridge High School (BHS) in San Antonio's Independent School District (SAISD) program began with a vision. SAISD's student population is 22% English learners, 90% economically disadvantaged, and 90% Latinx, and BHS mirrors those numbers. In 2017, part of the district professional development plan for DL was to provide campus and district leaders with opportunities to visit model DL campuses to see best practices in action. During a visit to Pfarr-San Juan-Alamo ISD (PSJA)—which had been implementing secondary DL for over a decade—Mrs. Cordova, then principal of BHS, decided she was ready to launch a DL program. The program would start with freshmen coming in from feeder middle schools (none of which were designated DL) and other campuses with a high percentage of bilingual students. Mrs. Cordova shared the vision with district leaders that, despite not having DL feeder schools, there were many students that would benefit from a DL program. Her students came from multilingual backgrounds, 21% of students

DOI: 10.4324/9781003240594-5

designated as English learners, the vast majority of whom spoke Spanish. The district was already engaging in a district-wide expansion of DL at the elementary level, and the collective sentiment was that there was no time—and no reason—to wait at the secondary level, especially not with a student population that could gain so much.

Case Narrative

The BHS DL program launched in the fall of 2018 with a cohort of nearly 70 freshmen (out of a typical class of approximately 350). Students came from campuses where they were either being served through an ESL Pullout program or monitored after reclassification. The BHS DL implementation process with no feeder program was led with the support of the district Dual Language, ESL, and Migrant department. District DL support staff included the following: secondary bilingual coordinator, Esmeralda Alday (co-author); DL director, Dr. Mario Ferrón; advanced academic director, Elizabeth Ozuna; DL coordinator, Monica Valderrama; five bilingual specialists; and dual credit coordinator, Dr. Annelise Vela. The DL district staff worked with Mrs. Cordova and enlisted a committee of campus stakeholders to create a timeline for student and family recruitment, professional development, and summer bridge planning. All educators involved in the program implementation engaged in critical consciousness including acts of critical listening, engaging with discomfort, interrogating power, *acompañamiento*, and affirming identities.

How Were Students Recruited? Critical Listening and Engaging With Discomfort

Students were recruited by district DL staff via intensive community outreach, which involved critical listening and engaging with discomfort. The district's Research and Evaluation department provided the DL department a list of all eighth-grade students in the district with a code of "01" (Spanish) on the initial home language survey. The district's DL team made phone calls to parents of these students and coordinated meetings at all 6th–8th grade campuses. Students at each campus took a short Spanish reading test to gauge proficiency. Students who scored proficient at the 50% or above mark were invited to participate.

Some parents and students were excited to receive the opportunity. Most recent immigrants were immediately on board. However, the recruitment process included pushback necessitating critical listening and engaging with discomfort. Many students indicated they had no interest in the DL program or developing their home language in content-area classrooms. A handful of students did not claim Spanish when invited to take the exam, despite their Spanish language heritage. One student threw the test back at the administrator and said, "*¡Que no hablo español! ¡Te digo!* [I told you I don't speak

Spanish!]" Some students appeared to fail the test on purpose. There was some hurt and anger around the question, "Why are you bringing me back now?" In a particularly memorable interaction, one Spanish-speaking parent observed his daughter's resistance to learning Spanish and just lamented that it was too late because she had not had any Spanish through middle school. The recruitment process entailed many side conversations addressing fears and concerns. In order to reach students and parents, district leaders had to own and acknowledge historical injustices in students' schooling experiences.

How Do You Structure a High School DL Program? Interrogation of Power Structures

The BHS DL model offered the students the following four courses in Spanish:

- Biology
- Algebra II
- World Cultures
- Spanish AB

Furthermore, the English I and English II pre-AP class were taught bilingually and explicitly fostered cross-linguistic awareness.

The inclusion of Biology as a core DL class reflected critical consciousness through interrogation of power structures. In short, BHS's DL program changed current policy by ensuring students' access to Biology in ninth grade. Over 50% of the new DL students would not have been eligible for freshman Biology because they had not met the standard on the eighth-grade science State of Texas Assessment of Academic Readiness (STAAR) exam. Failing that exam would have placed students into Environmental Systems instead of Biology. However, students in the DL program were placed into Biology, regardless. Ultimately, 69% of them coded as English learners passed the high-school STAAR Biology exam, despite the fact that the majority of them had not passed that eighth-grade exam.

How to Select and Train Teachers? Acompañamiento

The five teachers selected by Mrs. Cordova were all current Latinx teachers and either immigrants or children of immigrants who embodied *acompañamiento* or the centering of marginalized students to uplift their experiences. Two of them were soccer coaches in addition to being math and social studies teachers and mentioned using Spanish with their students in class and on the field. The Biology teacher (Ms. Orenalas; *testimonio* follows) was already using Spanish to clarify content and provide access to recent arrival students in her classes. The English teacher (Ms. Uribe; *testimonio* follows), like her peers in the program, was the daughter of immigrants and believed strongly in bilingual education. Teachers were provided "Dual Language 101" professional development during late spring and summer before the 2018 fall program launch. Three teachers went back to visit the Pfarr-San Juan-Alamo schools. Teachers received job-embedded coaching with the district's secondary DL coordinator throughout the first year of the program and were offered curriculum writing compensation via extra-duty pay.

Teacher Testimonios*: Affirming Identities*

Ms. Ornelas (DL Biology Teacher)

Ms. Ornelas is the middle daughter of Mexican immigrant parents with four siblings. Her mother is from Coahuila and her father is from Jalisco. Ms. Ornelas was born in Milwaukie, Oregon, but grew up across states wherever there was work for her dad until they settled close to her grandparents in San Antonio. Ms. Ornelas almost was a college dropout until her college Biology professor "*me vino a rescatar* [came to rescue me]" and invited her to participate in a research study in a lab. She views her position as a high-school biology teacher in the same high-stakes way it was to her; a teacher has the power to change a student's life.

Ms. Ornelas was immediately interested in the idea of teaching Biology in Spanish, but it also made her nervous. Ms. Ornelas had been in a transitional bilingual program as a child, and she was exited in elementary school. The summer before teaching, Ms. Ornelas participated in a teacher/research exchange program at Iowa State University. She explained the intensity:

> I would finish working at the lab and I would literally just read it aloud, the Spanish biology book. I was worried about not knowing all the terms and I would just sit on my bed and I would read the book aloud so that I could hear myself and I could practice the pronunciation.

Ms. Ornelas said that everything changed for her when she actually began teaching. The school gave her an extra prep period to work on translations and Spanish Biology materials. She described, "Once it started, I just loved it. It was the best thing that could have happened. It's so different from the other classes." Her first year teaching DL Biology she had students from El Salvador, Honduras, Nicaragua, Mexico, Brazil, and San Antonio; all students were at different levels in both English and Spanish. Her fears teaching such a linguistically diverse class quickly diminished:

> I was a bit nervous *porque dije pos como voy a dar esta clase si todos están en diferentes niveles. Pero en verdad ya cuando estamos en clase, todos se sienten muy agusto. Desarrollamos sistemas para que puedan ayudarse ellos mismos y pues en verdad ha tenido mucho éxito el programa.* [I was a bit nervous

> because I said how am I going to teach this class with everyone at different levels. But really when we are all together in class everyone feels comfortable. We develop systems so that they can help themselves and the truth is the program has had a lot of success].

The program changed her linguistic and professional identity. She explained, "Every single dual language class is always my favorite class, hands down. I like the participation, the culture . . . I don't want to speak English anymore!" She has frustration towards the circulating beliefs about English learners and their abilities. Teaching DL Biology transformed Ms. Ornelas's identity, and she felt the program similarly transformed the scholarly identity of her students:

> This idea behind the student not having the capacity to pass this biology exam is a complete lie. You just need to be there to support them and to guide them because they have it. They are so bright. The dual language program really offers them the opportunity to shine. I'm thankful that I'm able to help facilitate this program because it really helps them see how bright they are and they see that they can be very successful. Some of them have never passed the STAAR exam. There is all of this negativity towards this test because students think 'I'm not going to pass it. I've never passed it' and then they're given this opportunity and they see how successful they can be. It's a huge boost for them.

Ms. Ornelas tried to explain exactly what it is that makes students "shine" in the DL secondary program. It all comes down to giving her students a space with a voice, a space that affirms identities through *acompañamiento*:

> I know that the program is very effective because in my classroom, they are willing to speak up. I can literally see it within the school year, even within the day. When I go to the restroom, I'd see them (her students) in another class, and they're quiet. They're quiet. They're just sitting there like "*no, pos,* Miss, *ni entiendo,* I don't understand [no, well, Miss, I don't even understand, I don't understand]." It's upsetting to see that because it's literally night and day. You see them in my class and they're so energetic and they're so happy to be here, and they have that sense of community and they feel *bien agusto* [very comfortable]. What do they need to shine? I feel like they need that space, I feel like they need the support, and the encouragement.

Ms. Uribe (Dual Language English 1 & pre-AP English 2)

Ms. Uribe is a first-generation Mexican American. Her parents are both from Jalisco, Mexico. She grew up in California and San Antonio and is trying to embrace a Chicana identity. Ms. Uribe is the first person in her family to graduate from high school and go to college. Similarly to Ms. Ornelas, Ms. Uribe said it was her English teacher in high school that prevented her from dropping out and developing her love for linguistics. She is currently doing a master's program for English with a concentration in rhetoric and composition.

When Ms. Uribe was told about the DL program during a faculty meeting, she reacted strongly: "I need to do this. I want to be part of this. I had no idea what dual language was. I'm bilingual, dual language sounds great." Immediately following the meeting, she approached the associate principal who signed Ms. Uribe up for summer training. At the start of the new school year, she began teaching dual-language pre-AP English 2.

Similarly to Ms. Ornelas, Ms. Uribe described teaching in the DL program as transformational because of how participating in the program affirms identities and creates community through *acompañamiento*. She explained:

> The first day that I had class, you already feel like family. It doesn't matter if they're from Mexico or Honduras. I had Ryan who is from Brazil and there's already like this rapport that is unspoken. I don't even know how to explain it, you just, it's almost trust. You kind of trust the students more. They trust me knowing that we have similar backgrounds. Right? Maybe. I didn't immigrate from another country like they did, but my parents did and I understand a little bit of what that's like. And to speak Spanish when they don't feel comfortable speaking English.

Ms. Uribe felt that this trust and vulnerability directly connected to linguistic flexibility or translanguaging in the class. Ms. Uribe agreed with Ms. Ornelas that the students in her DL classroom participated and spoke more than they did in their non-dual language classes:

> Speaking is always the back burner out of the four modes of language, and so, in the classroom, being able to speak—acknowledging that even if they answer in Spanish that "yes, that's correct," instead of saying "sorry I didn't understand you, so you're getting it wrong"—being able to understand them in both languages, and that they can be correct in both, is just very powerful.

The powerful classroom community and experiences Ms. Uribe has built with her DL students has made her a strong advocate and believer in the program. She explained how it is the structure of DL that she believes makes them able to succeed:

> It's just the opportunity to be in a dual language classroom. A lot of these students would typically be placed in ESL. To be in the same classroom as students who speak more English or to be put in a Pre-AP class,

like, just a class being labeled Pre-AP. "What am I doing in a Pre-AP class when I was in the back room in ESL?" . . . I guess it's the structure of the program . . . making the students know that their knowledge, whatever it may be, whether they have schooling, traditional schooling, or not . . . just giving them that power. Letting them know they have that power, not giving them it, they already possess it.

Teaching Notes

Research highlights the academic and sociocultural benefits of secondary DL programs (Faltis & Ramirez-Marin, 2015; Przymus, 2016; Salerno & Kibler, 2017), but additional research is needed. This chapter describes the creation of a high school DL program with no feeder program that began with a shared vision and critically conscious educators at the school and district levels. The district Dual Language, ESL, and Migrant department staff members were able to assist in recruiting students, providing professional development, and training/supporting teachers. The teacher's *testimonios* illustrated the impact. Ms. Ornelas and Ms. Uribe taught different content areas in a different target language, and yet, their stories overlapped. For both teachers the program was transformational for their teaching identities and teaching in the DL program became their favorite part of their job. Ms. Ornelas expressed no longer wanting to teach in English and Ms. Uribe felt a sense of community and vulnerability with her DL students that she did not feel with other classes.

Ms. Ornelas and Ms. Uribe both described the DL program as transformational because students had a voice in their classrooms. They both expressed that this did not happen in other classrooms. The explanation of student participation was directly connected to linguistic flexibility and students' opportunities to draw on their full linguistic repertoire or translanguaging. Substantial research affirms that power of linguistic flexibility for positive student academic experiences (García, 2009; Durán & Henderson, 2018), and the teacher *testimonios* in this chapter support this research.

Furthermore, the *testimonios* of Ms. Ornelas and Ms. Uribe illuminate the potential for secondary DL programs to disrupt and challenge the negative academic identities English learners and bilingual students have developed over years of schooling that label and position them in deficient ways (Valdés, 2001; Valenzuela, 2010). Both teachers described their classroom as a place where newcomers, immigrants, and heritage speakers "shined." Students in their classrooms shifted their academic identity from "never passing the STARR" to "passing the Biology STARR" as well as from "long-term English learner" to "Pre-AP English." Students carry these labels and experiences with them as both Ms. Ornelas and Ms. Uribe—both almost school dropouts had it not been for an invested teacher—can attest. Through critically conscious actions, teachers can transform spaces for emerging bilingual students.

Discussion Questions

1. Reflect on the context and case narrative: what stakeholders were involved in implementing a high school DL program with no feeder program? What would happen if one of these stakeholders did not support the DL program? Do you think the program could be implemented without the support from one of these stakeholders? Why or why not?
2. The DL high school program started with a vision by the principal. What is your vision for critically conscious school programming in your context? What could be one step that would work in the direction of this vision?
3. Ms. Ornelas and Ms. Uribe created classroom spaces in which culturally and linguistically students had voices and "shined." How was this afforded by the DL program? Could the teachers have created this classroom space without the DL program? How and in what ways?

References

Durán, L., & Henderson, K. I. (2018). Pockets of hope: Cases of linguistic flexibility in the classroom. *EuroAmerican Journal of Applied Linguistics and Languages, 5*(2), 76–90. https://doi.org/10.21283/2376905X.9.156

Faltis, C., & Ramirez-Marin, F. (2015). Secondary bilingual education: Cutting the gordian knot. In W. Wright, S. Boun, & O. Garcia (Eds.), *Handbook of bilingual and multilingual education* (pp. 336–353). Wiley-Blackwell.

García, O. (2009). *Bilingual education in the 21st century. A global perspective*. Wiley-Blackwell.

Przymus, S. D. (2016). Challenging the monolingual paradigm in secondary dual-language instruction: Reducing language-as-problem with the 2-1-L2 model. *Bilingual Research Journal, 39*(3–4), 279–295. https://doi.org/10.1080/15235882.2016.1220995

Salerno, A. S., & Kibler, A. K. (2017). Building bridges: A dual-language experience for high-school students. In E. Barbian, G. C. Gonzales, & P. Mejía (Eds.), *Rethinking bilingual education: Welcoming home languages in our classrooms* (pp. 136–142). Rethinking Schools.

Valdés, G. (2001). *Learning and not learning English: Latino students in American schools*. Teachers College Press.

Valenzuela, A. (2010). *Subtractive schooling: US-Mexican youth and the politics of caring*. SUNY Press.

4 Centering Immigrant Voices and Experiences in a Dual Language Bilingual School

Teachers as Critical Pedagogues and Policymakers

Dina López and Tatyana Kleyn

Context

Entre Mundos (Between Worlds, a pseudonym) is a public elementary school in New York City (NYC). The school is housed in a bustling neighborhood that is full of bodegas, street vendors selling treats that range from empanadas to tamales de mole y pollo to fresh cut mangoes and stores whose wares spill over into the sidewalks. The aromatic smells of delicious foods and fruits intermingle with the pungent exhaust trailing behind city cabs and buses. The neighborhood moves to the beat of reggaeton, cumbia, and bachata that's played on the streets and escapes open apartment windows, the sounds of dominoes being slammed onto folding tables and businesses proudly displaying flags from Mexico, the Dominican Republic, and Puerto Rico. Spanish can be heard more than English, and if you listen closely, you will hear Arabic, Mixteco, and Russian mixed into the local soundscape. Spanish and English are the two most visible languages; storefront posters promote local candidates as well as information about elections that take place abroad for people who hold (dual) citizenship in their countries of origin and participate in politics across borders.

But things are changing in this multilingual and multiethnic immigrant-origin community of mostly Brown and Black people. There are more white people moving into the neighborhood, people whose ways of speaking, eating, and living in the community differs from the largely Latinx population that has been there for decades. Stores have started popping up that are not reflective of the local culture, since they simultaneously displace local businesses who are not able to pay the increasing rents. The same has happened with family housing units, where long-time locals are being pushed out after their lease expires and rents are inflated out of their range.

The gentrification of the neighborhood is not surprisingly making its way into Entre Mundos elementary school. Although it is predominantly made up of Latinx and Afro-Latinx students (85%) with a small percentage of

DOI: 10.4324/9781003240594-6

Asian and African American Black students (5%), there is a growing number of white students who attend the school (10%). Entre Mundos is unique compared to many schools in NYC that house a bilingual program, in that the entire building (Pre-K to grade 5) is a dual language bilingual school. Within this approach, it is the norm for everyone to become bilingual and biliterate, with students who come from multilingual homes, or with mainly Spanish or English-speaking families. This environment creates opportunities for students to not only learn *about* people from different backgrounds, but to learn *with* them as well. However, it also creates a context in which societal inequities can make their way into classroom lessons, which can result in some families experiencing discomfort with discussing real world issues that impact certain students and community members more than others.

Case Narrative

The curriculum at Entre Mundos is one that develops critical consciousness and is responsive to issues that are relevant to their larger community. This includes discussing difficult topics, even with younger students, in age-appropriate ways. Teachers at Entre Mundos have created units on anti-racism and the Black Lives Matter movement, translanguaging and linguicism, and LGBTQ+ communities. These thematic units encompass the core subject areas as well as art, dance, and technology. During the Trump administration, the teachers knew that they needed to address immigration issues with their students. Some students and their families were living the consequences of the anti-immigrant policies while others were hearing about them on the news, unclear as to why such things could be happening. Responding to this national context, local experiences, and questions from their students, the first-grade teacher team came together to plan a unit on current immigration issues.

The unit centered the stories of immigrant families who were in the US from different parts of the world. The classes read about undocumented, mixed-status, and refugee families. They tracked the journeys of the people in the books on a large map in their classroom and identified the languages they spoke too. They listed the different reasons people came to the US and discussed the difficult journey many made to arrive in this new land via land, water, and air. They talked about the treatment immigrants received when they looked and sounded different from others, and how policies or rules on how immigrant belonging didn't always seem fair, and sometimes seemed wrong. Some even shared about the migration experiences they or their families had lived through, whereas others didn't feel comfortable to share (and weren't forced to do so either).

One of the stories read to the first graders in Mx.[1] B's class was *Mama's Nightingale: A Story of Immigration and Separation* by Edwidge Danticat (2015). It is about a mixed-status Haitian family in the US. The mother, who did not have papers, was detained at her job and sent to an immigrant detention center. Her young daughter, Saya, became distraught about her mother being taken away and held in a prison-like setting. Saya and her father were able to visit weekly. They wrote letters to push for her mother's release and freedom. As Mx. B read the book, they paused to ask questions, but also allowed students to share their connections. One child shared that they had a very similar experience with their father, who was also taken away by the "immigration police" because they weren't allowed to be in the US. They shared how hard that was, how it made them very sad, and how much they missed their father. They also shared how angry it made them that their father was being treated so badly in the place where he lived and worked. Other students who hadn't lived a similar experience shared empathy for Saya and their classmates in similar situations because their parents do so much to take care of them, play with them, and love them every day. Mx. B had students think about why the rules allow some people to belong while punishing others in the same communities who are also living their lives.

The next morning when Mx. B—a US-born, mixed-race Latinx and white teacher—was picking up their class at the courtyard to start the day; a parent asked to speak with them privately. They were able to have their paraprofessional take the class up to the classroom while they engaged in a brief conversation with the mother, who shared that her daughter was very upset by the story that the class had read the day before. Her child came home afraid that her mother would be taken away. As a result, she demanded that books that addressed difficult topics such as family separation and immigration detention not be read to the first graders. She didn't want her daughter exposed to such topics and would escalate her concerns if Mx. B did not agree with her request. Mx. B reflected on the background of this parent, a white, middle-class woman who was born in the US. Then they contrasted this with the student in their class who sat right next to this woman's child and not only had to listen to this story but lived this experience with her father. Mx. B thought about the inequity of how immigration policies tear some families apart while other families object to the telling of these experiences for fear of upsetting their children whose privilege protects them from these realities.

Mx. B listened to this parent, but then explained that teaching children to be part of a society is not about shielding them from difficult realities but explaining them in ways that help young children make sense of the world. They told the mother they would continue to teach immigration in ways that address real-world issues—which are being lived by her child's peers in the class—so that her daughter and others would be better prepared for the world that awaits them. Mx. B wanted all their students to know that some people have to struggle in ways that others do not because of differences in migration status, language, race, gender, and more. And they recommended that the parent remind her child that because they are US-born citizens who are also white, their family is not at risk of being detained.

The response of Mx. B was not what the parent wanted to hear, and as a result they reached out to the principal to continue to demand that books such as *Mama's Nightingale* be cut from the school's curriculum. However, the principal also took a firm stance that the role of the schools is not to shield students from the world, but to prepare them to critically engage with privilege and inequity. The principal also called a faculty meeting to share these concerns and how gentrification was changing not only the faces in their school, but how families responded to Entre Mundos's responsive and critically conscious curriculum. A school-wide decision was made to put out a statement about their stance on bringing in current issues that may be contentious or difficult into their classrooms for students to address through age-appropriate and thoughtful approaches. Mx. B led the development of this statement, which was translated into the languages of the families and posted on the school's website and on a bulletin board at the school entryway to make the school's stance clear to all in their learning community.

Teaching Notes

Teachers as Policymakers

Policy-as-practice scholarship has troubled the notion that the investigation of policy is merely an analysis of policy texts. It shifts analytical attention to the interaction and intersections between texts and the actors who interpret and give meaning to them across educational contexts (Levinson et al., 2009). In the case of dual language bilingual education, it means that school leaders, teachers, and families should be seen as important policy actors who may be interpreting and enacting policies in diverse and unanticipated ways. Valdiviezo's (2009) work examines local teachers' responses to national bilingual and intercultural education (BIE) policy in Indigenous Quechua communities in Peru. She found that teachers' beliefs and practices "often replicated the contradictions and exclusionary ideologies present in official BIE policy discourse" (p. 161), but teachers also critiqued official policy and appropriated it in innovative and creative ways that "used indigenous worldviews as teaching resources" (p. 158). In a US-based qualitative study, Dorner (2011) brings to light the ways in which immigrant families and community members participated in local debates about dual language education, and ultimately, how mostly white English-dominant participants succeeded in making their voices heard to persuade policymakers to enact their preference of dual language class implementation throughout the district, rather than in specific sites as advocated by immigrant families. Dorner's research illustrates how these programs are inextricably bound up with issues of power, language, identity, and what local actors value vis-à-vis schooling.

According to the NYC Department of Education, the goal of dual language programs is "for students to learn how to speak, read, understand, and write in two languages, and also learn about and appreciate other cultures"

(NYCDOE, 2021). This mandate is taken up very differently across programs throughout the city. For school leaders and teachers at Entre Mundos, the mission of their bilingual school encompasses a critical understanding of power and the centering of immigrant families and students in their curriculum. Mx. B's decisions about the authentic literature they would use—to not only engage in meaningful literacy practices, but also discuss an important issue that affect many of their immigrant-origin students—reflect a particular interpretation of policy and what it means to be a bilingual teacher. Their response to a white middle-class parent's discomfort with their curricular choices illuminates how bilingual teachers negotiate policies across educational contexts and bring them to life in their classrooms (Menken & García, 2010; Varghese & Stritikus, 2005).

Developing Critical Consciousness and Embracing Discomfort

Entre Mundos is a bilingual school committed to addressing issues of community gentrification through a critical and transformative curriculum that not only develops the bilingualism and biliteracy of its students, but also their critical consciousness—all within an approach that centers the voices and lived experiences of immigrant and minoritized students and families. Within the context of dual language bilingual education, Palmer et al. (2019) have elaborated four key elements of critical consciousness: interrogating power, historicizing schools, critical listening, and embracing discomfort. We will use this framework to understand the policy and curriculum decisions made by Mx. B, their colleagues, and the principal at Entre Mundos.

The project of education is never neutral and always political (Freire, 1970). Thus, if dual language programs are to support equity, then an interrogation of power relations and how they manifest at the school and classroom level is imperative. Since its founding, Entre Mundos has always been committed to social justice, but the 2016 US presidential election brought these issues to the fore since a large percentage of their students were deeply affected by the ensuing anti-immigrant rhetoric, government raids, deportation, and family separation. During this time, the school made the decision to support their most vulnerable students in holistic ways, while also taking the opportunity to draw on their experiences and elevate their voices within the curriculum. The first-grade unit on immigration was a result of thoughtful, responsive, and critical dialogue among teachers and families. In addition to interrogating power, this called for a historicizing of narratives of immigration from the perspective of local communities and shedding light on the legacy of US colonialism and racism.

According to Palmer et al. (2019), "Critical listening seeks to engage students, educators, and families with others for meaningful and transformative connection, and it embodies a relation of curiosity and attention, sharing, caring, reciprocity, and responsivity toward others" (p. 126). Mx B's choice of text, *Mama's Nightingale*, for their first-grade bilingual classroom read aloud was based on this kind of critical listening to their students' concerns, and experiences during a particularly terrifying time for undocumented and mixed-status immigrant families. The book was used as a problem-posing prompt to generate meaningful dialogue among all their first-grade students and though the discussion was inclusive of all students' perspectives, the focus was on understanding the impact of family separation from an immigrant child's perspective.

The ways in which Mx. B responded to a white parent's complaints about this text illustrates how bilingual teachers can productively engage with and embrace the discomfort that can result from interrogating power and challenging the status quo through their pedagogy. Much research has pointed to the importance of critical approaches to education, but the reality of what this means for teachers who take a firm stance is often missing. The pushback from privileged families who often feel entitled to a prominent voice can put pressure on teachers to accommodate their requests or compromise their principles. We believe this aspect of developing critical consciousness—embracing discomfort—is understudied and underappreciated, particularly within the context of dual language bilingual education. Problematizing white supremacy will likely be uncomfortable for those in positions of privilege, but highly necessary for ensuring equitable practice (Burns, 2017). It is important to note that the unwavering support from their principal was a key factor in Mx. B's confidence in their response and firmness in their political and pedagogical stance. The teacher's actions led to a whole-school conversation, which then led to sharing with the wider learning community. Thus, school leaders must be willing to make their commitment to equity and social justice explicit and must stand behind and beside their teachers.

Discussion Questions

This case can help bilingual educators and school leaders think critically about the overarching goals of their programming, the ways in which they enact policies in their local school environments, how immigrant students and families are positioned and participate in school activities, and how the curriculum relates to broader community issues. Specifically, the case highlights the role of the teacher in engaging in critical literacy activities that center the voices of immigrant-origin students and how they productively deal with pushback from a white middle-class parent.

1. This case took place during a turbulent historical moment in the wake of the 2016 US presidential election. However, immigration has always been a politically contentious issue in this country that has affected bilingual education in multiple ways. Think about your local community as you answer the following questions:

    a. How do immigration issues figure into the local history and public discourse?

   b. What are the dominant narratives of immigration that prevail?
   c. How are immigrant families and communities positioned in these narratives?
   d. What is the relationship between immigration and what happens in schools?

2. In this case, the teacher used a developmentally appropriate and relevant story about immigration to engage their first-grade class in a discussion about issues that were affecting many students including detention, deportation, and family separation.

   a. Do you think first graders are too young to be discussing these issues? Why or why not?
   b. In addition to a read-aloud, what are other ways a teacher might engage in critical consciousness raising with their students?

3. Mx. B's response to a white middle-class parent's complaint about the text was firm and confident. Not all bilingual teachers would have responded this way.

   a. How do you think other bilingual teachers might have responded? Why?
   b. What do you think "embracing discomfort" would look like in your own educational setting? What are the possible opportunities? What are the possible challenges?

4. The teachers and families at Entre Mundos have the support of a principal who is committed to equity and social justice. As a result of Mx. B's interaction with this parent, the school put out a unifying statement on their stance on addressing relevant contemporary issues that impact their school community—regardless of how contentious they are—through classroom instruction.

   a. How else might school leaders support bilingual teachers in developing critical consciousness through their instruction?
   b. What kind of professional development is needed for bilingual teachers to effectively and confidently engage in this kind of equity-oriented practice?

Note

1. Mx. is an honorific that is used by individuals who do not associate with a specific gender in place of Ms., Mrs., or Mr.

References

Burns, M. (2017). "Compromises that we make": Whiteness in the dual language context. *Bilingual Research Journal, 40*(4), 339–352.

Danticat, E. (2015). *Mama's nightingale: A story of immigration and separation.* Dial Books.

Dorner, L. M. (2011). Contested communities in a debate over dual language education: The import of "public" values on public policies. *Educational Policy, 25*(4), 577–613.

Freire, P. (1970). *Pedagogy of the oppressed.* Continuum International Publishing Group.

Levinson, B. A. U., Sutton, M., & Winstead, T. (2009). Education policy as a practice of power: Theoretical tools, ethnographic methods, democratic options. *Educational Policy, 23*(6), 767–795.

Menken, K., & García, O. (Eds.). (2010). *Negotiating language education policies: Educators as policymakers.* Routledge.

New York City Department of Education. (2021, August 13). *Programs for English learners.* www.schools.nyc.gov/learning/multilingual-learners/programs-for-english-language-learners

Palmer, D. K., Cervantes-Soon, C., Dorner, L., & Heiman, D. (2019, January 1). Bilingualism, biliteracy, biculturalism, and critical consciousness for all: Proposing a fourth fundamental goal for two-way dual language education. *Theory into Practice, 58*(2), 121–133.

Valdiviezo, L. (2009). Bilingual intercultural education in indigenous schools: An ethnography of teacher interpretations of government policy. *International Journal of Bilingual Education and Bilingualism, 12*(1), 61–79.

Varghese, M., & Stritikus, T. (2005). "Nadie me dijó [Nobody told me]": Language policy negotiation and implications for teacher education. *Journal of Teacher Education, 56*(1), 73–87.

5 "Shifting Lenses Instead of Always Grinding Forward"

Using Ethnography to Challenge Raciolinguistic Ideologies in Dual Language Education

Karla Venegas, Nelson Flores, and Jennifer Phuong

Context

This case study draws from a nine-year-long ethnographic study at Dual Language Charter School (DLCS), a K–8 school with the explicit goal of graduating students that are bilingual and biliterate in English and Spanish. The school was created in collaboration with a local community organization and is located in a low-income, hypersegregated, and longstanding Latinx neighborhood of Philadelphia. In line with the broader neighborhood demographic, almost all of the students are Latinx and/or Black with about a quarter of the student population classified as English learners (ELs). Because the community is a longstanding bilingual community, most of the students come to the school with at least some exposure to bilingualism from their community. This makes it difficult to characterize the school as two-way in the sense that it is challenging to clearly demarcate students as "English-dominant" or "Spanish-dominant." Simultaneously, it is also difficult to characterize as developmental bilingual education since many of the students are characterized by their teachers as "English-dominant," despite having a range of bilingual competencies.

The in-between status, which we—as community research partners—have tried to capture with school staff and collectively dubbed the "1.5-way," offers unique challenges that lie at the nexus of one- and two-way programs. On the one hand, they confront some of the challenges of one-way programs that serve racialized bilingual students in which questions are often raised as to whether "these students"—typically labeled as "ELs"—should be developing bilingualism rather than focusing on English. On the other hand, the linguistic heterogeneity of their classrooms that include students with a range of previous experiences with both English and Spanish aligns with the typical expectations of a two-way program. Ultimately, without existing models to inform their program—and in relation to broader national discourses that often position two-way programs as the gold standard for bilingual education—the school sought to shape itself as a two-way program. To this effect, the school assessment policies and practices

DOI: 10.4324/9781003240594-7

sorted students as either "English-dominant" or "Spanish-dominant." This effort to align school policies to dominant notions of what two-way programs "should be" inadvertently erased students' dynamic bilingualism and perpetuated discourses of languagelessness across the school. Labeling students as dominant in one language suggested that many students were not dominant in *any* language, with one such category being students who were simultaneously classified as English learners and English-dominant (Flores et al., 2020).

As researchers who are interested in challenging raciolinguistic ideologies that frame the language practices of Latinx and other racialized students as deficient and in need of remediation (Flores & Rosa, 2015), we were troubled by these discourses of languagelessness. We were also troubled by our complicity in reproducing them through our use of the student categorizations in our conversations with teachers and school leaders. We began to think about ways we could use the ethnographic data that we had collected as part of our collaboration with the school to challenge these raciolinguistic ideologies. For us, ethnographic data involved the process of collecting (counter)stories, *testimonios* (Bernal et al., 2012), moments of joy (Love, 2019), language stories (España & Herrera, 2020), and moments of complexity and discomfort (hooks, 2001). We recognized how engaging in this data would propel us and the school to enact our shared commitment to affirming, building on, and extending students' existing cultural and linguistic knowledge and genius (Muhammad, 2020). We reflected on the practice it would take collectively—and as co-intellectuals—to use the rich narratives embedded in the data to (re)imagine new ways of listening to the language practices of our bilingual Latinx students.

In the following, we describe a leadership meeting, which was our first attempt at engaging in this conversation. Although we didn't name it at the time, we were collectively seeking to enact critical consciousness and would soon engage in a praxis cycle that would require us to critically listen and engage with discomfort so that we might move toward policies that captured the fluid bilingualism of Latinx students in ways that institutions have never been designed to do.

Case Narrative

Our meeting with the DLCS leadership team has been on the books for weeks now. Children and adults are milling about the lobby, as the school safety team orchestrates this last part of the day. Our team (Nelson, Karla, and Jenn) weaves our way through the lobby and into the main office, which is bustling with copiers going and phones ringing. Conversations weave in, through, and across Spanish and English. All in all, it is a typical Thursday afternoon dismissal.

The school principal waves us over and into the conference room where the school leadership team is busy opening laptops, responding to calls on their walkies, and chatting about the day. The leadership team includes

Marcy (the CEO), Yesenia (Principal), Hester (Dean of Language Services), and Matt (Assistant Principal). For the past four years, members of our research team have observed eight focal students who are now in fourth grade and have had the opportunity to create case studies on each student based teacher interviews and detailed notes on their language practices.

After introductions we dive into an activity that asks us to critically listen and interrogate whose bilingualism is valued and why. We begin the conversation by discussing a meme that applauds the bilingualism of Princess Charlotte. This activity sparks conversation because of how blatantly it shows that society values certain types of bilingualism over others and certain bilinguals over others. Although this activity is brief, it prompts moments of collective discomfort and outrage as we listen for, recognize, and name whose voices are silenced and erased by this meme—namely the stark juxtaposition of the praise that the princess receives for speaking two languages at the age of two and the institutionalized policies that seek to erase the bilingualism of our Latinx bilinguals when they show up in kindergarten. In retrospect, this activity serves as our entry point into enacting critical consciousness in that it primes us to critically listen.

For the next part of our conversation we share with the leadership team quotes from teachers describing three focal students who are classified as both English learners and English-dominant. We ask the leadership team to use the three guiding questions as a way to reflect on the quotes pulled from the case study of the three focal students:

1. How are the language practices/bilingualism of the student being discussed by teachers?
2. What factors might be influencing the way they speak about the student?
3. What implications does this have for you in your role as a school leader?

Case Study #1: "A Spanglish kid"—Javier

> "I can always see a million wheels spinning in his head, and I feel like they are like English and Spanish all spin together, and that's why [communication] is harder for him."
>
> (06/12/2015)

> "I'm pretty sure from the last IEP meeting, they were saying that it could be either one, the speech is making it, that he's saying it, out of order, or the fact that it's the Spanish going into English. So they're not really sure which one it is. It could be both."
>
> (06/08/2018)

Jenn reads the quotes in this text box from an interview with Javier's kindergarten and fourth grade teacher respectively. She then leaves space for folks to reflect and respond. Marcy begins the conversation. She states the teacher seems to be implying that students in a dual language school have a harder time developing communication skills because of the two languages. She follows up by saying this is a narrative she has heard from Javier's teachers since kindergarten, and more broadly, this is a narrative she hears from many teachers daily. She adds teachers often seem invested in the narrative that their Latinx student population have a hard time receiving instruction in two languages and wind up being "low" in both languages. She asks the team what actions they think it would take to change the school culture away from the narrative that "this two-languages thing is too confusing for these kids." After a pause she remarks, "Ultimately, how do we influence the bigger conversation so that we don't feel like outliers when we talk like that?"

Her questions are far from rhetorical. Through her questions she is helping her team recognize that enacting critical consciousness requires critical listening. She is inviting her leadership team to critically listen as a way to recognize and name the narrow ways in which broader language education policies frame the bilingualism of their students. She is asking her team to develop the ability to challenge deficitizing narratives through action (Hornberger & Cassels Johnson, 2010). And she is holding space for the concerns, contradictions, and complexities that arise when you challenge dominant narratives in ways that position you as an "outlier."

Case Study #2: "She's not perfectly there yet"—Alejandra

Alejandra's reading level "[was] actually above what she [was] supposed to be at for English" (Interview, 06/08/2018).

> "Alejandra is really amazing how, it's (Spanish) clearly not her first language and she's like on level."
>
> (Interview, 06/12/2015)

> "Alejandra must have not passed (the English learner reclassification test), because the test must have had a lot of inferential learning and maybe she just wasn't there yet in third grade but hopefully after this year she'll be there for that? But I don't know. **She's not perfectly there yet.**"
>
> (Interview, 06/08/2018)

To continue the conversation, we introduce more quotes, about another student, Alejandra. Hester, the dean of language, begins the reflection process more cautiously. She wonders if teachers have a lack of knowledge or understanding of what it means to be an "EL" and, therefore, take on a deficit mindset as default. For example, in the quote in the text box, Alejandra's fourth-grade teachers are simultaneously saying she is reading above grade level in English and in Spanish and yet rationalize why she has not tested out of her EL designation, specifically pointing to her inability to make inferences. Yesenia, the school principal, lingers on "not perfectly there yet" and points out that there almost seems to be a "finish line" teachers are striving for but states "it's like a finish line that keeps moving." While literacy assessments deem Alejandra right on track for the finish line, the reclassification exam moves the finish line to an unknown location that has nothing to do with her language practices nor does it even account for her dynamic bilingualism.

After more conversation, Hester articulates, "I think as a whole, like being an EL, having that label in our system is a deficit." Hester is calling attention to a very specific and poignant way in which race and language has and continues to be co-constructed within the US schooling system in ways that frame the bilingualism of Latinxs and other racialized communities as deficient and in need of remediation. Teachers are expected to get students to the finish line. Yet, even though those finish lines don't exist, the narrative of their existence continues to be peddled as the sole narrative available for teachers to rely on and gaslights educators who begin to see the contradictions in the policies. Marcy wonders out loud what it would take to break the hold these narratives have on teachers. She is asking how we might transform the discourses of languagelessness that shape the education of Latinx students to capture their fluid bilingualism regardless of what institutional categories might suggest.

A member of the leadership team jumps in to say, "Yeah, teachers need to get better at not thinking these negative things about their students." As the conversation begins to head into the realm of teacher-blaming, Yesenia stepped in to remind her team that it is their responsibility to support teachers in developing alternative narratives to describe their students. Nelson iterates this by pointing out that the classification of "English-dominant English learner" would be confusing for anyone. He suggests they begin to work on developing new narratives by taking a closer look at the language practices of their students. In turn, the research team introduces data collected of a focal student during their literacy block the previous week.

In the first example, Karla asks Dominic, a fourth-grade focal student, in Spanish, what he's up to and he responds by saying, "I was just drawing. I'm about to draw . . . wait wait what is this? *Un charco* (a puddle)." Then Karla asks him what else he drew; he says, "*Un rio*," and goes on to read the descriptor of *el rio*: "*Un rio es un desembolcan . . . no . . . una corupta de agua que va a desembocar en un lago o mar* (a river is a body of water that empties into a lake or the ocean)." Then he quickly takes more interest in Karla's soccer jersey and asks her, "Miss is this a jersey?" Karla explains that it is a "*futbol*" (soccer) jersey asking him if he knows about "*futbol*" (soccer). He responds, "I don't play," but another classmate interrupts to say, "Yeah you do play, you play American football." Dominic defensively responds, "Yes, I play that," in a tone that implies he is annoyed that she didn't recognize he meant he didn't play "*futbol*," as in soccer.

The leadership team erupts into excited conversation because they immediately identify the student and are genuinely intrigued by his understanding of *futbol*, football, and soccer and his ability to communicate with the research team member. Dominic is one of the small number of Black students in the dual language program. He is typically positioned, as observed through copious fieldnotes, conversations, and interviews, as not knowing any Spanish despite being part of the dual language program since kindergarten. In student interviews, he also positions himself as solely an English speaker.

Matt comments that this particular student routinely finds ways to evade the classroom during Spanish instruction. He states that this student often and adamantly proclaims the reason he "acts out" during Spanish class is because he doesn't understand Spanish and can't speak it "the right way." A quizzical look takes over Matt's face and he states how ridiculous it is to continue to assume Dominic doesn't understand Spanish in light of what they just heard. He wonders where Dominic picked up the notion that he doesn't fit the image of what a Spanish-speaking emerging bilingual student looks and sounds like. In response, Hester contemplates how collecting more examples of dynamic language would help illustrate the vibrant language practices of all their students, including students, like Dominic, whose bilingualism is commonly overlooked and discounted. She proposes this process would help shift the assumption that their students are always lacking in some way.

Yesenia lets out a sigh and states that this sort of shift would be dependent on "how willing we are to facilitate a conversation like this one that might shift our perspective but also it might be uncomfortable." Hester, as if speaking to the work this shift would require, asserts, *Right—shifting lenses instead of just grinding forward.*

Yesenia's sigh and Hester's assertion speak to a collective understanding in the room that engaging with student data in this way necessitates engaging with our own discomfort. We witness a collective understanding of Dominic's complex and dynamic language practices. We witness Matt describe Dominic as someone only known for his recurrent behavior issues during Spanish class and in the same breath recognizes how dynamic Dominic's understanding of Spanish truly is. Finally, we witness Hester engage with moments of discomfort as she asks what their role might be in collecting new data that captures more examples of these language practices. This speaks to the realization that they have been missing out on opportunities to listen for and leverage the translanguaging practices of students like

Dominic. This is especially poignant because reimagining new school policies involves admitting and leaning into the discomfort that the way current policies describe students is negligent. Bilingual school leaders are supposed to be data-driven instructional leaders; therefore, recognizing that the data on which they so often rely is limited and does not work to affirm or leverage the practices of their students is understandably uncomfortable.

Hester's comment about shifting lenses instead of grinding forward speaks to the action that engaging with discomfort ultimately requires. We collectively recognize the awkward, messy, uncomfortable commitment it would require to change school policies that have long worked to modify and obscure the dynamic bilingualism of children. However, in that discomfort there is joy in imagining new possibilities.

Teaching Notes

This case study provides a window into the educational landscape that school leaders of racialized bilinguals navigate. This landscape holds school leaders accountable to outcomes and metrics rooted in raciolinguistic ideologies that frame the language practices of Latinx bilingual students as inherently deficient and in need of remediation while positioning them as complicit in enacting these oppressive and dehumanizing policies and practices (Venegas et al., 2021). Yet, this case study also provides a lens into the work of school leaders who are willing to leverage ethnographic data as a way to call out and begin to challenge pervasive mainstream discourses that harm racialized bilinguals.

Javier's institutional designation of EL and literacy assessments position him as someone with language skills that are "low" in both English and Spanish—speaking to raciolinguistic ideologies that frame bilingual Latinx children as languageless. Alejandra's dynamic language practices and her English and Spanish literacy assessment achievements are incompatible with her institutional designation of English learner—speaking to raciolinguistic ideologies that frame bilingual Latinx children as perpetually deficient despite clear evidence to the contrary. Dominic's conversation with Karla shows how dynamic and complex his language practices are, yet he does not see himself and or is seen by others as someone who can be bilingual—speaking to raciolinguistic ideologies that frame the bilingualism of Black children as unintelligible or unfathomable. By using ethnographic data, the researchers and school leaders in this space are able to name these pervasive raciolinguistic ideologies and begin to grapple with what actions would be necessary to challenge the policies that perpetuate these discourses. While gathering and discussing ethnographic data will not fundamentally transform the pervasive discourses of languagelessness, deficit, and erasure, it is a way to begin to create new ways of listening for the dynamic language practices of our students of color.

Teaching Activities

Activity #1: Whose Bilingualism Matters?

Compare and contrast the following six news headlines and accompanying images at the links that follow. Take note of what is resonating with you and what questions are emerging. Use the following questions to discuss.

- What do you notice about the way in which bilingualism is discussed?
- Where do you think these ideas about bilingualism come from?
- In what ways do you see or think that these same ideologies are embedded in educational policies and practices in your school or in other educational contexts you've experienced?

Headline #1: "Princess Charlotte can already speak two languages—at age TWO" www.mirror.co.uk/news/uk-news/princess-charlotte-can-already-speak-11848448

Chapter 5—Venegas—QR Code 5-1

Headline #2: "Princess Charlotte is Already Bilingual at Age Two" www.independent.co.uk/life-style/princess-charlotte-bilingual-spanish-speaking-age-two-a8156511.html

Chapter 5—Venegas—QR Code 5-2

Headline #3: "Princess Charlotte Is 'So Polite and Very Confident,' Says Source—and Speaks Some Spanish!"

https://people.com/royals/princess-charlotte-is-so-polite-and-very-confident-says-source-and-speaks-some-spanish/

Chapter 5—Venegas—QR Code 5–3

Headline #4: "Two friends speaking Spanish were told to speak English"
www.cnn.com/2018/10/05/us/colorado-woman-defends-two-friends-speaking-spanish-trnd/index.html

Chapter 5—Venegas—QR Code 5–4

Headline #5: "Rising Number of ESL Students poses challenges for U.S. schools"
www.edweek.org/teaching-learning/rising-number-of-esl-students-poses-challenges-for-u-s-schools/2018/01

Chapter 5—Venegas—QR Code 5–5

Headline #6: "How can being bilingual be an asset for white students and a deficit for immigrants?"

https://hechingerreport.org/how-can-being-bilingual-be-an-asset-for-white-students-and-a-deficit-for-immigrants/

Chapter 5—Venegas—QR Code 5–6

Activity #2: Engaging with Ethnographic Data

Facilitate a collaborative discussion around the following pieces of ethnographic data. Read Amanda's case study and answer the questions in the text box.

Case Study #3 "Made in Puerto Rico but born in Philly"—Amanda

Amanda is a self-professed "fully" Puerto Rican student who was "made in Puerto Rico, but . . . born in Philly." Her teachers describe her as inquisitive, creative, and artistic. Her teachers characterize her as animated, perky, a bit eccentric, and excited about language and learning in general. She is often positioned as a "great talker" and "strong speaker" and as someone who enjoys playing, imitating, and presenting. Like the students in the case narrative, Amanda is considered English-dominant and an English learner. She speaks Spanish at home, which has been stated by the teachers, as well as Amanda herself; she says she learned Spanish because her mommy spoke to her in Spanish when she was still in her tummy.

Throughout her time at DLCS her Spanish teachers have commented that she is comfortable with Spanish, although her reading levels do not represent that throughout the school year. They have also mentioned that Amanda is able to easily translate and "go in and out" of the two languages. In first grade, Amanda was described as someone who can apply concepts from one language to another. All her English teachers remark that although she is not always able to move reading levels, she is someone who might "steamroll" someone in a conversation, in that if she has something she wants to share, she is focused on sharing that piece instead of listening and responding to her interlocutors. Amanda loves storytelling and for her third grade project even wrote a play with dialogue in Spanish and English. The following is a snippet from an interview with Amanda's second grade teacher:

> So she is just like an English language learner from almost like a deprivation sense, like she didn't hear enough of this at home or she doesn't know enough of that. With Amanda, I think it's really probably just a maturity and attention level thing (pause). But she has this EL label for some reason that she, and I believe, would suit somebody else better. But, I mean, I also think that with her, with all things that she has going on, that extra attention is not anything that's gonna hurt her. Right? So, I am ok with that, but, yeah . . . we have the WIDA scale and she's middle on all of the standards, like in speaking and listening and pretty low on decoding but, she does a lot of reversals so I think that's another issue too . . . So I don't think that she actually is truly like an EL.
>
> (Fieldnote_06/13/2016)

Approach Amanda's case study using an ethnographic lens. Ask your team to engage in critical listening and to lean into their discomfort as they make sense of the case study. Have your team engage in a conversation using the following questions as a point of entry:

1. How are the language practices/bilingualism of Amanda discussed by her teacher?
2. What factors might be influencing how her teacher talks about Amanda?
3. What are some of the raciolinguistic ideologies—or the conflation of Black and Brown bodies with perceptions of linguistic deficiencies—embedded in this case study?
4. What questions might you continue to ask in trying to understand the language practices of Amanda? What observations might you do? What kind of data might you collect during walkthroughs, classroom observations, student interviews, etc.?

References

Bernal, D., Burciaga, R., & Carmona, J. (2012). Chicana/Latina Testimonios: Mapping the methodological, pedagogical, and political. *Equity & Excellence in Education*, *45*(3), 363–372.

España, C., & Herrera, L.Y. (2020). *En Comunidad: Lessons for centering the voices and experiences of Bilingual Latinx Students*. Heinemann.

Flores, N., Phuong, J., & Venegas, K. (2020). "Technically an EL": The production of raciolinguistic categories in a dual language school. *TESOL Quarterly*, *54*(3), 629–651.

Flores, N., & Rosa, J. (2015). Undoing appropriateness: Raciolinguistic ideologies and language diversity in education. *Harvard Educational Review*, *85*(2), 149–171.

hooks, b. (2001). *All about love: New visions*. Perennial.

Hornberger, N., & Cassels Johnson, D. (2010). Slicing the onion ethnographically: Layers and spaces in multilingual education policy and practice. *TESOL Quarterly*, *41*(3), 509–532.

Love, B. L. (2019). *We want to do more than survive: Abolitionist teaching and the pursuit of educational freedom*. Beacon Press.

Muhammad, G. (2020). *Cultivating genius: An equity framework for culturally and historically responsive literacy*. Scholastic.

Venegas, K., Saldívar García, E., & Montes, I.R. (2021). Raciolinguistic perspectives in leadership development: Testimonios within and across bilingual education. In K. Pak & S. Ravitch (Eds.), *Critical leadership praxis for educational and social change* (pp. 87–100). Teachers College.

6 Using Critical Policy Analysis in Collaborative Professional Learning Communities to Enhance Dual Language Bilingual Educators' Critical Consciousness

Verónica E. Valdez, M. Garrett Delavan, and Juan A. Freire

Context

Teachers and school-level administrators may not often think of themselves as policymakers and policy analysts. Still, every time an educator teaches or makes a decision that shapes the direction of their students' experiences, they are, in effect, being policymakers (Menken & García, 2010). Many educators are constantly analyzing, critiquing, and selectively embracing or resisting top-down educational policies in their classrooms through their bottom-up efforts. We believe top-down and bottom-up policymakers need to hold one another accountable to achieve more equity for historically marginalized communities. Dual language bilingual education (DLBE) educators can develop critical consciousness by speaking back to top-down policies when they do not sufficiently promote equity (Menken & García, 2010).

As DLBE programs have increased in the last two decades, the number of state, district, and school DLBE policies (directives and actions on how DLBE teaching and learning should happen and for whom) have also risen. Whether these policies are explicit or implicit, they impact how marginalized students benefit from DLBE programs compared to Whiter and wealthier students. Understanding the nature and impact of educational policies is particularly important because DLBE is often uncritically portrayed as a panacea for equity. Yet, researchers continue to find examples of program demographics and prioritization of group interests that resemble the gentrification of urban neighborhoods by Whiter and wealthier inhabitants (Bernstein et al., 2021; Dorner et al., 2021). The gentrification of DLBE gives a name to the increasing presence of privileged individuals and the pushing out of language-marginalized students, their families, and their communities (Valdez et al., 2016). Understanding how DLBE policies

DOI: 10.4324/9781003240594-8

marginalize certain students is necessary for critical consciousness development. Professional learning communities (PLCs) are groups of practitioners who organize formally or informally to make ongoing improvements in student learning through collaboration, reflection, and fine-tuning of their practices. Educators' engagement in critically analyzing DLBE policies within PLCs facilitates their development of critical consciousness—the foundational orientation needed to successfully enact DLBE's core student learning goals equitably for all students.

In this chapter, we provide a PLC-oriented critical policy analysis process grounded in Palmer et al.'s (2019) framework (see Chapter 1), which can be utilized in different school settings to support the development of critical consciousness through the examination and changing of policies that impact student learning goals. Teachers engaged in this work can benefit from conscientization calls, which refer to the personal experiences and observed inequities affecting marginalized populations that raise critical/sociopolitical consciousness (Freire, 2021). The PLC-oriented critical policy analysis process we propose follows these four steps:

1. *Identify*: Notice policy issues with power implications that would benefit from being interrogated in the PLC.
2. *Dialogue*: Regularly interrogate and analyze policies collectively using critical listening, conscientization calls (lived or observed injustices), and the embrace of discomfort by comparing the status quo to historical patterns and structures.
3. *Envision*: Envision fairer policies in order to plan and revisit actions beyond the group.
4. *Act and Reflect*: Accomplish and reflect collaboratively on an action step outside the group toward those fairer policies.

We will illustrate this four-step process by discussing how Andrea, a composite character of a DLBE educator, enlisted her colleagues to join a PLC to critically analyze DLBE policies in ways that developed their critical consciousness. This case study is based on our experiences and collaborative efforts working with educators in DLBE contexts. Although based on our work in Utah, the implications of this chapter can be extrapolated to other contexts.

Case Narrative

SkyLane, a Utah K–6 elementary school with 25% Latinx and 70% White enrollment, has 10% of students designated as English learners. Andrea, a Chicana bilingual Spanish/English teacher in SkyLane's Spanish-English DLBE strand, became aware of equity issues affecting the DLBE program and its racialized students. What follows is how Andrea worked toward raising critical consciousness collectively with her DLBE colleagues.

Sharing Equity Issues with Colleagues

Andrea started a new job as a fifth grade DLBE Spanish teacher when conscientization calls, drawn from her personal, professional, and collective experience as a Chicana, began to lead her to want to identify, understand, and analyze DLBE inequities. Andrea had immediately noticed that only about 25% of students in SkyLane's two-way program were Spanish speakers upon entering the program (despite the recommendation that two-way programs enroll equal numbers based on language dominance). Andrea discussed this concern with Kim, her partner English teacher. Kim's background as a White working-class individual allowed her to be sympathetic to issues of equity yet uncertain about the reasons behind inequities in this context or how best to address them. Kim asked, "Why do you think our school doesn't do a better job of recruiting Spanish-speaking families?" Kim wondered if it was about keeping the English-speaking parents feeling like they're still safely in the majority. Kim drew on a conscientization call explaining how she had grown up seeing her working-class parents deal with a similar dynamic when middle-class families got more attention from teachers and administrators. In further conversations, Kim and Andrea agreed that the school tended to focus more on the White middle-class families enrolled in DLBE programs, further perpetuating the DLBE gentrification issue.

Andrea and Kim talked about whether there was anything to be done, or whether they should keep their questions to themselves and just be thankful they could empower at least a few working-class, Spanish-speaking families. Then they came upon the idea of strength in numbers. Andrea said, "What about a study group or a professional learning community of as many teachers as we can get interested in local DLBE equity? We could let teachers discuss what you and I have discussed thus far, and maybe even discover more problems with school, district, or state policies as we go along."

Formalizing the Collaborative Professional Learning Process

With administration approval, Andrea and Kim sent invitations to their colleagues and posted a flyer in the faculty lounge. They got ten teachers and the assistant principal to show up at the library after school near the beginning of October. Andrea suggested that perhaps they should call themselves the DLBE Equity PLC. The group would meet monthly to dialogue, examine, and report progress on equity concerns raised in previous PLC meetings. They also planned action steps for improving these equity issues over time. Although three teachers quietly stopped attending, those who remained frequently expressed how empowered they felt to do something about equity issues. Several testified to getting better at detecting inequities they hadn't been in the habit of seeing before. Ultimately, the year turned out like this:

October. *The crucial benefits of DLBE for marginalized students.* Andrea and her colleagues identified that DLBE marginalized students were not receiving equal attention as policy beneficiaries. The group historized bilingual education and its effects on DLBE through a weekly reading of selected chapters from *A History of Bilingual Education in the US* by Moore (2021) about the civil rights era history of bilingual education and *Dual Language Education for a Transformed World* by Thomas and Collier (2009) on the identity, heritage, linguistic, academic, and equity benefits of DLBE for marginalized students. They agreed that while DLBE was good for all students, it was gap-closing for students whose language and/or heritage was related to Spanish. They also read how students labeled "special education" should not be excluded in Cioè-Peña's (2021) chapter *Dual Language and the Erasure of Emergent Bilinguals Labeled as Disabled (EBLADs)*. Several teachers owned that they had unquestioningly believed DLBE was closer to a gifted program that was not for everyone. Two teachers argued that more Whites in DLBE programs made sense since more Whites lived within the school boundaries. However, they seemed swayed by others' arguments on how DLBE enriched marginalized students' educational experience in ways that resulted in the narrowing of educational gaps while White, English-speaking, middle- and upper-middle-class student enrollment in DLBE worked against this equity goal. This helped the team envision and start focusing on marginalized students more consciously. The October discussion led to planning the next meeting around interrogating student representation in the program. Andrea and Kim ended the meeting thanking the group for their courage to disagree while critically listening to one another respectfully and remaining open to having their minds changed by others' thinking.

November. *DLBE enrollment data.* Per faculty request, the assistant principal brought the enrollment data for the DLBE and mainstream programs to the November meeting. They identified and discussed the DLBE gentrification pattern and drew on conscientization calls of how some students who should be in the program were not participating or had been pushed out. Although there was discomfort for teachers who had participated in this gentrification process, they collectively brainstormed and envisioned how the school could recruit more Spanish-speaking families. They decided actions such as posting Spanish recruiting signs in the front office and adding a Spanish DLBE informational sheet and registration form to the registration packet would advance this effort. They also scheduled a meeting with the principal about changing the DLBE student enrollment and recruitment procedures to be more inclusive.

January/February. *DLBE enrollment and recruitment materials*. The meeting with the principal planned in response to the PLC's enrollment data discussions turned out to be positive. The principal agreed to have Andrea translate English parent materials into Spanish. In the process, Andrea began to feel uncomfortable with the equity implications of some of the ideas in the flyers and forms, which reminded her of newspaper articles on DLBE she had previously read. She proposed that the January and February meetings examine their school and district websites and newspaper articles for similar issues. Each teacher was assigned to report on a school or district website document or video and bring a news article to co-analyze with the group using a document camera to project it for everyone to view. After critically listening and sharing, they came to a consensus that most of the DLBE-related news articles had a similar message as the DLBE promotional materials on the school and district websites. Messages about intergenerational language loss and the heritage, identity, and equity benefits of DLBE for language marginalized students and their families they had previously read in the historical literature about the reasons for founding bilingual programs were absent or peripherally addressed under vague economic and cognitive benefits for "all," namely the interests of English-speaking parents. Additionally, the district and state websites set student ability and behavior expectations that promoted elitism and gentrification within DLBE. The group envisioned fairer materials and proposed to the principal a reworking of the school webpage and flyers to create Spanish and English versions that were explicit about the benefits for marginalized populations. They decided to communicate with the district and the state about the needed changes to the district's DLBE website and flyers. A teacher proposed to write an op-ed to the local paper problematizing news discourses and highlighting DLBE for language-marginalized students.

March. *DLBE teacher qualifications*. Kim had previously disclosed to Andrea her feeling of inadequacy and lack of training to teach students designated as English learners. Kim and Andrea proposed that the PLC group analyze DLBE teacher qualifications at the March meeting. They made copies of the teacher state qualifications policy and shared them with the group. Everyone was surprised to find that an English DLBE teacher did not need an English as a second language (ESL) endorsement. In contrast, the Spanish DLBE teacher was required to do extensive coursework in second language learning, including a DLBE endorsement, which was usually taught from a world/foreign-language perspective that paid less attention to the needs of students designated as English learners. There was a high level of discomfort in the meeting because two English DLBE teachers felt at first that the discussion singled them out as somehow less qualified. However, others critically listened to the English DLBE teachers' concerns and persuaded them it was not a personal attack but a criticism of the state's choice in creating a double standard. The group ultimately agreed that airing and addressing this discomfort was productive, and they agreed there should be equivalent preparation on both sides. The teachers and the school administrator decided to email district and state leaders to raise the problems created by the discrepancies in teacher qualifications, hoping more voices would have a more significant impact.

April. *Program model constraints*. Faculty had to show fidelity to the strict language separation policy in the DLBE program, with which teachers and students can only communicate in the respective language of the day. Marcos, one of the Spanish teachers, mentioned that his Spanish-speaking students tended to translanguage (the act of moving across named languages employing their full linguistic repertoire) and that he always felt discomfort in not letting them use their full linguistic repertoire for academic purposes. After some dialogue, the team envisioned a fairer pedagogical approach. They proposed to the principal and were approved to remove the strict language separation policy for the rest of the school year (see Chapter 24).

May. *Reflecting and moving forward*. After classes were over, the team held their last meeting for the school year and reflected on their collective process. Although reflection had occurred throughout the school year, in this meeting they analyzed and evaluated the progress they had made and got ready to continue their work for the next school year.

Teaching Notes

This case illustrates how DLBE teachers can implement a local PLC-oriented critical policy analysis process to facilitate critical consciousness development and engage in activism in a DLBE context. In this PLC, Andrea's and Kim's conscientization calls were essential. These types of PLC activities can affirm marginalized individuals' conscientization calls and lead to activism and change (Freire, 2021). Observing and analyzing inequities by exploring DLBE policies can be used as a tool to foster critical consciousness development, as illustrated in this PLC. Discussions raising critical consciousness allowed teachers to realize how DLBE policies affected their students, including issues of gentrification in DLBE. Teachers were able to analyze language education and its policies as sometimes benefitting some students more than others; they were then able to direct their efforts toward equalizing power differences resulting from how things were said and written inequitably, as well as how educational and economic attainment were inequitable.

This case demonstrates how critically analyzing specific DLBE data with other practitioners can develop DLBE educators' critical consciousness, which will ultimately benefit their students and communities. The actions of Andrea and the PLC constituted growing collective critical consciousness and change. First, drawing on her own experiences and critical consciousness calls as a Chicana Spanish-speaker, Andrea immediately noticed the low number of Spanish speakers in her program and the imbalanced requirements in the teacher qualification policy (Freire, 2021). In turn, Andrea and her colleagues engaged in four additional critical consciousness actions (see Palmer et al., 2019). Together they committed to developing similar habits of *continuously interrogating power* during regularly scheduled PLC gatherings where they reviewed DLBE policy information on program aspects whose fairness they questioned. Second, the group *historicized schools* in DLBE by looking backward at the history of bilingual education to have a larger sense of the possibilities for focusing on the civil rights era issues still at play in the current DLBE climate. Third, the group engaged in *critical listening* as they encouraged one another to be courageous and calmly express disagreement when necessary as they made different arguments for what constituted fairness. Finally, teachers got better at *engaging with discomfort.*

The case points to areas of discussion for educators who are embracing DLBE. Although the case presented may not resemble all DLBE programs, we encourage readers to pose similar critical questions to ensure equity in the distribution and implementation of DLBE programs in their area. Many DLBE teachers may find themselves unprepared for the instructional, sociopolitical, and community debates surrounding DLBE programs and the particulars of the model their school may be implementing. Learning in a supportive PLC with compassionate colleagues like Andrea can fill some preparation gaps. We have showcased an ideal PLC process that we understand might be challenging and much messier to replicate, perhaps due to teacher or administrative resistance or other barriers. The purpose of the narrative is to share ideas of how teachers can organize themselves to develop critical consciousness collectively, engage in activism, and produce change. We call for practitioners to feel empowered throughout their careers to critically analyze DLBE policy-related data and its equity implications.

Teaching Activities

1. Try developing a PLC-oriented critical policy analysis process in your context. First, bring colleagues together to work collectively.

    - *Identify* and locate the school, district, and state policy documents and other materials related to your DLBE program. In addition to the documents reviewed by the PLC in this chapter, you might look at state bills or local school and district DLBE practices that are not formalized in policy. Data can also include where the DLBE programs are geographically located in relation to school demographics of race/ethnicity, socioeconomic status, and students designated as English learners.

- Use *dialogue* to analyze the policy documents collectively. Review using key questions and conscientization calls to identify equity patterns across the data reviewed. Consider the implications of the findings for a) students designated as English learners and their families and b) English-speaking students and their families.
- *Envision* alternative DLBE policies and plan actions that respond to the data you analyzed in the PLC, particularly the implications of the equity patterns affecting marginalized students and the key persons, departments, or institutions involved.
- *Act and reflect* to change inequitable DLBE policies and raise the critical consciousness of others, i.e., proposing changes to administration. Your PLC can also reach out to a non-DLBE school colleague or group, such as a faculty meeting, to share your findings and help your colleagues critically explore DLBE policy issues. These actions can provide an opportunity to build allyship (constructive bridges) with school colleagues and discuss points of tension in DLBE policy not visible to the general school community while also opening space for discussion of other school policies that intersect and impact DLBE. Continuously reflect on the results of your actions and plan your next steps.

References

Bernstein, K. A., Alvarez, A., Chaparro, S., & Henderson, K. I. (2021). "We live in the age of choice": School administrators, school choice policies, and the shaping of dual language bilingual education. *Language Policy*, *20*(3), 383–412.

Dorner, L. M., Cervantes-Soon, C. G., Heiman, D., & Palmer, D. (2021). "Now it's all upper-class parents who are checking out schools": Gentrification as coloniality in the enactment of two-way bilingual education policies. *Language Policy*, *20*(3), 1–27.

Freire, J. A. (2021). Conscientization calls: A white dual language educator's development of sociopolitical consciousness and commitment to social justice. *Education and Urban Society*, *53*(2), 231–248.

Menken, K., & García, O. (2010). *Negotiating language policies in schools: Educators as policymakers*. Routledge.

Palmer, D. K., Cervantes-Soon, C., Dorner, L., & Heiman, D. (2019). Bilingualism, biliteracy, biculturalism, and critical consciousness for all: Proposing a fourth fundamental goal for two-way dual language education. *Theory into Practice*, *58*(2), 121–133.

Valdez, V. E., Freire, J. A., & Delavan, M. G. (2016). The gentrification of dual language education. *The Urban Review*, *48*(4), 601–627.

Section II

Leadership and Critical Consciousness

7 The Convergence of Critical Consciousness and Culturally Sustaining Leadership Practices in Dual Language Bilingual Education

Sandra Leu Bonanno

School and Leadership Context

Angela Davis Elementary School is nestled in an urban neighborhood amongst rows of brick *carnecerías* or butcher shops and a striking mural portraying a Latina with script that proudly stating, "*Este barrio, no se vende* [This neighborhood is not for sale]." The principal, Amy Howards, describes the school community as intergenerational, in which some "first-grade teachers [were] teaching the grandchildren of former students." The school employs a Spanish and English bilingual dual language program that serves a predominantly 74% Latinx[1] student population with students who also identify as White, Pacific Islander, Multiracial, Asian, and Black. Walking down the hallways, one might hear and see a mixture of Spanish and English, noting adorned walls with bilingual quotes and flyers. Though the dual language program is a strand model, meaning only two classrooms per grade officially participated in both Spanish and English instruction, numerous teachers, students, and families across the dual language or English programs unofficially speak in multiple languages throughout all classrooms.

Amidst national and state-level trends of implementing one-way enrichment dual-language programs for English-speaking students (Flores & García, 2017; Valdez et al., 2016), Principal Howards intentionally coordinates outreach to local Latinx families to provide continued access to bilingual programs and the maintenance of heritage culture and language in a schooling environment. Principal Howards understands the interconnected and fluid nature of community culture and language and its role in shaping bilingual programs. She expresses that "bilingual education should try to maintain fluidity in our children so that they can go face the world non-rigidly" rather than the elitist enrichment program it had been before. The school leader had spent her "entire career in bilingual education" across multiple states, stating that bilingual education was "just kind of where my heart and soul is." She identifies as a White ally with familial connections to the Latinx culture and spoke both Spanish and English fluently, which affords her a deeper level of communication and connection

DOI: 10.4324/9781003240594-10

to the Latinx stakeholders with whom she works. She often draws upon her bicultural and bilingual knowledge, sometimes switching to Spanish when explaining her advocacy and allyship for minoritized students. In turn, teachers and students choose to work at and attend Angela Davis Elementary because of the school's commitment to bilingualism and sense of community.

When Howards first began as an assistant principal at Angela Davis Elementary School, there was a deep divide between teachers and students who operated in the bilingual strand and monolingual strand. She also faced resistance from teachers who in name supported the bilingual and bicultural direction of the school but struggled to envision how social justice and equity melded into the DLBE program and school. Being a White cisgender female[2] leading a predominately Latinx school community, Principal Howards drew from her knowledge of critical consciousness, awareness of self-identity, and culturally and linguistically sustaining democratic practices as she transitioned into the position of principal. Critical consciousness, in this case narrative, refers to the reflexive practice of knowing one's own identity in relationship to the community they serve as well as an understanding of societal and historical injustices that impact diverse students in schools. This following narrative documents her overarching interpersonal and institutional practices that exemplify critically conscious leadership by way of sustaining the rich cultural and linguistic knowledge of the DLBE school community.

Case Narrative: Interpersonal and Institutional Leadership Practices for Fostering Critical Consciousness

Throughout her tenure as a school leader at Angela Davis Elementary, Amy Howards maintains a relationship with the local university and its professors, the institution where she completed her doctoral degree. Through her interactions with the university as a school-university partnership, influences of Mentors of Color,[3] and life experiences, Principal Howards upholds a strong sense of personal identity and how this identity influences her leadership in a predominately Latinx community. She describes her approach as follows: "I think part of social justice is recognizing like okay, I don't know everything. . . . Especially for White people, there is this protection that I've been afforded, and so I don't know your experience." This awareness of identity and privilege acts as a catalyst for Principal Howards to honor the voices of Students and Teachers of color and to foster their own critical consciousness. "I think you have to listen to kids . . . they already know they're Brown and bilingual." She elaborated, "If you listen to them and develop [their] sense of self then they'll tell you as an adult when you're kind of messing up." Principal Howards's critical consciousness prompted the fostering of Students of Colors' own sense of identity and critical consciousness of self and society, which she hoped would cyclically inform her leadership practices.

Initially, teachers, even those in the DLBE program, questioned, "When is it too early to talk to children about race?" Inherently, Howards realized that their hesitation stemmed from an inability to first openly speak and ponder about their own racial and linguistic identities before implementing similar conversations with students in the classroom. Principal Howards first instituted conversations about race and language in whole-faculty professional developments, including topics about identity, culture, and systemic racism through professional development funds. For two years, she hired an outside consultant who was trained in Courageous Conversations to lead a book study with teachers and to foster their critical consciousness, so that they might recognize how Black and Brown children already think and talk about race in their daily lives. Ultimately, this work culminated in a shared vision and language about equity in DLBE for culturally and linguistically diverse students. While developing critical consciousness remains a continuous process, this is one such example of how Howards drew from her critical consciousness and recognized that, as a white cis-gender female, she needed diverse and collective voices to establish and shift the school-wide momentum towards equity.

After paving an initial vision of equity for DLBE, Howards continues to *interpersonally* model bilingual and bicultural norms that mirror the lifeways of the community to disrupt English-centric norms and hierarchy often present in school. Intentionally centering ways of being that reflect the school community in interpersonal interactions, the DLBE model, and the curriculum support the development of critical consciousness of students in the program. One kindergarten teacher recalled the conscious efforts of Principal Howards to elevate the importance of Spanish in their school climate. She stated, "Several years ago . . . we would have conversations about the importance of Spanish, because the kids weren't feeling it as much at the time. And they weren't wanting to speak Spanish." Even though over half of the population attending Angela Davis identified as Latinx, students refused to draw from their linguistic strengths in the classroom and throughout the school.

To combat the internalized racial and linguistic strata in schools, Principal Howard consciously elevates and models bilingualism by speaking Spanish first in announcements and in formal assemblies. She also utilizes translanguaging—the full usage of an individual's linguistic repertoire, to connect with families and students and to affirm the community's linguistic use (García & Wei, 2014). In parent teacher conferences, she states, "I just saw that. *Felicidades* [Congratulations]. *Cien por ciento* [100%] on your reading, that's important," or during assemblies, "I forgot that *tenemos que decir bienvenidos a nuestras familias* [we need to welcome our families]." These interpersonal interactions compound with more institutional practices, such as the symbolic representation of both languages in school announcements and signs, encourage the staff and students to question the centrism of English and take pride in their bilingualism and biculturalism.

In addition, Principal Howards draws from her critical consciousness to *institutionally* challenge the English and Eurocentric ways of schooling in DLBE programs. A few years prior the school had opted to adhere to the state model of 50/50, half the day in English and half of instruction in Spanish to gain more financial and professional learning support. However, she recalled, "[The state model] just has some things about it that we did not agree with and so we withdrew from the program." Together she and the faculty agreed that the strict recommendations of language separation contradicted their philosophy about bilingualism and biculturalism. Fighting to maintain such norms as resistance to ideologies of dual monolingualism purported by the Utah state model, she stated,

> I think the most offensive thing to me was that I'm the principal and everyone knows I'm bilingual. Am I supposed to choose a language I speak to parents in because that's what [the recommended dual-language model] was asking teachers to do? Like if you are the Spanish teacher, you only speak Spanish even if everyone knows you speak English, too. I just find that offensive and the total opposite point of becoming bilingual.

In the classroom, numerous teachers now parallel a culturally and linguistically sustaining approach to DLBE instruction and classroom environments. Teachers co-create shared norms in the classroom—such as collectivity, *la familia*, and community—that affirm students' cultural ways of knowing, implement units for students to study their own familial histories to understand migration, and often utilize translanguaging themselves. Such examples continue blossoming because Howards maintains interpersonal and institutional opportunities for the school community to collectively validate the ties amongst language, culture, and identity.

Drawing from critical consciousness, Principal Howards also understands that her efforts alone cannot sustain biculturalism as a part of the school culture. Thus, she *institutionally* initiates shared governance to distribute power and privilege, providing leadership positions to teachers and community members that incorporate their culture and language into professional roles.

At times, this democratic approach empowered school members to create equitable change and alter the major structures or policies of the school. In one example, Principal Howards collaborated with the school community council chair to rename the school after a more socially just role model that better represented the Angela Davis population. One second grade teacher described this endeavor as "a big part of her legacy" in which the principal discovered through a school climate survey that Students of Color at Angela Davis Elementary did not want to identify with a school named after a white US President who had enslaved the Black community. This led to supporting a community leader who spearheaded the renaming of the school. She stated,

> We were going to various events and holding so many meetings about how this is our current student population and this is how they're feeling. This is how they voted on our surveys. They want to identify with somebody that is not this president. When [the sixth graders] started researching like who [he] was they asked, "Why would you name the school after them?"

Principal Howards guided her decision-making by the students' voices and provided the support and resources for the chair to initiate a change that was culturally sustaining to him and the students. As a Parent of Color, he helped bring in a needed perspective to reevaluate the school structures and identity that mirrored the community.

Taken together, Principal Howards endeavored personally, interpersonally, and institutionally to cultivate critical consciousness for herself and for the school community. In addition to shifting mindsets, she implemented actionable change prompted by critical consciousness that prompted culturally and linguistically sustaining education and democratic structures that encouraged the school community to draw on their cultural and linguistic identity to institute social justice change in DLBE.

Teaching Notes

This case briefly narrated the multiple influences and experiences Principal Howards underwent to examine her identity in relationship to the social order and to the school population. Beyond her own critical reflection, she also ensured that faculty across DLBE and non-DLBE departments cultivated a shared nomenclature for how their school engaged in social justice work. Setting this foundation emboldened the collective efforts of all stakeholders to sustain bilingualism and biculturalism in DLBE as one form of educational equity for themselves or the CLD communities they served.

The Critical Consciousness of White Allies

In DLBE, principals who maintain a level of privilege (whether socioeconomic, racial, linguistic, or otherwise) must first critically analyze their position in the social order (hooks, 1994). Similar to studies of white allyship or the social justice journey of white people, school leaders must remain cognizant of their historically situated positionalities as white and middle-class and how their identities may inhibit understanding the inequities experienced by marginalized communities (Blumer & Tatum, 1999; Erskine & Bilimoria, 2019). Here, it is helpful to draw from Dantley (2010), who frames critical consciousness as simultaneous acts of critical reflection and deconstructive interpretation in which school leaders grapple with how their own personal assumptions and values intersect with the ethical considerations of schooling. This identity work is necessary before collectively fostering critical consciousness or social justice change on an organizational level. Under this assumption, critically conscious DLBE principals might then engage in disrupting unilateral power dynamics and leverage democratic structures that frame Communities of Color as experts of their own language and culture. Diemer et al. (2021) argue that these dual components of critical reflection and critical action carry equal weight since critical consciousness raising is only as effective as the action it produces to transform inequitable social structures.

Critical Consciousness as a Catalyst for Sustaining Language and Culture: Culturally and Linguistically Sustaining School Leadership

One way to analyze the role of critical consciousness—with simultaneous nods to critical reflection and action—is through the framework of culturally and linguistically sustaining school leadership (CLSL; Leu Bonanno et al., 2019).

In this model, fostering critical consciousness for self and for the school community remains at the center of leadership action. Because schooling has traditionally reified White norms and English-dominant narratives sometimes even in dual-language models (Flores & García, 2017; Valdez

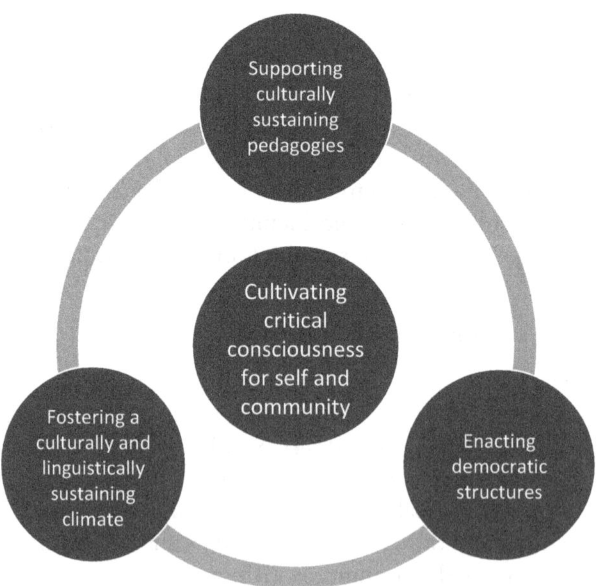

Figure 7.1 A Culturally and Linguistically Sustaining Leadership Model

et al., 2016), sustaining the cultural and linguistic lifeways of Communities of Color is one way to ensure social justice in DLBE. The other three leadership dimensions of the framework operate in tandem—based in the foundation of critical consciousness—to sustain students' capacity and experiences in schools, fostering a culturally and linguistically sustaining climate, supporting culturally sustaining pedagogies, and enacting democratic structures.

This case narrative documented the culturally and linguistically sustaining leadership of Principal Howards. In relationship to the framework, she first drew from her critical consciousness to then develop the critical consciousness of stakeholders through democratic structures and fostered a culturally and linguistically sustaining climate that more closely mirrored the community in a school setting. Her interpersonal linguistic modeling encouraged teachers to promote bilingual and bicultural pride to challenge the linguistic hierarchies felt by students. Drawing on institutional democratic structures, Principal Howards empowered school members to draw from their cultural and linguistic knowledge as strengths to shape school norms and even the school's name. Ultimately, these CLSL practices ensure that DLBE schools are not erasing the community knowledge and wealth with colonizing tactics. Rather, CLSL is one way in which principals might cultivate permeable boundaries between the school and community so that one is inextricably connected to and influenced by the other.

Teaching Activities

Readers might utilize these questions to examine their own positionalities in the social order as well as determine ways in which they can adopt interpersonal and institutional practices in the CLSL framework in their own role.

1. Dissect your own positionality and the multiple identities that make up who you are as a person and educator. How do these multiple identities engage with the traditional hierarchies of power and privilege in society? What identities do you share with dominant or marginalized populations? How might you be critically conscious of these identities and the implications they have for serving the DLBE school community?
2. How might you interpersonally and institutionally adopt the stance of a co-learner alongside the teacher, student, and family populations you serve?
3. Supporting biculturalism and bilingualism does not mean we automatically engage in equity or social justice work. How does your leadership interpersonally and institutionally push back against systems of oppression in DLBE? How does social justice intersect or not intersect with your school's mission?

4. List out and analyze the formal and informal structures that you have for gathering feedback from stakeholders. What types of institutional structures or interpersonal interactions do you have each year for gathering what is culturally and linguistically important for the learning and teaching of students? Do any of these structures disrupt traditional hierarchies of power and privilege?
5. Ask about the cultural and linguistic backgrounds of stakeholders in your school community. What are some professional passions and initiatives central to their identities that you may be able to support with time, resources, or a leadership platform?

Notes

1. Latinx is an inclusive, gender-neutral term referring to communities or persons with Latin community or heritage connections.
2. Cis-gender refers to a person whose gender corresponds to their assigned sex at birth.
3. The narrative includes intentional capitalization of Communities of Color, including Students, Teachers, and Mentors of Color as a reference to and honor of racialized populations or groups of people.

References

Blumer, I., & Tatum, B. D. (1999). Creating a community of allies: How one school system attempted to create an anti-racist environment. *International Journal of Leadership in Education, 2*(3), 255–267.

Dantley, M. E. (2010). Successful leadership in urban schools: Principals and critical spirituality, a new approach to reform. *The Journal of Negro Education*, 214–219.

Diemer, M. A., Pinedo, A., Bañales, J., Mathews, C. J., Frisby, M. B., Harris, E. M., & McAlister, S. (2021). Recentering action in critical consciousness. *Child Development Perspectives, 15*(1), 12–17.

Erskine, S. E., & Bilimoria, D. (2019). White allyship of Afro-Diasporic women in the workplace: A transformative strategy for organizational change. *Journal of Leadership & Organizational Studies, 26*(3), 319–338.

Flores, N., & García, O. (2017). A critical review of bilingual education in the United States: From basements and pride to boutiques and profit. *Annual Review of Applied Linguistics, 37*(1), 14–29.

García, O., & Wei, L. (2014). Translanguaging and education. In O. García & L. Wei (Eds.), *Translanguaging: Language, bilingualism and education* (pp. 63–77). Palgrave Pivot.

hooks, b. (1994). *Teaching to transgress: Education as the practice of freedom*. Routledge.

Leu Bonanno, S. L., Ynostroza, A., & Alejandre, E. (2019). Standardized testing and mariachi: Dilemmas of a culturally sustaining dual-language principal. In E. Crawford & L. Dorner (Eds.), *Educational leadership of immigrants: Case studies in times of change* (pp. 48–57). Routledge.

Valdez, V. E., Freire, J. A., & Delavan, M. G. (2016). The gentrification of dual language education. *The Urban Review, 48*(4), 601–627.

8 The Power of *Plática*

Expanding Dual Language Bilingual Education at the District Level with a Bilingual Redesign Committee

Olivia Hernández and Kathryn I. Henderson

Introduction

"You have to go deep into the hopes and dreams of educators, students, and the community to expand dual language programs in a school district," reflects Dr. Olivia Hernández, assistant superintendent and co-author of this chapter, when recalling her experience shifting the district's bilingual education programs from transitional bilingual education (TBE), programs that transition students to English-only instruction, to dual language bilingual education (DLBE), programs that develop student bilingualism, biliteracy, and biculturalism. Her reflection articulates the transformational ideology that paved the way for her Texas school district's aspirational journey through their bilingual education redesign process. In this chapter, we share a case of mutual self-discovery that brought together community members in a bilingual redesign committee (BRC)—including teachers, administrators, parents, and other stakeholders—to profess their *testimonios* (testimonies) and reflect deeply on personal experiences, language policies, and issues regarding language acquisition and teaching. We will demonstrate how the format of the BRC interrogated power structures and historicized schools, and how the BRC process involved critical listening and engaging in discomfort reflecting a critically conscious approach. Throughout this chapter, we integrate pragmatic examples of Dr. Hernández's fellow educators' and administrators' path to foster communal assets and critical consciousness to develop and implement DLBE.

Context

HISD (pseudonym), an urban school district in south central Texas, educates over 50,000 students in 90 campuses. The student population is 91% Latinx, 90% economically disadvantaged, and 22% emergent bilingual (EB) students. A great number of students in the district are Spanish-speaking or Spanish heritage speakers and embrace bicultural identities (i.e., Mexican American). The district's Bilingual Department provides state-approved

DOI: 10.4324/9781003240594-11

bilingual/ESL programs for more than 10,000 EB students across the district. In 2015, district leaders in HISD convened to discuss concerns about standardized assessment scores of EB students. District leaders and stakeholders discussed the possibility of implementing DLBE programs to meet the academic, linguistic, and socio-cultural needs of their EB students.

District leadership was receptive to feedback from teachers and stakeholders and hired a new assistant superintendent, Dr. Olivia Hernández, to lead the Bilingual Department in assessing the current bilingual programs and creating a plan to change the academic trajectory of EB students in the district. Dr. Hernández immediately began her work building a bilingual redesign committee (BRC) to identify the best bilingual programs to implement and how to tailor them for the following school year and beyond.

From the beginning, Dr. Hernández resolved to lead the BRC in a manner devoid of top-down mandates. This format reflected critical consciousness in its disruption of traditional power structures. She wanted BRC members representing diverse community voices to arrive at an informed decision to expand the implementation of DLBE programs because they genuinely wanted to, not because it was being forced. An informed decision could only be possible through historicizing the district's bilingual education policies and interrogating current state policy, further reflecting a critically conscious approach. She knew her leadership needed to unite and organize teacher leaders and stakeholders, to rebuild trust, and to light the spark that would set her plan in motion. It would be necessary for her to lead a grassroots approach that put the needs of the district front and center in order to build continuous stakeholder buy-in from the inside out.

Case Narrative

"I was beyond excited to begin our first BRC meeting," Dr. Hernández recalls. "I couldn't wait to get everyone together and leverage the assets of teachers, principals, district administrators, university partners, and community members to redefine what bilingual education would look like in the district." She worked with the Bilingual Department, including the bilingual director and coordinators, to build a timeline and objectives based on a problem of practice and a theory of change to align research, policy, and practice (García & Kleifgen, 2010). As Dr. Hernández recalls,

> The tighter research, policy, and practice are, the more sustainable the program is. We may have a good program model, but what's happening in the classroom could be totally different. I wanted everyone in the BRC to genuinely understand how important this is.

The first BRC meeting got off to a fantastic start. All committee members were present and morale was high. After a quick ice breaker, Dr. Hernández began presenting the research, policy, and practice construct; the charge of the group; the theory of change; and the BRC objectives. The group was receptive and engaged, and supplied pertinent feedback.

The first hiccup to the meeting occurred when Dr. Hernández transitioned into presenting on the different bilingual programs under Texas Education Code Chapter §89.1210 (Adaptations for Special Populations, 2020). Dr. Hernández recalls:

> I was well into introducing Chapter 89 when a member in the front row raised his hand and asked what an English learner is. That's when I first realized that I probably needed to slow down a little to ensure everybody was understanding. I then went into what were the bilingual programs that we have in Texas, and not many people were able to name them. There were a slew of questions, clarifications, doubts, and ideas. I remember thinking that we would need to do something to address the different levels of knowledge.

Dr. Hernández convened with the Bilingual Department the next day to plan a more meaningful activity to better help BRC members historicize, analyze, and internalize Texas bilingual program policy. The subsequent brainstorm was fruitful, but the ideas were not immediately accepted by everyone on the team. As Dr. Hernández recalls:

> Not everyone in the team was happy about the idea of spending extra time to go over policy. We were actually going to have to squeeze in an extra meeting, and people were eager to move on to dual language already. One member of the team was pretty adamant that the extended focus on reviewing policy would be, in her words, "a big waste of time." Based on previous experiences leading a redesign team, I knew we didn't have any other choice but to go deeper for the sake of all BRC members, and ultimately the team decided to go in this direction.

At this point, Dr. Hernández identified BRC members who were more knowledgeable and experienced in bilingual education to serve as group leaders during breakout discussions. This strategy proved beneficial to generate great discussion that went beyond policy. Dr. Hernández explains:

> Discussion can be a double-edged sword. I've experienced the snowball effect where one deficit comment spawns another and, before you know it, the entire discussion becomes negative, bitter, and fruitless. You really need a balance of problem- and solution-oriented discourse for discussion to be successful. My hope for the BRC was that having experienced leaders in each of the small groups would help other members lean towards an asset-based perspective during discussion.

As BRC members worked in groups to come up with recommendations, they organically began to practice the social pedagogy of *pláticas* (dialogues), in which multidimensional conversation is shaped by listening, inquiry, storytelling, and story making (Guajardo & Guajardo, 2013).

When discussing late-exit bilingual programs, which have the goal of transferring students to English-only instruction, members innately began to compare what they were reading to what they were experiencing in the classroom. They recognized that a true late-exit model means that Spanish instruction continues through the fifth grade, and this was not happening in their classrooms. This led to *pláticas* about how language was lost and how the bilingual program wasn't being implemented well. This process involved critical consciousness as educators listened critically and engaged in uncomfortable conversation. Conversations took place about how some of the members had lost their Spanish language and worked on regaining it as bilingual teachers. They began talking about their families and the language they spoke at home. They shared how they grew up learning two languages and how well-implemented bilingual programs such as DLBE could benefit students who are growing up the same way.

The trend of *pláticas* continued, especially when discussing difficult topics such as language ideologies and state assessments. BRC members shared anecdotes to express their legitimate concerns about topics related to language of instruction or language of assessment if DLBE were to be implemented. This required a nuance of vulnerability and further discomfort for those sharing stories of their experience because they had to be critical of the bilingual education research being presented. The BRC provided a safe space for this to occur.

Teachers liked the idea of extending native language instruction, but it scared them. They had doubts about teaching in Spanish in the testing grades, which would be required in DLBE. Dr. Hernández elaborates:

> Some members thought there were going to be learning gaps if we alternated teaching content areas in a different language each grade level. Some were not familiar with the concept of "transfer" and were understandably concerned about students not passing the state assessment. This is why we need the *pláticas*. We need stakeholders to be able to voice their concerns and share their experiences in order to build solidarity and find meaningful solutions when implementing bilingual programs.

The combination of *pláticas*, juxtaposed with exploring the research, created a powerful force that grew as the BRC meetings progressed. Conversations continued to intensify during the last meetings as participants were excited about the possibility of expanding the implementation of DLBE programs in the district. But at the same time, there remained a sense of *inquietud* (uneasiness) reflected in the discomfort of critically conscious conversations. Bilingual teachers had a lot of questions because they were very accustomed to implementing transitional models when they only had EB students in their classrooms. The transition to implement DLBE incorporating monolingual students would require new scheduling, simultaneous literacy, and updated language of instruction guidelines. The *pláticas* helped authentically address the concerns teachers had about these new structures in a manner that genuinely considered a variety of real-world perspectives from educators positioned as leaders with meaningful contributions.

In the end, the beauty of the BRC's work was the true collaboration that built the two-way DLBE program model for the district from the ground up through authentic conversations, critical listening, and engaging in discomfort with topics that historicized bilingual education (i.e., conversations about loss of Spanish from schooling) and surfaced power structures (i.e., TBE versus DLBE models). Within three years, fifty schools in HISD were implementing the new DLBE model. The BRC members all had new skills and knowledge to be DLBE leaders in their communities and continue to meet twice a year to evaluate and monitor the implementation of the program. Parents and students are invited to these meetings to share detailed accounts of their experiences in the DLBE program, and their voices help sustain the program into the future.

Teaching Notes

Bilingual education policy and programs can be *additive (pluralist)* in nature—developing student bilingualism and biliteracy—or *subtractive (assimilationist)*—transitioning students to English (de Jong, 2013; Lambert, 1975). The assimilationist beliefs and ideologies entrenched in TBE program models, whose ultimate goal of transferring students to English-only instruction often comes at the expense of their native language, reflect the historical and still-present linguistic oppression and racism experienced by linguistically minoritized and ethno-racially diverse communities in Texas (Flores, 2016; Valenzuela, 1999). We, as educators, advocates, community members, and mothers, have personally witnessed this loss of language, culture, and identity too many times.

DLBE, with the aim to develop student bilingualism, biliteracy, and multiculturalism, provides an additive program policy and model in contrast to TBE (Baker & Wright, 2017). Teachers, parents, and community members have long fought and created spaces to implement bilingual programs that reflect the linguistic resources of the community, which, in the context of Texas, include language practices associated with Spanish, English, Spanglish, Tex-Mex, or Spanish of the Southwest (Sayer, 2013; Toribio & Bullock, 2016). This endeavor for linguistic and cultural equity in education has long been valiantly taken up by leaders and educators in their schools (Degollado et al., 2021), by parents in their homes, and by advocates within linguistically diverse communities (De La Trinidad, 2015; Flores, 2016).

The power of the BRC came from a model of community learning exchange (CLE) that utilized a theory of change and social pedagogy to facilitate and document the learning and development process of participants and organizational engagement with community (Guajardo et al., 2016). The meeting topics and structure which allowed for participants to shift in and out of leadership roles disrupted a traditional power structure and opened the opportunity to historicize schooling. The BRC created safe spaces where district staff and community members could share stories of language, teaching, and culture through *pláticas* involving critical listening and engaging in discomfort. Throughout the entire BRC process, the stories shared enhanced members' empathy and re-affirmed their identity, providing a catharsis to the *herida abierta* (open wound) and leveraged the power inherent in their linguistic and cultural identity.

Teaching Activities

Activity A: Bilingual Redesign Committee Objectives

In October of 2016, the BRC was created with the goal of redesigning the district's bilingual programs to better serve their learning community. More than thirty educators and student advocates met for nine consecutive months to plan the improvement of educational experiences for emergent bilingual students across the district.

The charge of the BRC was to accomplish the following:

- Evaluate the existing bilingual education models, including the early- and late-exit transitional models and DLBE models, based on research, policy, student achievement data, teacher surveys, and principals' input.
- Develop an effective DLBE program model that meets the specific needs of EB students in the district.
- Determine the elements that are essential to the implementation of the DLBE program model and the late-exit model that would be phased out.
- Establish district-wide systems to ensure an effective and efficient implementation of DLBE in the district.

Significant outcomes and products produced by the BRC during the planning period included:

- DLBE program model
- DLBE program guidelines
- essential program elements
- program goals
- program model phase-in process
- roll-out plan
- references and definitions central to DLBE implementation

- well-implemented program indicators
- three-year professional development plan

Take a moment to reflect on these objectives. What might be the charge of your committee, department, or district? What could be some possible outcomes and products you produce?

Activity B: Planning Bilingual Redesign Committee Meeting Agendas

The BRC served multiple purposes in the district, including representing multiple voices and stakeholders in DLBE implementation, providing professional development for stakeholders on foundational knowledge including national and state policies connected to DLBE, and building relationships and local leaders for sustainable implementation.

Examine Table 8.1 outlining topics that were discussed during each of the BRC meetings that took place over a nine-month period.

Fill in the areas to indicate the topics and activities your district would implement for each of the nine meetings.

Table 8.1 Bilingual Redesign Committee Meetings Planning Tool

Meetings	*Topic*	*Activities*
Meeting 1 **September**	**HISD BRC Topic:** Setting the Stage	**HISD BRC Activities:** • Identify problem(s) of practice • Create a theory of change • Review state and district policy • Review bilingual program student data • Review DLBE education research • Establish a timeline
	Your district's topic:	***Your district's activities:*** • • •
Meeting 2 **October**	**HISD BRC Topic:** A Close Look into Transitional Bilingual Education	**HISD BRC Activities:** • Analyze bilingual programs as described in state policy • Analyze discrepancies between policy and practice regarding district late-exit model • Identify key elements required for a successful and sustainable implementation of a transitional late-exit model
	Your district's topic:	***Your district's activities:*** • • •

(*Continued*)

Table 8.1 (Continued)

Meetings	*Topic*	*Activities*
Meeting 3 November	**HISD BRC Topic:** Wrapping up Transitional Bilingual Education	**HISD BRC Activities:** • Review Charge of BRC • Review EB student data • Review BRC member feedback
	Your district's topic:	***Your district's activities:*** • • •
Meeting 4 November	**HISD BRC Topic:** Wrapping Up Transitional Bilingual Education Continued	**HISD BRC Activities:** • Review charge of BRC • Refine existing district late-exit model to meet state definition • Establish essential elements for a successful transitional late-exit model
	Your district's topic:	***Your district's activities:*** • • •
Meeting 5 December	**HISD BRC Topic:** Setting the Stage for Dual Language	**HISD BRC Activities:** • Review charge of the BRC • Review DLBE state policy • Identify similarities and differences between one-way and two-way DLBE programs
	Your district's topic:	***Your district's activities:*** • • •
Meeting 6 January	**HISD BRC Topic:** A Closer Look into Dual Language	**HISD BRC Activities:** • Review charge of the BRC • Review DLBE implementation in similar urban districts • Identify characteristics and benefits of 50/50, 80/20, and 90/10 DLBE models
	Your district's topic:	***Your district's activities:*** • • •
Meeting 7 February	**HISD BRC Topic:** Redefining the District Dual Language Programs	**HISD BRC Activities:** • Review charge of the BRC • Determine the DLBE program model to be recommended and implemented in the district • Develop a tentative five-year plan to expand DLBE
	Your district's topic:	***Your district's activities:*** • • •

Meetings	*Topic*	*Activities*
Meeting 8 March	**HISD BRC Topic:** Solidifying the Dual Language Redesign Program	**HISD BRC Activities:** • Review charge of the BRC • Vote on late-exit model and DLBE model to be implemented in the district • Map out which schools would implement DLBE
	Your district's topic:	***Your district's activities:*** • • •
Meeting 9 April	**HISD BRC Topic:** Wrapping Up Dual Language	**HISD BRC Activities:** • Review charge of BRC • Finalize five-year plan to expand DLBE • Create mission and vision statements for DLBE
	Your district's topic:	***Your district's activities:*** • • •

References

Adaptations for Special Populations. Chapter §89. (2020). https://texreg.sos.state.tx.us/public/readtac$ext.ViewTAC?tac_view=4&ti=19&pt=2&ch=89

Baker, C., & Wright, W. E. (2017). *Foundations of bilingual education and bilingualism* (6th ed.). Multilingual Matters.

de Jong, E. (2013). Policy discourses and U.S. Language in education policies. *Peabody Journal of Education, 88*(1), 98–111.

De La Trinidad, M. (2015). Mexican Americans and the push for culturally relevant education: The bilingual education movement in Tucson, 1958–1969. *History of Education, 44*(3), 316–338.

Degollado, E. D., Bell, R. C., & Salinas, C. S. (2021). "No había bilingual education:" Stories of negotiation, educación, y sacrificios from South Texas escuelitas. *Journal of Latinos and Education, 20*(4), 397–411.

Flores, N. (2016). A tale of two visions: Hegemonic whiteness and bilingual education. *Educational Policy, 30*(1), 13–38.

García, O., & Kleifgen, J. (2010). *Educating emergent bilinguals: Policies, programs and practices for English Learners.* Teachers College Press.

Guajardo, F., & Guajardo, M. (2013). The power of *plática*. *Reflections, 13*(1), 159–164.

Guajardo, M., Guajardo, F., Militello, M., & Janson, C. (2016). *Reframing community partnerships in education: Uniting the power of place and wisdom of people.* Routledge.

Lambert, W. E. (1975). Culture and language as factors in learning and education. In A. Wolfgang (Ed.), *Education of immigrant students: Issues and answers* (pp. 55–83). Ontario Institute for Studies in Education.

Sayer, P. (2013). Translanguaging, TexMex, and bilingual pedagogy: Emergent bilinguals learning through the vernacular. *TESOL Quarterly, 47*(1), 63–88.

Texas Education Code: Chapter 89. §89.1210. Adaptations for special populations. Subchapter BB. Commissioner's rules concerning state plan for educating Limited English Proficient students.

Toribio, A. J., & Bullock, B. E. (2016). A new look at Heritage Spanish and its speakers. In D. Pascual y Cabo (Ed.), *Advances in Spanish as a Heritage Language* (Vol. 49, pp. 27–50). John Benjamins.

Valenzuela, A. (1999). *Subtractive schooling: US-Mexican youth and the politics of caring.* SUNY Press.

9 Dual Language, Dual Purposes

A Community in Conflict

David DeMatthews and Leyla Olano

Context

Central City Independent School District (CISD) is an urban school district located in a southwestern US state. CISD has more than 75,000 students and serves a majority Latino/a community (60% Latino/a, 5% Black, 25% White, and 5% Asian, with 5% Pacific Islander, two or more races, and American Indian). Half of CISD students are classified by the state as "economically disadvantaged," and one third are classified as English learners (EL). CISD has a long history of racial segregation and underserving Black and Latino/a students. The city's master plan in the 1920s promoted racial segregation. In the 1970s, CISD was ordered to implement mandatory busing to meet federal desegregation requirements. The legacy of the master plan and racial segregation remains intact because most low-income Black and Latino/a students attend the same schools.

Recent growth has led to considerable gentrification primarily concentrated in Black and Latino/a communities. The increased integration has created tensions. Black and Latino/a residents often feel like they are losing control of their community as more affluent, mostly White residents move in. The significant increase in housing prices has pushed many Black and Latino/a families out, which translated into anger and resentment. Demographic shifts have also created a call for school consolidation by district-hired efficiency experts, pitting low-income families of color against district officials. CISD's recent move to promote dual language bilingual education (DLBE) was related to a need to value the cultural and linguistic assets of Latino/a students, given growing frustrations. DLBE also attracted affluent families into racially diverse schools

Case Narrative

Haynes Elementary School

Principal Reveles of Haynes Elementary School (ES) is a campus leader in a divided community. Principal Reveles is a Latina woman who has worked

DOI: 10.4324/9781003240594-12

in CISD for over twenty years. She is knowledgeable about reading instruction and has a passion for DLBE, especially since she is bilingual and was an EL student when she attended public school. She is beginning her first year as principal at Haynes ES and her fourth year as a principal overall. When she interviewed for the position, she learned that longtime residents felt the school was "a community centerpiece" that was "historically committed to a family-like atmosphere." Haynes ES was not described as a community school going into the new school year. Instead, the community was divided and had little trust in Principal Reveles. The recent demographic shifts in the Haynes ES community contributed to decreasing enrollment, which put the campus on the verge of closure. To attract new families and retain existing families, CISD tasked Principal Reveles with designing and implementing a DLBE model for EL students.

The PTA Meeting

Before Principal Reveles' arrival, the parent teacher association (PTA) came together to discuss the development of the DLBE program. A one-year planning process commenced, and CISD expected families to be part of the planning process. The PTA president was Mrs. Parker, an influential community member and parent. Mrs. Parker is a Black woman who was born and raised in the community. She attended Haynes ES as a child and was trusted in the community and known for her advocacy. Mrs. Villanueva, a parent and community activist for Spanish-speaking families, was PTA vice president. She served with Mrs. Parker for the past two years. Although Mrs. Parker and Mrs. Villanueva did not always see eye to eye, they shared a mutual respect, because they were fierce community advocates. A growing contingent of White parents were vocal in the PTA. Most parents felt DLBE was an excellent opportunity and expected a rigorous and challenging program that would benefit all students. However, the details of the program were not revealed. The assistant principal, serving as interim principal while Principal Reveles was transitioning from her prior campus, and other teacher leaders were present to share updates about DLBE. For the upcoming year, the assistant principal announced: Haynes ES will be a DLBE campus proceeding a one-year planning period and will include multiple language options – French, Spanish, and Chinese."

Some of the PTA members, who identified as Latinx Spanish speakers, preferred Spanish as the sole language of choice. Mrs. Villanueva was upset to learn that French and Chinese would also be offered. A Latina parent shared the following: "Given all the change [in the community], it's like a slap in the face to not focus entirely on English and Spanish." She added that an emphasis on Spanish could promote Latino/a culture in the school and allow the newer White families to adapt to the school's community-oriented nature. Another Latino/a parent said, "Chinese and French? That's just going to increase gentrification. . . . Why is the district supporting this?"

Most of the PTA felt that Chinese and French were unique options, and provided better opportunities for their children. A parent supporter of Chinese and French language options noted, "Yes, it's about giving our children every advantage, but it's also preparing them to live in a multicultural and multilingual world."

The staff were divided. A veteran teacher stated, "Spanish is an integral part of the community's history and that should be our focus." Another teacher agreed, "Adding Chinese and French would send the wrong message to Latino/a families." Mrs. Parker and Mrs. Villanueva shared some additional context with the PTA. Several years ago, the Latino/a families pushed for a Spanish DLBE program with the previous district administration and principal but did not receive support. Mrs. Villanueva said, "A few years ago, we were entirely shut down. What's changed? I think I know what's changed," alluding to the demographic changes in the community. The PTA meeting became tense and some members felt "racial tensions were high." Some Latino/a parents reflected that CISD did not care about their community and only pushed initiatives to attract and benefit White families. Some White families sensed this frustration and understood the need to focus on Spanish, while others disregarded the racial dynamics.

Principal Reveles Arrives

During Principal Reveles's first week on campus, she scheduled one-on-one teacher meetings, a staff meeting, and a community meeting. She realized she inherited a divided community with little confidence in her abilities. The one-on-one teacher meetings gave her insight into staff dynamics. Most staff were pleasant. They were concerned about enrollment and creating a DLBE program for all students. Several vocal teachers expressed their concerns at every chance. One said, "What are you going to do about enrollment? Our last principal didn't do anything." Another said, "We have a divided community, and now yet another principal." Veteran teachers witnessed the impact of gentrification. They observed a shrinking of the Latino/a Spanish-speaking community over the past decade and the prior failed attempt to create a Spanish DLBE program. One veteran teacher said, "Now that there is a need to find a program to boost enrollment, the community is suddenly interested in their support. When they needed help for their cause, they were not met with a listening ear." Newer teachers did not have the same attachment to the community, but they were invested in its future.

The first staff meeting indicated what the team dynamic was like and which teachers were the most vocal and influential. Principal Reveles started her staff meeting by sharing her racial autobiography and a brief story about her experience as an EL student. She stated that she was hopeful about the school's future and the shared work ahead. She then opened the meeting to answer questions. One of the veteran teachers, Ms. Williams, wanted to know more about the principal's credentials. Her candor was on full display:

> We are so glad to have a principal who grew up as an English learner, and thank you for sharing your story. With all due respect, we do not know much about your experience. This place is different and rapidly changing. We have been the pillars of this school, and we genuinely understand what is going on. The district is out of touch with our students' needs and only caters to wealthy White families. They did not ask us for our input, so we are not really sure what to expect from you. How are you going to help us?

Principal Reveles gave a diplomatic response, thanked her, and assured her that she was invested in the children. Her mission was to build trust and bridge all the divisions. She also stated that she was ready to take on the challenges. One newer teacher, Ms. Scott, raised her hand and spoke:

> I just think that some things need to be said and that we need to address the elephant in the room. Spanish is not going to get us anywhere in terms of enrollment. The cost of living is high, and we have seen a decrease in our Black and Latino/a population. Whether we like it or not, we must think about the families moving in. It's sad, but if we want to keep our school open, we must think about the people who will be here down the road. Chinese is a better option because it is what the new families want.

Ms. Scott added that as a newer teacher, she was worried that her position would be one of the first to be cut if enrollment continued to decline. Principal Reveles was beginning to recognize the significant tensions on the campus. She could hear whispers among the groups along with several looks of disapproval.

Resistance and Opportunities

Principal Reveles needed to create a structure for planning the DLBE program. The plan would have to help teachers learn about DLBE, cultivate appropriate resources, and make decisions about program components, values, and goals. In addition, Principal Reveles recognized a need to build consensus among teachers and families. In speaking with her mentor principal, she recognized that the school's shifting demographics could significantly complicate family relationships. Her mentor noted, "In schools with shifting demographics, and with DLBE too, unequal power dynamics can emerge and fracture not only the community, but also the teachers."

She was determined to bring her teachers together because they were the ones who would carry the program. She decided to schedule planning meetings to start. She sought a diverse group of teachers and family members as well as the PTA leadership to plan. In her review of reform literature, she read about the importance of creating school-community teams to make decisions. She decided to establish a bilingual leadership team composed of the principal, bilingual teachers, general education teachers, special education teachers, a district administrator, PTA president and vice president, and a diverse group of family members. She also recognized a need to set two non-negotiables: first, the DLBE program would be developed to prioritize the needs of EL students and be based on research; second, the bilingual leadership team would be inclusive of diverse perspectives and consider the school's past, present, and future.

At their first meeting, Principal Reveles gathered her teachers and began to share her why with her new team:

> The first thing to remember is we are ultimately here to do what is best for children. The second is that what we do in the planning stage will set the tone for the future. It's important for teachers to have input. It's also imperative for me to entrust you to make sound curricular and instructional decisions. We must learn together. We don't have all the answers but engaging in professional development and touring campuses will help us make the best decisions. I'd like us to use this time to create a plan. I want to leave this meeting with individuals who are interested in forming the bilingual leadership team. This team will consist of individuals who will help us plan for our future and make student-centered decisions.

Some teachers were surprised by Principal Reveles's open approach. Principal Reveles sensed a shift among veteran and novice teachers. Then, Ms. Scott raised her hand and said, "Gentrification is still a major issue and I just want to make sure that we still remember what is going on. I'm open to dialogue, but I won't accept outsiders dictating what happens or going to the superintendent behind our backs." Immediately after Ms. Scott shared, Ms. Williams asked if she could contribute. She said, "I also like that we are forming a decision-making group that isn't so top-down. We have to make sure we don't continue pushing away and hurting our Latinx families because they are just as important too." Another parent asked Mrs. Williams, "What are you insinuating? Accusations aren't the way to start a dialogue." Principal Reveles respectfully acknowledged and validated each statement. She knew she had a long road ahead.

Teaching Notes

Many states, districts, and schools struggle to provide a high-quality education that meets the needs of students from diverse backgrounds, particularly students of color whose first language is not English (DeMatthews &

Izquierdo, 2016). DLBE has often been viewed as a model to bridge these divides by valuing the cultural and linguistic assets of EL students, yet such models have sometimes been developed and implemented in ways that continue to marginalize EL students. DLBE tends to resemble two primary models: 50:50 and 90:10. In a 50:50 model, curriculum is provided in Spanish and English throughout all grades. In the 90:10 model, kindergarten students receive 90% of instruction in Spanish, with the percentage of Spanish dropping to 50% by fourth or fifth grade. DLBE often has three primary goals: (1) to support emergent bilingual children with learning English, succeed in schools, and continue language and academic development in their family's language; (2) to help English-proficient students learn a second language, including academic language; and (3) to promote linguistic, cultural, and racial/ethnic equity and social justice for all students, families, schools, and communities. DLBE thereby values diversity and maintains a vision defined by acceptance. Research focused on cognitive and academic functioning has documented the enhanced benefits of DLBE (Bialystok, 2007; Collier & Thomas, 2004). EL students instructed in English and their primary language have been found to achieve at or above their peers on standardized tests while emergent bilingual children in traditional English immersion programs lose or do not make progress in their family language (Genesee et al., 2006).

Principals, teachers, staff, families, and students should work together to create an inclusive and welcoming school-community context. Since most teacher preparation programs and in-service trainings neglect bilingual education topics and teaching practices, teachers need to be provided with tailored professional development as well as collaborative and flexible planning time (Goodwin, 2017). A cultural shift is also necessary, because teachers and staff may need to be taught to see language diversity as an asset rather than a deficit. Thus, DLBE must include the development of critical consciousness to interrogate unequal power dynamics, reckon with problematic local histories, lift historically marginalized voices, and act in ways that promote social justice (Cervantes-Soon et al., 2017). Lastly, teachers need time and resources to develop curricula and learning experiences that are developmentally appropriate and attentive to context (Schachter & Gass, 2013).

Policies associated with DLBE instruction, accountability, testing, and teacher and leader evaluations often fail to promote a healthy and inclusive school environment. Palmer (2007) described an elementary school with a DLBE immersion program or "strand," which meant that only a small segment of the school population received access to DLBE while most of the school was English-only and devoid of any Spanish language. The small segment of the school dedicated to DLBE immersion was described as "small oases of Spanish in a vast desert of English-only" (p. 756). In this school DLBE did not change the language-as-problem orientation beyond the small group of DLBE classes, which allowed most teachers, staff, and students to continually view Spanish through a deficit lens. Parent groups from different social, cultural, linguistic, and economic backgrounds can also create complex and problematic power dynamics. In a study of DLBE implementation in a Chicago-area school district, Dorner (2011) found that White and Black monolingual English-speaking parents were more able to advocate for their children than Mexican American immigrants, which had implications for school and language policies.

Discussion Questions

1. How did Principal Reveles's identity and experience influence her leadership? How do your identity and experiences shape your decisions?
2. What types of support and resources does Principal Reveles need from CISD? How would you address concerns to district leadership? What kind of support and resources would you request?
3. How can Principal Reveles create a culture shift among veteran and novice teachers? Where should she start?
4. How can Principal Reveles engage in conversations about race, class, and gentrification to guide her staff? What professional learning activity can she design to help implement the four agreements and six conditions with her staff?

Teaching Activities

Knowing the Law

In 1975, the Texas legislature passed a law authorizing districts to deny enrollment to children who had not been "legally admitted" into the US. In 1982, the US Supreme Court ruled in *Plyler v. Doe* that the Texas law violated the Equal Protection Clause of the 14th Amendment. States cannot discriminate against undocumented children based on immigration status or deny them access to public education. The decision reinforced the prevailing notion that schools provide the primary means of preparing children with the tools to contribute to social, political, and economic life. Principals need to be knowledgeable about the implications of the *Plyler* decision, especially when designing DLBE models. Instructors can develop assignments focused on the implications of the *Plyler* decision:

- Collaborate with the district to issue a statement that articulates support for EL students.
- Strengthen teacher and parent training to support, advocate, and protect EL students and families.

- Collect and distribute information about community programs that address immigrant community concerns and ensure school personnel attend as a sign of solidarity.
- Audit school and district policies related to complying with the *Plyler* decision and the actions identified in this section.

Family Engagement

Principals need to be knowledgeable about available community resources and power dynamics in a diverse school community. Few principal preparation programs prepare leaders for effectively navigating these complexities. Students can be assigned the article *Parental Involvement in Children's Education: Considerations for School Counselors Working with Latino Immigrant Families* (Gonzalez et al., 2013). The instructor can also have students engage in a discussion using the following questions:

1. What are some of the potential challenges confronted by EL students and their families?
2. How can principals collaborate with other stakeholders to identify and address deficit-oriented views of Hispanic families?
3. What potential partnerships can principals identify to better support all families?
4. What professional development can be provided to teachers to better support EL students from Latinx communities?
5. How might these strategies be adapted to consider the dynamics at play in gentrifying school communities?

References

Bialystok, E. (2007). Cognitive effects of bilingualism: How linguistic experience leads to cognitive change. *International Journal of Bilingual Education and Bilingualism*, *10*(3), 210–223. https://doi.org/10.2167/beb441.0

Cervantes-Soon, C. G., Dorner, L., Palmer, D., Heiman, D., Schwerdtfeger, R., & Choi, J. (2017). Combating inequalities in two-way language immersion programs: Toward critical consciousness in bilingual education spaces. *Review of Research in Education*, *41*(1), 403–427. https://doi.org/10.3102/0091732X17690120

Collier, V. P., & Thomas, W. P. (2004). The astounding effectiveness of dual language education for all. *NABE Journal of Research and Practice*, *2*(1), 1–20.

DeMatthews, D. E., & Izquierdo, E. (2016). School leadership for dual language education: A social justice approach. *The Educational Forum*, *80*(3), 278–293.

Dorner, L. M. (2011). Contested communities in a debate over dual-language education: The import of "public" values on public policies. *Educational Policy*, *25*(4), 577–613.

Genesee, F., Lindholm-Leary, K., Sanders, B., & Christian, D. (2006). *Educating English language learners: A synthesis of research evidence*. Cambridge University Press.

Gonzalez, L. M., Borders, L. D., Hines, E. M., Villalba, J. A., & Henderson, A. (2013). Parental involvement in children's education: Considerations for school counselors working with Latino immigrant families. *Professional School Counseling*, *16*, 185–193.

Goodwin, A. L. (2017). Who is in the classroom now? Teacher preparation and the education of immigrant children. *Educational Studies, 53*(5), 433–449.

Palmer, D. (2007). A dual immersion strand programme in California: Carrying out the promise of dual language education in an English-dominant context. *International Journal of Bilingual Education and Bilingualism, 10*(6), 752–768.

Schachter, J., & Gass, S. M. (2013). *Second language classroom research: Issues and opportunities*. Routledge.

10 Black and Bilingual

Challenges in Decentering Whiteness in Dual Language Bilingual Education

Rhonda J. Broussard, Faith R. Kares, Nicole Caridad Ralston, and Maria Patrizia Santos

Context

Contributors to this anthology are part of a wave of scholar-practitioners centering equity in dual language bilingual education (DLBE) and calling for critical consciousness as a core value. Critical consciousness refers to liberatory educator and Brazilian philosopher Paulo Freire's (2021) process of "learning to perceive social, political, and economic contradictions, and to take actions against the oppressive elements of reality." Leadership and policy scholar Angela Valenzuela (2016) defines critically conscious educators as "a voice that courageously and intelligently stands up against injustice and does so from a culturally and community-anchored standpoint" (p. 5). We propose these definitions warrant closer examination of the role of Black leadership in decentering whiteness in DLBE. The case narrative depicts how one Black school leader engaged in efforts to disrupt whiteness in DLBE. The Black administrator featured here was the only BIPOC school leader at the French-language, open-enrollment charter school located in the Gulf Coast. The charter management leadership included two Black women and a Black man. Victor's efforts to promote critical consciousness emerged out of his own experiences of microaggressions and observations of how teachers and staff treated the predominantly Black student body. This chapter examines challenges he encountered in advancing critical consciousness, leading to his decision to eventually leave his post as principal. Given that research on the impact of Black leadership in DLBE remains limited, this case study begins to fill this gap by offering a counter-narrative centering a Black administrator as driver of equity efforts. Strategies to activate critical consciousness in DLBE must therefore include deliberate policies and practices to hire, promote, and retain Black leadership at the school building level.

Case Narrative

Literature across disciplines and fields (e.g., Positive Youth Development [PYD]) shows how adults have a tremendous impact on youth development,

DOI: 10.4324/9781003240594-13

identity, and learning.[1] This case narrative features Victor, the founding principal of a French-language, open-enrollment charter school in a Gulf Coast state, who was emphatic: "Language is intimately tied to identity." He recognized how his identity as a Black bilingual person is key to decentering whiteness in bilingual education. As he put it,

> I think just having that person in the building who shares an identity with the students, but also is demonstrating this skill, this thing that is not typically associated with our group because of stereotypes and all these negative ideas about us. I always thought that that was important.

Victor reflected how Black people have historically been excluded from DLBE spaces:

> Immersion education was not for Black kids. I guess the stereotype was that . . . our kids need so much support in reading and math and English. . . . And so I think, for me, it's about shifting mindsets about who the program is for and what the benefits of the program can be, and who it can benefit.

Previously, Victor never considered himself in an administrative position. He was simply excited about the prospect of helping to build an open access French school. As he put it, "It just seemed very exciting to help envision a model where French and the whole child model would be accomplished together." Additionally, as a Black man who learned French as a second language, he was drawn to the idea of "going back to the community that we served." Indeed, nearly 75% of the students served at Victor's school were Black.

From the outset, Victor and his leadership team, comprising two white women, encountered obstacles. First, it was difficult to find both French-speaking and whole child model trained teachers. Second, as any public school is, they were held to end-of-year standards. "We could never let gaps in the language become an obstacle to students mastering academic content." He explained,

> A student could come to us in third grade, fourth grade, or fifth grade when they got there, at any point having no background in French at all. And so the system had to be set up to where those students would be integrated into the culture of the school and be introduced to the language in a way that was at their level, while still accessing academic content.

Thirdly, Victor depicted a "fixed mindset" among the majority of his staff.[2] He added he observed this among both white and Black teachers. He expressed frustration that they were unable to recruit more Black American teachers whose experiences reflected those of the students. He elaborated, "The Black American experience, for example, is very different from a Black teacher who comes from Togo, or a Black teacher who comes from Algeria." Victor's recognition of the nuances of identity politics reflects the important role of critical consciousness in countering white supremacy culture (WSC), which may be internalized in non-white bodies. In many ways, these teachers from the African and Francophone diaspora held similar racist beliefs as white teachers.

Of all the challenges Victor encountered as principal, he spoke most passionately about language and Black youth identities. He explained the majority of students were from the surrounding Black neighborhoods and would arrive speaking at school the way they speak at home. He observed that teachers and staff disapproved of Black English. He put it, "Black English has a stigma of being an unintelligent, broken form of English." But because language is tied to identity, when adults in the school framed students' home English as "incorrect" they simultaneously communicated that there was also something fundamentally wrong with them [students].

> I think I tried to undo, in conversations, this idea, because I often heard the way children were redirected in language. "Don't say it like that. That's the wrong way to say this, or that's the wrong way to say that." And so when you start there, and you start being critical of someone's language within an academic setting, you're also in some way communicating their place at all altogether in school. "This is the way that I naturally speak, and it doesn't fit here. That's not affirming to my identity within the context of school. I feel like I may not belong here at all" . . . And I felt like that was an obstacle to getting teachers to speak more French, because they [teachers] heard how they [students] spoke.

After a few years, Victor left his post. He identifies three factors contributing to his departure: (1) personal circumstances; (2) COVID pandemic, which was draining to manage; and (3) he found it increasingly difficult to shift mindsets among his colleagues. Victor emphasized the difficulty surrounding shifting mindsets was what primarily fueled his departure. He reflected,

> I found it exceedingly difficult to shift mindsets around cultural things regarding Black students. Our school was 75% African American. And I would hear things constantly that, as a Black school leader, it drains you to hear the way that some of the adults in the building would talk about students' home language, about Black English. And just how close-minded they were and limited they were in their understanding or willingness to try to understand the experiences of these students.

Victor elaborated how both white and Black adult views of Black children impeded the potential for the school to provide the safe space necessary for young people to take risks, like learning a new language.

In addition to shifting mindsets pertaining to Black students, he also encountered some resistance in his own leadership as a Black man. In describing his working relationship with the two white school leaders with whom he primarily worked, he conveyed that his identity caused lack of confidence in his leadership.

> There were times when I often felt like who I was caused a lack of confidence in my decisions or the way that I perceived certain situations. I often think that's true of my role now, too, as a head of a school . . . if I were an older white man or an older white woman, I might not get so much pushback on certain decisions that I make, [they] would be more trusting of my judgment calls whenever I have to make them.

Victor's experience, and his critical analysis, reflects how whiteness was centered. Effective leadership was presumed as white whereas Black leadership held contradiction and tension. It is also important to point out here that Victor held a doctorate while his white women colleagues did not. This speaks to the racial inequities frequently surrounding hiring, retention, and promotion—namely, white people with far less experience and training more quickly advance in an organization and/or are viewed as exemplary leaders despite their disparate credentials compared to their Black counterparts.

Victor identified constructive feedback as an important part of his role as a leader. However, his identity as a Black man made it difficult for some staff to accept his feedback. He surmised, "I think they were just so blinded by who I was." Over time, self-doubt emerged. Victor commented, "I did often ask myself that, like, 'Am I not doing a great job of sharing the vision? Am I not communicating this well?'"

> Because the whole child model and French have a history of being elitist models that are typically for white, upper-class students and affluent families, I wanted to change that . . . I realized later on, though, that there were actually teachers within the school who needed that, to have their mindset changed, and needed to be shifted internally. And that had to happen first.

He referred to the major roadblock: "I think folks' imagination, hope, flexibility, and tolerance for building a process that's not always super linear or clean." Victor attempted to shift mindsets by soliciting and offering feedback and creating an environment in which anti-racism commitments were openly discussed. However, many adults in the school still grappled with being able to see the vision of a whole child model French language school with a majority Black student population.

Teaching Notes

Scant research exists on the role of Black leadership in DLBE. The literature examining the role of Black professionals in DLBE is limited to the experience of Black *teachers* in the model of bilingual education prescribed by the 1968 Bilingual Education Act, focusing on transitional bilingual education rather than the enrichment of bilingual education. A study of Black teachers identified limitations to this model, including not enough support to encourage adequate instruction in the students' native language; lack of teacher training; and lack of clear goals regarding bilingual-education policies and procedures (Cooper, 1999). Other studies that focus on the contemporary model of DLBE—which positions biliteracy as enrichment versus remediation—address experiences of Black students and families, but still excludes Black leaders. Within those studies, Black families named that DLBE schools should offer better professional opportunities for their children and provide cross-cultural education (Palmer, 2010). However, without explicit, ongoing anti-racism training for teachers and staff in DLBE, Black children still experience discrimination as they would in a traditional monolingual school. While teacher preparation and family input are fundamental to driving the shift toward critical consciousness in DLBE, equal attention must be paid to administrators who play a pivotal role in driving equity decisions and policies. If Black leaders are not adequately supported and/or if they are the only ones attempting to advance critical consciousness in schools, then they risk burn-out and leaving.

Key elements of Victor's approach to school leadership reflect antidotes to white supremacy culture (WSC) and therefore ingredients to advance critical consciousness in DLBE. Tema Okun (2021), one of the authors of *Characteristics of White Supremacy Culture*, describes culture as being pervasive yet invisible. Elements of WSC include but are not limited to perfectionism, sense of urgency, quantity over quality, defensiveness, either/or thinking, paternalism, fear of open conflict, individualism, objectivity, and the right to comfort.

Victor's approach to leadership challenged many WSC traits. For instance, he believed in normalizing feedback, wherein feedback was not merely provided during an annual performance review but as a regular practice. This normalization of feedback was for Victor also an important way to cultivate a growth mindset. However, he received a great deal of defensiveness. Many of his staff and teachers were uncomfortable with the messiness intrinsic in trying something new (e.g., joining the whole child model methods with deep language immersion). Victor's growth mindset countered perfectionism as well as "only one right way" thinking. Whole child development embraces a learner-centered approach, valuing the experiences and knowledge each young person brings into a learning space. These experiences must be honored and recognized in order to meet children where they are at, and this certainly includes home languages, beliefs, and practices that may differ from adults or even other children at their school. Aside from his supervisor who was a Black woman, who largely worked outside the physical school building, Victor had very little support in his work of shifting mindsets: namely, getting all schoolteachers, staff, and even members of his own leadership team to view Black students as capable of acquiring French as a second language *and* to view Victor himself as a Black man as capable of serving as a leader. Indeed, Victor's story is a cautionary tale of DLBE programs that do not center, hire, promote, and retain Black leaders. Without adequate supports, Black leaders who are critical to advancing antiracist practices in DLBE will burn out and ultimately leave.

Discussion Questions and Activities

This chapter demonstrates the vast opportunity to learn more about Black administrators in DLBE and their impact on Black students and their families. Such work may advance certain fields such as PYD, and answer calls to build on literature examining the relationship between language and identity in DLBE spaces (Alfaro, 2019). The rich case narrative outlined in this chapter has clear implications for practice and research. Regarding practice, these preliminary observations provide rich material to leaders who are looking to center policies and practices that de-bias their talent strategies to hire, promote, retain, and support Black leaders.

Hiring

Questions to ask:

1. How does and *can* your hiring process reinforce commitment to racial equity, diversity, and inclusion?
2. What structures or shifts are necessary to advance hiring practices from a racial equity, diversity, and inclusion perspective?
3. What barriers present themselves?
4. What additional resources might you require?

Points for consideration:

- Review WSC characteristics to determine which are heavily weighted in hiring rubrics.
- Identify bias in hiring systems by disaggregating demographic data. When in your process are Black candidates being released (e.g., resume review, team interview, supervisor interview, CEO interview, etc.)? Once you identify where the bias is occurring, narrow your strategies.

- Market DLBE roles in traditional Black education programs, professional organizations, and universities.
- Have your hiring team take implicit association tests and discuss biases prior to the search. Hold each other accountable when biases creep in.
- Survey candidates between the final interview and offer period to capture their experience in your process.
- Prepare team members to address why racial equity, diversity, and inclusion are important to your team in introductions. Ask team members to model vulnerability and be honest about the team's and their personal growth areas. This will signal to your candidate that your team is willing to be vulnerable, model imperfection, build relationships, and have the difficult conversations necessary to advance racial equity.
- Assess each candidate for alignment to your racial equity, diversity, and inclusion goals by embedding key questions throughout the interview process.

Promotion

Questions to ask:

- How does and *can* your performance management and promotion process reinforce commitment to racial equity, diversity, and inclusion?
- What structures or shifts are necessary to advance performance management practices from a racial equity, diversity, and inclusion perspective?
- What barriers present themselves?
- What additional resources might you require?

Points for consideration:

- Review WSC Characteristics to determine which are heavily weighted in performance management and promotion process.
- Mitigate bias in performance management by grounding performance and promotion reviews in competencies, job responsibilities, documented behaviors/actions, dedication to dismantling White supremacy culture, and forwarding racial equity.
- Ensure performance reviews involve multiple stakeholders by utilizing a 360-degree review.
- Carve out space for managers to align on performance review processes and check each other's reviews for bias.
- Disaggregate data to determine how advancement and promotions play out in your organization by race and other demographic markers.

Pertaining to research, we amplify the call for mixed methods and longitudinal research on how Black school administrators lead DLBE programming. Indeed, most empirical work on DLBE has used qualitative approaches (Cervantes-Soon et al., 2017). Moreover, as scholars and practitioners call for a shift toward critical consciousness in DLBE, the case narrative offered in this chapter indicates that Black leaders are already at the forefront of advancing such practices but need more support. By conducting more research on the experiences of Black leaders in DLBE, administrators may gain greater understanding into how schools and programs may best support them as well as recognize them for their efforts in advancing equity and antiracism.

Notes

1. For instance, within the context of STEM wherein girls and BIPOC students frequently experience exclusion and a lack of belonging, BIPOC adults and women who lead STEM programming or teach STEM courses have a positive influence on the youth with whom they interact (DeWitt et al., 2011). "By observing staff that look and talk like them, young people may be able to envision themselves one day occupying similar roles of power and authority" (Price et al., 2019).
2. "In a fixed mindset, people believe their basic qualities, like their intelligence or talent, are simply fixed traits. They spend their time documenting their intelligence or talent instead of developing them. They also believe that talent alone creates success—without effort" (Dweck, 2006).

References

Alfaro, C. (2019). Preparing critically conscious dual-language teachers: Recognizing and interrupting dominant ideologies. *Theory into Practice*, *58*(2), 194–203.

Bilingual Education Act of 1968, Public Law 90–247, 81 Stat. 816 (1968).

Cervantes-Soon, C. G., Dorner, L., Palmer, D., Heiman, D., Schwerdtfeger, R., & Choi, J. (2017). Combating inequalities in two-way language immersion programs: Toward critical consciousness in bilingual education spaces. *Review of Research in Education*, *41*(1), 403–427.

Cooper, T. E. (1999). *Community in conflict: Black bilingual teachers in bilingual education programs*. California State University.

DeWitt, J., Archer, L., Osborne, J., Dillon, J., Willis, B., & Wong, B. (2011). High aspirations but low progression: The science aspirations—careers paradox amongst minority ethnic students. *International Journal of Science and Mathematics Education*, *9*(2), 243–271.

Dweck, C. (2006). *The new psychology for success*. Random House.

Freire, P. (2021). *Education for critical consciousness*. Bloomsbury Publishing.

Okun, T. (2021, May). White supremacy culture—Still here. *Dismantling Racism*. www.dismantlingracism.org/uploads/4/3/5/7/43579015/white_supremacy_culture_-_still_here.pdf

Palmer, D. (2010). Race, power, and equity in a multiethnic urban elementary school with a dual-language "strand" program. *Anthropology & Education Quarterly*, *41*(1), 94–114.

Price, C. A., Kares, F., Segovia, G., & Loyd, A. B. (2019). Staff matter: Gender differences in science, technology, engineering or math (STEM) career interest development in adolescent youth. *Applied Developmental Science*, *23*(3), 239–254.

Valenzuela, A. (2016). *Growing critically conscious teachers: A social justice curriculum for educators of Latino/a youth*. Teachers College Press.

11 Vietnamese Dual Language Immersion

Commodifying an Uncommodified Language and Culture

Michael Bacon and Vân Truong

Context

Dual language education began in Portland Public Schools (PPS), a major urban school district in the Pacific Northwest, over 35 years ago as magnet programs began to attract and retain students in public schools. As innovative educational programs, these initial one-way foreign language immersion programs focused on languages and cultures (i.e., Spanish, Japanese, and Mandarin) and have become coveted and commodified by English-speaking families. Strong interest in these initial programs, along with concerns about saving specific neighborhood schools and with dwindling enrollment, pushed the district to implement lotteries and establish wait lists that continue today. However, in PPS and the education field in general, the advent of two-way dual language immersion (DLI) programs[2] were viewed as effective educational programs to close the gap for emergent bilinguals (EBs),[3] in particular for Spanish-speaking EBs, and began to take hold in the late 1990s. The district then initiated two Spanish DLI programs at schools with significant Spanish-speaking populations in 1994 and 1997. These programs aimed to serve EBs and were initiated by an innovative principal or the ESL department, who tapped into grants or federal funding rather than through the district's general funding as the district had done with the earlier "magnet" one-way foreign language immersion programs.

The two new DLI programs were successful. They were developed according to preliminary research from language education scholars Thomas and Collier (2002). However, there were concerns that a growing Spanish-speaking student population in other parts of the city were not being served by these two small programs. The grassroots-based Latino Network also advocated to expand the number of DLI programs. This led to an initial proposal from the community in 2003 to implement more Spanish DLI programs as two-way programs to serve Spanish-speaking EBs. The next year the district initiated a task force to expand DLI programs to meet the needs of these students and the community. The task force noted in their recommendations the significant size of the Vietnamese EB population, the second largest in PPS, but the task force did not recommend Vietnamese

DOI: 10.4324/9781003240594-14

as a DLI program language. One of the original task force members concluded, "We did not think we could make the case for Vietnamese, because we could not make it sustainable without having a large number of English native speakers to make it a Two-Way program."

The task force's view that Vietnamese DLI programs would not be sustainable coincided with shifts in state school funding policies and economic woes; district budgets were being slashed, and DLI programs with low enrollment were being heavily scrutinized. The district superintendent's chief of staff at the time pointed at an FTE allocation formula and stated, "DLI programs are no different than other educational programs. Student enrollment must generate the classroom teacher FTE. Otherwise, we will need to cut them." When asked about challenges the community faced in working with the district to propose a Vietnamese DLI program, a Vietnamese community advocate noted,

> One of the key issues the district administrators had was saying we can't get enough English-speaking families to join the program so we can't have a two-way program. Not enough interest from non-Vietnamese. I suggested that the other half could be 2nd and 3rd generation Vietnamese (who speak English as their first language). "Not American enough" means not white English speakers. Don't look "American" enough. They said these things to us many times.

Time and again, district administrators turned a deaf ear to the Vietnamese community with a mindset that DLI needed to be sustainable for white English native speaker enrollment.

In the mid-2000s, the district began investing in system-wide racial equity work using Glenn Singleton's book *Courageous Conversations* and guidance from his Pacific Education Group (PEG). The framework provided by PEG set the stage for district employees, families, and community members to engage in both personal reflection and a critical examination of the impact of systemic racism on the outcomes of students of color. Regular and explicit conversations about equity took place at all levels of the organization and relied upon all stakeholders, from leaders to teachers, to engage in issues of race. In 2011, the school board passed a Racial Education Equity Policy that guided district employees in examining desegregated data and seeing race as a key factor in every district matter, from budget and school boundary changes to the transfer policy, student discipline, achievement data, curriculum, teacher and principal reviews, and day-to-day teaching. With this racial equity work, PPS employees PPS at all levels of the organization began applying a racial equity lens to decisions and deliberations, raising critical consciousness, and shifting many long-standing biased practices and policies.

A newly appointed DLI director, in collaboration with other key district stakeholders, recognized the importance of aligning the DLI department priorities to the district's Racial Education Equity Policy and moving the department's goals from the classic three pillars of dual language education: 1) academic achievement, 2) bilingualism and biliteracy, and 3) cross-cultural competence to close the opportunity gap for historically underserved EB students. This shift in stance pushed the DLI department and the district to examine carefully many policies and practices around DLI that often set up barriers for EBs in accessing DLI programs, such as the enrollment lottery process that failed to hold slots for EBs in all programs despite the academic necessity of DLI programs for their academic success.

As the district continued to work with PEG in engaging in racial equity, a number of important shifts occurred that seemed to facilitate DLI being recognized as a lever in equity work. Initially, Singleton's work seemed to focus primarily on the impact of systemic racism on Black communities, but as PEG engaged with this district and many others, the racial groups widened to include Latinx, Asian, and Indigenous peoples. PEG presenters and facilitators working with the district diversified in their racial makeup accordingly. As the work evolved, nuances were added to the racial equity framework, such as consideration of immigrant populations, even if they were white (i.e., Russian) and being racialized by holding on to their language and culture. Racial equity leaders began seeing the incredible diversity and differences of Asian Americans, many of which suffered from being lumped all together and masked or hidden by the high-performing Japanese and Chinese Americans. This work laid the foundation for both the district and community members to be open to engaging in the idea of starting a Vietnamese DLI program in PPS.

Case Narrative

"Why the hell are you starting a Vietnamese program? You should be doing Mandarin!" boldly stated the irritated white father in front of a large crowd of fellow parents at a district DLI parent information meeting in spring of 2014. After a brief moment of silence, the DLI assistant director leading the meeting circled back to the main driver of DLI: to close the opportunity gap for emergent bilinguals (EB). Vietnamese EBs had been and continue to be the second largest EB population in the district. The DLI assistant director noted the achievement gap these students face. As early as 2001, the Vietnamese-speaking EB student population was already the second largest in the district with the city, becoming one of the top ten cities in the US in terms of Vietnamese American population (US Census Bureau, 2010). Sandy Boulevard, a major thoroughfare in the city, became colloquially known as "Saigon Boulevard" because it served as the hub of a thriving Vietnamese American community with businesses, restaurants, and churches.

When making the internal case for Vietnamese DLI, the ESL director clearly remembers meeting with the newly appointed director of DLI to share the demographic and academic data on Vietnamese EBs. "You're advocating for Vietnamese DLI, because you're Vietnamese!" the director of DLI pushed back. The DLI director was against the idea of initiating a Vietnamese DLI program, believing the district should expand Chinese DLI to meet the demands of English-speaking parents instead of starting a new program which presented many hurdles, such as sustainable enrollment. Vietnamese was not "marketable." As a public school system heavily invested in equity, DLI serves as a lever in closing that gap. Yet, this same commodification, or lack of commodification, of certain languages and cultures, also permeated the thinking of key educational leaders within the district. The DLI department was no exception, despite its explicit role of expanding DLI to meet the needs of EBs.

Finally, in 2013 and in alignment with this district's Racial Education Policy, which included specific reference to "linguistic equity"—and in the face of compelling long-term national research on the potential of DLI in closing the achievement gap for EBs—the school board charged the district's Department of Dual Language with identifying and recommending potential expansion sites for Spanish and other language immersion programs. DLI programs were to align to meet the linguistic, cultural, and academic needs of native-speaking populations throughout the district. With closing the achievement gap as the primary aim, the department focused on minority language populations that demonstrated significant populations to support sustainable dual language immersion programs, which included Vietnamese.

As the Department of Dual Language team, in collaboration with key stakeholders both inside the district and in the community, began to move the recommendation forward to the proposal stage, resistance with seemingly logical rationales for not starting a Vietnamese DLI (VDLI) surfaced regularly and at all levels. Several principals in Title I schools with Vietnamese EBs claimed that the Vietnamese students were already doing well so why direct scarce district resources to starting a VDLI program? Many people, including the principal of the school where the program eventually landed, expressed the age-old concern that English-speaking parents would not enroll their children in the program. Subsequent concerns of racially segregating Vietnamese American children also popped up. Human resources, principals, and the district's Office of Teaching and Learning staff worried that the district lacked teachers who could teach in the program, and the schools would struggle to find or develop curriculum materials aligned to state and district standards. Monolingual English-speaking teachers at the identified school also shared their fears of losing their jobs. Further, the scattered population of Vietnamese-speaking students across a wide expanse of the outer east side of the city made identifying a centrally located school challenging. Transportation would be required. The long litany of seemingly valid reasons for not doing VDLI tested many in the work.

Simultaneously, PPS superintendent, in alignment with the equity work, looked to diversify district senior leadership. This diversification included a number of Black and Latinx senior leaders—but almost no representation by

Asian leaders. After four ESL directors left the district central office for various reasons within five years, one of the first Vietnamese American educational leaders in the district, Dr. Tran, was recruited to be ESL director. Dr. Tran was reluctant to accept the promotion, however, because of the stigmatization that she suffered earlier as an ESL student coming to the United States. However, she accepted the position, recognizing that with her lived and professional experiences, she could advocate for EBs and specifically for Vietnamese-speaking students just as Black and Latinx leaders do.

As interest grew in the Vietnamese American community and with advocacy from leaders in several community organizations led by Asian Americans, Vietnamese Americans, and people of color, in May of 2013, district leadership presented the concept of a VDLI program to a room of over 300 Vietnamese American community members at one of the major Vietnamese Catholic churches found along "Saigon Boulevard." The presentation was met with strong interest, but also with an understandable and undeniable skepticism given the community's sense of being ignored and neglected by the district for so many years. One Vietnamese community leader pointed to the district leaders at the meeting and pronounced, "I am going to hold you accountable for following through on the Vietnamese DLI program."

Beyond the lack of trust between the Vietnamese community and district leadership, more work was needed to understand the intense and challenging politics and trauma centered on a war-refugee community that continues to vilify and fear the government of their homeland. Words and dialects directly or indirectly associated with the Vietnamese Communist regime stirred up deep rooted pain for those traumatized in the war and as they fled their country. This trauma, passed on generationally along with a strong tradition of filial piety in Vietnamese culture, often keeps language issues at the center of controversy in the program's teachers and curriculum. Learning Vietnamese language is certainly not just a simple commodification for economic gain or travel. Learning Vietnamese comes with complex emotions and perspectives in the community. Despite these challenges, Vietnamese American community members continued to advocate for VDLI, including testifying at the school board meeting in July 2013 and collecting over 700 signatures on a petition submitted to the superintendent that fall.

Internally, as the Department of Dual Language drafted and submitted a proposal to design, plan, and implement a Vietnamese DLI program to senior leadership, questions of viability surfaced again. One key senior leader vocalized, "What if we fail? We will lose all trust with the community." This fear seemed to be based once again on the idea that "families" will not buy into Vietnamese language and culture. Budget concerns also plagued the effort to move the proposal forward. Purchasing, developing, and translating curriculum materials into a language that almost no American publisher supported would require much institutional and financial commitment. A culminating meeting with the chief academic officer resulted in a key advocate for the program walking out in the middle of the meeting and others leaving in tears of frustration. Yet, after continued advocacy appealing to the district's racial equity policy and a successful application for a state equity grant that specifically supported the design and development of DLI programs, district leadership finally approved the program. VDLI was finally implemented nearly nine years after the initial discussions. VDLI finally moved from invisibility to a top recommendation based on large numbers, need, and community advocacy.

Teaching Notes

The case narrative demonstrates how parents can "commodify" languages as they seek skills to ensure their child's future job prospects, language usability in the local community, travel, and the perceived prestige of language and culture. A Google search on "important languages to learn," for example, cites increased salaries for those who speak certain languages as a top reason. However, presumably in the mind of the father who attended the DLI information meeting mentioned earlier, he, like many others in the community, viewed DLI as a highly effective way to learn a second language and culture. Selecting a partner language that mainstream America views as "valuable" is an important part of the decision for a parent to enter their five-year-old into a K–12 DLI program. Questioning the purpose of DLI, and raising awareness of how DLI is a critical lever in closing the opportunity gap and a necessity for EBs rather than a "nice to have" for the already empowered English native speaking families, are essential for challenging this commodification.

In advocating for and implementing a two-way dual language immersion program, a critical principle is to develop a high level of bilingualism and biliteracy in addressing the inevitable lower status—in this narrative, Vietnamese—of the partner language or the L1 of EBs (Hamayan et al., 2013). Addressing the inequities of status outside the classroom necessitates emphasizing and protecting the partner language time in the classroom as well as throughout the school culture. In the US context, Spanish has historically been a particularly low-status language (García, 2014). However, one might argue that Spanish is a fairly "commodified" language in the greater US social context since the number of Spanish speakers in many communities—and specifically workplaces—promotes a higher value on employees who can communicate in Spanish. Vietnamese, on the other hand, may fall into an even lower status given the lower number of immigrants across the US and workforce and its subsequent lack of "practical" application.

Research has also found that two-way dual language immersion programs tend to emphasize furthering higher-income students' multilingual skills to compete in the global economy (Palmer, 2009), rather than supporting minoritized students' home languages. To this end, Vietnamese as a language not typically seen as a critical language in international trade plays a critical role in whether or not district leadership prioritizes the implementation of such non-commodified languages. As Palmer et al. (2019) stated (referencing Cervantes-Soon, 2014), "Specifically, the individualistic, depoliticized, competition-based, and market oriented ethos of neoliberal ideologies can result in contexts that lack a sense of obligation toward minoritized students, that commodify bilingualism, and that prioritize human capital accumulation." (p. 121)

In advocating and implementing a less commonly taught language (LCTL) such as Vietnamese, the four elements of critical consciousness in two-way dual language ([TWDL]; Palmer et al., 2019) become particularly pertinent to even achieving approval, let alone success. The four following strategies can help districts and leaders approach implementing LCTL programs. First, the *continuous interrogation of power holders* in all levels of the organization, even those who seemingly stand for TWDL, is essential for an LCTL that is often primarily associated with war and nail salons. Second, *historicizing schools and educational policy context* and leveraging district leaders and parents who are members of the dominant community who acknowledge the history and rights of language minority children to act as allies and advocates (Palmer et al., 2019). Those with more privilege need to recognize when to refrain from speaking and when to stop others from dominating the discourse, especially with a language and culture that is typified by not questioning those in power and respecting elders. Third, they must employ *critical listening*. Fourth, and finally, those in power must experience *discomfort* as they invest in a language and culture that may not bring them benefit and praise from the mainstream power holders.

Teaching Activities

Activity A: Surfacing Hurdles Both Above and Below

Roleplay one of the key district leaders (i.e., ESL director, DLI director, chief academic officer, superintendent chief of staff, etc.) in the narrative individually or in small groups. Use the following questions as potential prompts:

- *Identify the major hurdles above and below the surface for proposing and implementing a DLI program in a "less commonly taught language" such as Vietnamese.*
    - What hurdles are easiest to overcome and why?
    - What hurdles are most difficult to overcome and why?
    - In your role, what steps would you take to address these hurdles? What additional information would you need?
- *How would you in your role work to "commodify" Vietnamese language and culture with district leadership? With your school board? With your school leaders? In the Vietnamese American community?*

- *Using a critical consciousness lens how would you define "commodification" and both its positive and negative effects on efforts to serve EBs?*

Activity B: Unpacking Quotes

Select one of the quotes from the case narrative to respond to the following questions in writing:

- What is their perspective on the commodification of Vietnamese language and culture? How do you know that?
- What is the role of "Whiteness" or privilege in the perspective shared in the quote?
- How might district leaders respond to the quote?
- How might members of the Vietnamese American community respond to the quote?
- How would you respond to the quote?

With a partner do the following:

1. One partner shares their quote and their responses.
2. The other partner asks only clarifying questions first.
3. The other partner then asks probing questions.
4. Switch roles and repeat 1–3.
5. As partners, identify an "aha" and a wondering question to share with the whole group.

Notes

1. One-way foreign language immersion: dual language immersion programs primarily serving English native speakers (majority language speakers) to learn a second language.
2. Two-way dual language immersion: dual language immersion programs serving both partner language native speakers and English native speakers (majority language speakers).
3. Emergent bilingual (EB): This term is used by the district as a more appropriate term than LEP or ELL, because it points to possibilities of developing bilingualism rather than focusing on language limits or deficiencies (García, 2009).

References

Cervantes-Soon, C. G. (2014). A critical look at dual language immersion in the New Latin@ Diaspora. *Bilingual Research Journal*, *37*(1), 64–82. doi:10.1080/15235882.2014.893267

García, O. (2014). *The sociolinguistics of Latino Diasporas: Latino practices, identities, and ideologies*. Routledge.

Hamayan, E. V., Genesee, F., & Cloud, N. (2013). *Dual language instruction from A to Z: Practical guidance for teachers and administrators*. Heinemann.

Palmer, D. (2009). Middle-class English speakers in a two-way immersion bilingual classroom: "Everybody should be listening to Jonathan right now . . .". *TESOL Quarterly, 43*(2), 177–202.

Palmer, D. K., Cervantes-Soon, C., Dorner, L., & Heiman, D. (2019). Bilingualism, biliteracy, biculturalism, and critical consciousness for all: Proposing a fourth fundamental goal for two-way dual language education. *Theory into Practice, 58*(2), 121–133. doi:10.1080/00405841.2019.1569376

Thomas, W. P., & Collier, V. P. (2002). *A national study of school effectiveness for language minority students' long-term academic achievement.* Center for Research on Education, Diversity and Excellence, University of California-Santa Cruz.

U.S. Census Bureau. (2010). *QuickFacts: Portland City, Oregon.* www.census.gov/quickfacts/portlandcityoregon

12 *De La Lucha a La Victoria*

The Journey to Save a Dual Language Bilingual Education Teacher Preparation Program

Cristina Alfaro

Context

In thirty years of K–20 teaching and educational leadership, I learned that the most impactful bilingual education champions sooner or later must take on a *lucha* (fight) en route to discovering their voice and the ideological clarity they will need to overcome obstacles. I realize now that before I took on formal leadership roles, I exercised my leadership at a very young age. My *lucha* began in a kindergarten classroom, where I became an unlikely activist refusing to acquiesce to the dangerous English-only, anti-bilingualism ideologies carried out by well-meaning but oblivious teachers since the sixties. I was an energetic five-year-old, the daughter of proud Mexican immigrants. Spanish was the language of our heritage, the language we spoke at home, the only language I knew. On the first day of school, I waltzed into my rural classroom in Southern California, unaware that Mrs. Spencer, my new White teacher, was a staunch "English-only" advocate. "If you're going to speak," she declared, "you must speak English."

"*¿Qué dijo la maestra?*" ("What did the teacher say?") I asked the girl sitting next to me, unaware that Mrs. Spencer was already walking in my direction. All eyes on me, I was about to become her sacrificial lamb to illustrate what would happen if anyone else dared to break her rule. She grabbed me by the arm and walked me to the corner of the room, where she deposited my tiny frame in front of a desk next to the door. Ceremonially, she grabbed a set of felt paper donkey ears from a shelf and placed them on the desk, signaling with her hands for me to put them on my head. Time froze. I stared at the donkey ears, then scanned the room full of stunned faces until my eyes rested on the open door next to me. I took a big breath and ran through the classroom door, then through the school's gate to the street, until I found refuge behind a large tree in the field across the street. Fortunately for me, after a policeman returned me to the school's office, I never returned to Mrs. Spencer's classroom, thanks to my father. Despite the communication barriers between him and the school principal, he demanded that I should be placed in a different classroom. The experience stayed with me.

DOI: 10.4324/9781003240594-15

When I received my bilingual teaching credential twenty years later, I invited the newly retired Mrs. Spencer for coffee. Though she didn't remember me, she accepted. During our time together, I recounted the humiliating moment and how it had been the first of many jarring and emotional moments that reinforced the cognitive dissonance that began in her classroom. I also shared how I had finally understood, through my study of language policy and bilingualism/biliteracy as an asset, why so many students are often impacted by dismissive pedagogical practices that disregard and devalue students' native cultural identity and linguistic background (Macedo et al., 2003). I believe this was a pivotal moment for both of us, but especially for Mrs. Spencer, who humbled herself to engage in critical listening and immense discomfort. With tears in her eyes, she apologized. "I was wrong," she said. "It was my sincere belief that the sooner my students stopped speaking Spanish, the faster they would learn English, which would increase their potential for personal and academic success."

Ideology, Ideological Consciousness, and Ideological Clarity

Mrs. Spencer, like other teachers, did not set out to be a cruel educator. Scholars suggest that educators' ideological consciousness—and the ideological clarity that emerges from self-questioning until we understand that our authentic values align with our practices—ultimately drive beliefs and attitudes about linguistically diverse learners and their families, which in turn impact how we lead, teach, and treat students and their families (Alfaro, 2019; Bartolome, 1994; Cervantes-Soon et al., 2017). The challenge is that educators' ideological consciousness is often hijacked by the stories we come to believe (Keckler, 2015), many of which are driven by political agendas and informed by colonized ideas and policies which perpetuate biases and oppressive pedagogical practices. Leaders and other K–12 educators who have not learned how to examine their pedagogical praxis (Freire, 1993)—or how their ideological consciousness informs their pedagogical practices inadvertently become Trojan horses introducing toxic and destructive classroom practices, not entirely unlike the ones in Mrs. Spencer's classroom.

De la Lucha a La Victoria: A Case Study

This chapter documents my *lucha* and seemingly endless journey as an educational leader determined to save the dual language English learner education (DLE) teacher preparation program under attack by anti-bilingual and anti-immigrant ideologies and the devastating effects of anti-bilingual education policies. *I will use "program" moving forward for simplicity.* I hope that as you read the various stories behind how this program re-emerged from near ashes to become the premier dual language bilingual education (DLBE) teacher preparation program it is today—providing inspiration at the state, national, and international levels—you will be encouraged to forge a journey of your own when your *lucha* arrives at your door. It will.

I was an associate professor and department chair in the College of Education (COE) at San Diego State University, leading the university's DLBE teacher preparation program. The passing of California Proposition 227 in 1998, which "Required English Instruction in Public Schools," was a violent attack on bilingual education, marking the beginning of a twenty-year battle to keep the program afloat. Enrollment plummeted almost overnight. My fellow faculty members began to retire or find alternative teaching and administrative assignments. Staff members were reassigned to other college departments. No one could deny that closing a program unsanctioned by the state that was bleeding resources was a sound business decision; yet, as a leader, I knew that as long as the program remained open, we would send a strong signal that we opposed an ill-conceived, politically motivated policy.

The question I often got was, "Where do you find the strength to stay the course?" Leaders must always be ready to rally the resilience nurtured over time. I was fortunate also to have developed ideological clarity. Gramsci (1971 [1935]) defined ideology as the power of ruling class ideas to overshadow and eradicate competing views, which can become the commonsense view of the world. On the other hand, ideological clarity is an individual's ability to see ideologies for what they are and to upend this "commonsense" view of the world. I was prepared with a foundational understanding of critical ideological consciousness inclusive of an assets-based vision of multilingualism and social justice education that comes from questioning other ideologies and our own, but ultimately by what we come to believe and practice. For example, throughout my thirty-year trajectory, my experiences were processed through the critical lens I gained en route to becoming an educational leader and researcher. I was continuously shaped by my ideology and, ultimately, my praxis, which is the intersection between ideological consciousness and educational leadership practices—or what I do to affect pedagogy, policy, and the environments that shape the future of our students. Without the guiding light of this well-developed critical ideological consciousness, I could have never stayed the course. Critical ideological consciousness is key to discerning the power structures that shape our realities—to read the word and the world (Freire, 1970). It brings humanity, empathy, autonomy, solidarity, and passion to a praxis framework that can transform our world into a more humanizing and liberatory education.

From Critical Ideological Consciousness to Praxis

Agency and urgency drive praxis. When the program became expendable, I could not ignore the extremely rapid growth of linguistically and culturally diverse students in our classrooms. The need for critically ideologically conscious and linguistically competent administrators and teachers was urgent. This urgency demanded that I assert my leadership like never before;

I could not ignore that San Diego State University (SDSU) was—and is—a large public Hispanic-serving institution (HSI) located on Kumeyaay land at the Mexico-US border. The process of historicizing decades of struggles demands that we learn from the stories and narratives that are habitually unexplored and unexplained in mainstream spaces. For decades and under different names, given the political climate and focus, the Dual Language and English Learner Education (DLE) Department in the College of Education has been the cornerstone of bilingual teaching credentials and MA degrees, historically serving a large Latinx, first- and second-generation immigrant student population. Still, I was not ignorant that this was a political fight, one that could be fought only through collective political action, which meant I could not win this one alone. Revolutionary leaders cannot think without the people, nor for the people, but only with the people (Freire, 1970).

My long-time mentor was one of the first voices that encouraged me, Dr. Alberto Ochoa. He walked through my office at the worst possible moment. "Cristina, *aquí estoy para apoyarte y ayudarte con cualquier cosa*," he said. "I'm here to support you and help you with anything." I must have looked pretty bad. Just that week, my husband Tony had also told me, "This is too much, Cristina! You have to give it up." Before Dr. Ochoa left my office, he said, "First, you need to take care of yourself." But, he paused, "Understand this—if you give up *la lucha* now, thirty years of the historical work that has been done before you will be lost forever." It was as if he was reading back to me the words I already knew, but I was afraid to admit.

When I got home, I told Tony what Dr. Ochoa had said. Tony, a dedicated high school principal, had also been in the trenches of educational *luchas* for as long as I. "Then," he said, "you have to fight."

With Tony and Dr. Ochoa in my corner, I knew that I would not abandon *la lucha* no matter what. I also knew that I needed more allies. I would need to galvanize community members, program graduates, faculty, bilingual teachers, principals, and superintendents who were ideologically aligned with the program's vision and mission. Around this time, I was awarded a fellowship from the Kettering Foundation, through which I learned to organize public forums on policy to answer the question, "What does it take for democracy to work as it should?" (*www.kettering.org*). Immediately, I began to organize a policy forum, calling on bilingual education advocates of influence who had a stake in the problem—district school leaders, teachers, parents, students, and policymakers. The forums had a three-prong purpose: to inform, educate, and inspire action.

As part of critical pedagogy discussions with my bilingual credential, master's, and doctoral students, I challenged them to critically interrogate the political power structures and become active agents of change. They were pivotal in mobilizing others by inviting forum participants to engage in the work while carefully examining who and what tends to get in the way of transformative action while working with, through, and around the political system. In many ways, this fight became a critical part of our collective ideological consciousness, a form of political awakening and energizing force of community activists and critically conscious educational leaders. Before long, these community members began to emerge as active and vocal activists, writing letters to SDSU's president, provost, policymakers, and the COE dean. For example, educational leaders spoke about the need for bilingual teachers to educate children with diverse cultural and linguistic backgrounds; community activists shared stories of how immigrant families and children continued to be invisible and devalued within schools and classrooms. We had created a movement through personal narratives, a collective praxis of active voices that would not stop.

By this time, I had started working closely with university senators who supported the need to continue to prepare bilingual teachers. After months of community dialogues and bridge building, the university senate voted unanimously to preserve our program as an autonomous department and afford the resources and bilingual faculty it would need to re-emerge and develop into what is now a model DLBE program in the state of California. Our mighty senate-sanctioned program continued to serve the needs of aspiring DLBE teachers who never lost hope that non-English languages and the cultures of those who speak them would once again be allowed and encouraged in California's classrooms, which is precisely what finally took place in 2016 after the passage of Proposition 58, California Non-English Languages Allowed in Public Schools Act (Senate Bill 1174), that repealed restrictive language policies. Today, the program prepares bilingual teachers and administrators in policy and practice to meet the needs of multilingual learners in diverse settings, from structured English immersion to DLBE programs promoting bilingualism, biliteracy, and global competence.

Teaching Notes

Language policies in the United States have always manifested ideologies (Alfaro, 2018). Whether they are assimilationist or pluralist, the ideologies, sociohistorical factors, and sociopolitical context behind education policies influence the educational treatment that extends to linguistically racialized students, the educators prepared to serve them, and ultimately the learning experiences in schools, homes, and communities which shape students' lives, perspectives, and future agency. We must remember this context before identifying the people who can join our *luchas*, because being ideologically aligned is vital.

Freire (1993) reminds us that teaching and learning in schools constitutes a political act tied to ideological forces operating on behalf of the dominant class. In short, education never is, has been, nor will be a neutral enterprise (Freire, 1993, p. 127). Freire's teachings, which extend to teacher education and leadership preparation programs—given that the curriculum and goals are typically based on dominant ideologies—remind us that teacher education and leadership preparation are not neutral enterprises.

As you consider how to find your critical ideological clarity, remember that you will not first locate it within the pages of textbooks or academic research. Ideological clarity and critical consciousness development begin by historicizing ourselves through the examination of your trajectory and the stories and counter-stories that have shaped you and your values and, in some cases, your acts of rebellion in the face of humiliation and injustice and a commitment to interrogating power as a critical step to undoing inappropriateness (Flores & Rosa, 2015). My research and that of many scholars have suggested that a teacher's and leader's critical ideological consciousness is often reflected in their beliefs and attitudes about linguistically diverse learners and their families, consequently affecting the way they teach and treat students (Alfaro, 2019; Alfaro & Bartolomé, 2017; Bartolomé, 1994; Cervantes-Soon et al., 2017; Friere, 2019). Reading, studying, and questioning one's emerging ideologies through the lens and work of influential scholars, activists, and trailblazers who have made an impact before us is a critical part of developing a mature ideological consciousness informed by one's ideological clarity—which ultimately fuels the resilience and integrity needed to enter the most daunting of fights.

A Reminder from My Heart to Yours

Whatever your background, experiences, or skin color, we need you. Invest in knowing what drives you. Interrogate your ideological consciousness, examining your experiences against those of others. Study the words and actions of scholars and activists who got us this far. Internalize their courage and empathy. Aim to understand their righteous indignation. Join a compassionate community that feeds you and nurtures you. And don't forget to practice self-care, because only a strong body and mind can withstand the fight. Lastly, share your story and lift others—and me.

Discussion Questions/Activities

Activity A: Reflective Practices to Develop Critical Ideology Clarity

Like the operating system in our computers, one's critical ideological clarity is ever present and constantly running in the background of our consciousness. Whether we realize it or not, it informs how we teach, lead, and make decisions. Long fights demand vulnerability and remembering "why" we do this. That's ideological clarity. Developing it requires a conscious and intentional self-interrogation discipline to evaluate, question, and analyze competing ideologies until we are clear about our own. Start with these questions:

1. Why am I doing this?
2. What is my intrinsic motivation for this work?

3. What personal experiences and stories have shaped my convictions?
4. What are the political aspects of *la lucha* I am embarking on?
5. How can I become more politically savvy and strategic?
6. How can I ensure I am physically and mentally fit for the long term (because if I collapse, the work stops)?
7. What mentors can help me remain grounded, point out my blind spots, and build me up when things get tough?

Activity B: Rallying Support and Facilitating Ideological Unity

As leaders, we need others to join the fight that will effectively affect meaningful change. Building trusting relationships—and honing people skills, communication skills, and the ability to persuade and move others to action—is vital for leaders like you and me. If taking the time to develop one's critical ideological clarity is the most crucial investment we can make, investing time in learning how to lead by reaching others' hearts and minds is a close second.

First, start with these questions:

1. What allies do I need to join the fight?
2. What skills do I need to develop to rally others' support and connect with their hearts and minds?

Second, organize and facilitate forums and dialogues that bring together stakeholders across disciplines and sectors. Freire (1993)'s words remind us that "*limit-situations*" do not create a climate of hopelessness, but rather we perceive them. Hence, using the problem-posing questions below, turn to your community and educational leaders for support and engage them in a strategic problem-posing process:

1. What is the problem/situation?
2. What is the context of the problem/situation?
3. What are the "limit" situations/barriers (historical conditions that prevent people from having freedom)?
4. Who are the potential aliases?
5. What are the resources available?
6. What are my limit-acts or actions? (Praxis)

References

Alfaro, C. (2018). The sociopolitical struggle and promise of bilingual teacher education: Past, present and future. *Bilingual Research Journal, 41*(4), 413–427.

Alfaro, C. (2019). Preparing critically conscious dual-language teachers: Recognizing and interrupting dominant ideologies. *Theory into Practice, 58*(2), 194–203.

Alfaro, C., & Bartolomé, L. I. (2017). Preparing ideologically clear bilingual teachers: Honoring working-class, non-standard language use in the bilingual education classroom. Special edition: Bilingual teacher education. *Issues in Teacher Education, 26*(2), 11–34.

Bartolomé, L. (1994). Beyond the methods fetish: Toward a humanizing pedagogy. *Harvard Educational Review, 64*(2), 173–194.

Cervantes-Soon, C. G., Dorner, L., Palmer, D., Heiman, D., Schwerdtfeger, R., & Choi, J. (2017). Combating inequalities in two-way language immersion programs: Toward critical consciousness in bilingual education spaces. *Review of Research in Education, 41*, 403–427.

Flores, N., & Rosa, J. (2015). Undoing appropriateness: Raciolinguistic ideologies and language diversity in education. *Harvard Educational Review, 85*(2), 149–171.

Freire, P. (1970). *Pedagogy of the oppressed*. Continuum.

Freire, P. (1993). *Pedagogy of the city*. Continuum.

Friere, J. (2019). Promoting sociopolitical consciousness and bicultural goals of dual language education: The transformational dual language framework. *Journal of Language, Identity, & Education, 19*(1), 56–71.

Gramsci, A. (1971). *Selection from the prison notebooks*. International Publishers (Original work published in 1935).

Keckler, M. (2015). *Bridge builders: How superb communicators get what they want in business and in life*. Morgan James Publishing.

Macedo, D. P., Dendrinos, B., & Gounari, P. (2003). *The hegemony of English*. Paradigm Publishers.

Section III

Families, Communities, and Critical Consciousness

Section III

13 Fostering Critical Consciousness with Immigrant Families

The Story of a Chinese Immigrant Mother in a Mandarin-English Dual Language Program

Wenyang Sun

Context

This case study takes place in a suburban college town located in the southeastern US, Spring Hill (pseudonym), a town with approximately 60,000 population, approximately 70% White, 10% Black, 6% Latinx, and 13% Asian. More than 20% of the Spring Hill residents speak a language other than English at home and 16% are considered foreign-born; both numbers are higher than the state average of approximately 10% and 8%, respectively. Partially due to the fact that Spring Hill is a college town, more than 75% of its population has a bachelor's degree or higher, a rate higher than the state average of 30%.

The school district located in Spring Hill, the Spring Hill City Schools (SHCS), has the lowest high school dropout rate in the state. According to the data from SHCS, Asian American students are the second largest minority group enrolled, constituting approximately 15% of the student population in local public schools. Linwood Elementary (pseudonym), a public elementary school in the SHCS district, houses a two-way Mandarin-English dual language (DL) program. The program is the only Mandarin-English DL program in the school district and one of the 19 Chinese-English DL programs in the state. Half of the classes in Linwood belong to the DL program, whereas the other half are traditional English-only classes. The DL program offers math and social studies in Mandarin Chinese, as well as science and language arts in English and seeks to enroll a balanced number of English-speaking and Chinese-speaking students. All the kindergarten-aged students in the SHCS district are eligible to apply and are admitted through a lottery system. According to previous conversations with Linwood administrators, the demand for the DL program was high, especially among English-speaking families. English-speaking children and Chinese-as-a-heritage-language children have separate lottery pools; since there are much fewer Chinese-speaking families than English-speaking families who

DOI: 10.4324/9781003240594-17

apply for the DL program, Chinese-speaking children are almost guaranteed a seat if they apply, whereas many English-speaking children are placed on a waiting list.

Based on the interviews with local community members and the nature of the area as a college town, the majority of Chinese immigrant parents living in Spring Hill are first-generation immigrants and middle-class professionals. Unlike regions with a long history of Chinese immigration, the Chinese population in Spring Hill has a scattered residential pattern. Parents exchange information through a few community centers, such as a Saturday Chinese heritage language school and churches. The Linwood DL program is well known in the community. From its inception, the DL program received support and advice on staffing and curriculum from the local Chinese immigrant community. In addition, the DL program has multiple collaborations with the local community-based Chinese heritage language school, because they shared information and hosted cultural events together.

Case Narrative

Aimei (pseudonym) immigrated from China to the US 12 years ago as a teenager to be united with her family members who immigrated earlier. Unlike many first-generation Chinese immigrant parents in Spring Hill who came to the US for graduate school or professional employment, Aimei finished one year of high school in New York City and moved to the Southeast ten years ago. She is currently a homemaker who takes care of her four young children, while her husband works in a local Chinese restaurant. Aimei's eldest daughter has been enrolled in the Linwood DL program for the past three years, and her second daughter is starting kindergarten in the same program. She plans to enroll her younger twin sons (age 4) in the DL program as well.

Critically Listening to Heritage Language Speaking Parents' Needs

Aimei is a fluent speaker of Mandarin Chinese and Fujianese, a dialect spoken by people living in Fujian, a province located on the southeastern coast of China. She describes herself as having limited English proficiency. Fujianese and Mandarin are the only languages spoken at her home, and all her children are very proficient in speaking either variety of Chinese. However, since they speak almost no English before starting school, Aimei is worried about her children's English development. Despite her concerns, she still makes active efforts in promoting her children's heritage language, by reading Chinese books with her children, playing Chinese cartoons, and sometimes assigning them Chinese-related homework. Although she believes that learning both Chinese and English benefits her children's future employment, the career benefit is not the primary reason that motivates her to keep her children's languages. She believes that building a good relationship with her children is crucial and is only achievable through speaking Chinese. She said,

> 我年纪再大，他们可能就跟我也会文化上各方面上不好沟通。他们可能会很努力跟你走近却走不近了，因为好像两个世界的人。我觉得他们会觉得好像爸爸妈妈远远得一样的。他们会懂得这边的文化，还能懂爸爸妈妈的这边会更好。 . . . 我觉得好处实在太多了，一定要学的。(When I am older, they will have difficulties in communicating with me at the cultural level. It is possible that they want to be close to you, but they cannot. Because . . . it's just like we are in two entirely different worlds. I think they will feel like their parents are far away from them. They will know the culture here, but not the culture of their parents. It will be much better if they can do both . . . I believe it [learning Chinese] has so many benefits. They must learn.)

Aimei shared that when she went to grocery stores with her children, she would ask them to talk with the cashiers by telling them, "妈妈英文不如你好。你能过去替我跟他们讲讲吗？ [Mom's English is not as good as yours. Could you please talk to them on my behalf?]" She believes that her children's abilities to speak both Chinese and English enable them to help their families and communities while also building their confidence. Her enthusiasm to maintain her children's heritage languages led to her decision to apply for the Linwood DL program when her eldest daughter reached school age. Aimei is generally satisfied with her eldest daughter's experience in the DL program. Although her daughter spoke little English when she started the program, she is very confident in her language abilities, and her Chinese proficiency is seen as an advantage. However, during the past few years as a DL program parent, Aimei also experienced moments of doubt.

Interrogating Power: Bilingualism for Whom in DL Spaces?

Many DL programs start with a 90:10 or 80:20 model with more instructional time in the non-English language during the first few years, and then transition to a 50:50 model. The Linwood Chinese-English DL program was proposing the 80:20 model in grades K–2, so that children would have more time immersed in Chinese from the beginning. However, due to the strong opposition from the Chinese families, the program kept the 50:50 model. Aimei said she would transfer her children out of the program if the program changes to the 80:20 model. Only 20% of English a day is far from enough for her children to learn English, she said, and that the 80:20 model is "太迁就 [too accommodating]" to the English-speaking children's needs.

Aimei also encountered other situations in which she felt that English-speaking children's needs are prioritized. In the Linwood DL program, students learn math exclusively in Chinese. However, students' math homework and exams are in English. When asked why, Aimei said,

> 因为他说方便其他别人中文看不懂。我觉得是更多给老外孩子。不然老外孩子拿回去，中文他就看不懂。 . . . 反正老师好像有讲过。毕竟美国可能以后考试什么都要用英文。(Because they said that it is for the convenience of those who cannot read Chinese well. I think it's for the foreigners' ["Laowai"] children. Otherwise, those children take the homework home, and they don't understand Chinese . . . Anyway, the teacher has said that. After all, the math tests in the United States are all in English.)

Aimei used the word "老外 (Laowai)," which is often used in China to refer to foreigners, to refer to the English-speaking parents in the DL program, who are mostly White. While her children learn math in Chinese, the fact that they need to do the homework in English for the ease of the Laowai's children and that all the math tests are in English send her a message that Laowai's children's needs are prioritized, and that English is the more valued language in school.

During last winter, due to the strong opposition from the neighborhood families and non-DL teachers in Linwood, the SHCS district had a public hearing regarding the future of the DL program. Aimei, together with other DL parents, attended the meeting to support the program and DL teachers. Parents, teachers, and community members who opposed the program also voiced their concerns in the meeting. Aimei shared,

> 我知道有[家长]我觉得是反对双语的。我觉得讲的也很对。那是这个学区的黑人爸爸。他说你们的这一批[双语项目的]人拿着国家的钱，剥夺了我们这一批孩子[的资源]。他说你们想学中文，请让你们去花钱去课外去学，他们言论就蛮激烈 . . . 我觉得的确他们说得是。我们是在美国，然后你们在美国你们就想着学中文，他们是这么讲，像你们中国人想学额外的中文，你们要花钱去搞课外，你们别把政府拨下的钱拿去搞这些。(I know there are [parents] who oppose this program. I think they are right. There was an African American father who lived in the same school zone. He said that all of you [DL parents] took the money from the government and deprived our children's resources. He said that if you want to learn Chinese, please pay a tutor and learn outside school. His words were pretty harsh . . . I think indeed, they are right. We are in the United States, and you want to learn Chinese in the United States—that's what they say—you Chinese want to learn more Chinese, then please do this after school. Don't use the government's money to do this.)

Aimei shared that SHCS's administrators and board members always applauded when the parents and teachers who objected to the DL program finished talking during the meeting, but rarely when pro-DL parents and teachers concluded their words. The tension during the meeting made Aimei worried about the program's future. In SHCS, Chinese American children are viewed as high-achieving and coming from affluent backgrounds. In the opponents' minds, these children have no needs in school and should not use public resources for enrichment purposes. On the other hand, Aimei's recollection also reveals the programs' lack of attention to other minorized communities, who feel excluded and believe that the DL program brings no benefit to their children. This hearing shows the importance of interrogating power and critically listening to all minoritized communities in Spring Hill and using the program to build solidarity among various minoritized groups.

The Linwood DL program webpage displayed reasons under the subheading "Why Mandarin?" all highlighting future employment and cognitive benefits. However, the needs for Chinese immigrant families to preserve their heritage are entirely missing. When the DL program is described as an enrichment program only, bilingualism becomes an added privilege, rather than a necessity for heritage language learners. This framing simultaneously excludes those who are less privileged and underserved, such as other minoritized communities in Spring Hill. Instead of constructing bilingualism as a bridge to build solidarity and meaningful relationships among diverse communities in Spring Hill, the discourses of enrichment result in Chinese families being accused of using public resources that could be allocated to other children in need. Aimei's children clearly benefit from this program because it helps build her children's confidence and positive cultural identities. Her children thrive in the DL program because they are not just labeled as English learners, but as experts in their heritage language and culture. However, these needs are missing in the debates, and parents like Aimei are pitted against the interests of other marginalized communities.

Teaching Notes

Learning one's heritage languages has a positive impact on immigrant children's cultural identity, academic achievements, and psychological wellbeing (Liu et al., 2009), whereas losing their languages could result in negative consequences for them, their families, communities, and the country (Li & Wen, 2015). Therefore, it is important to counter the hegemony of English and the linguistic assimilative forces in the US. Among all the linguistic-minoritized groups, Asian Americans are especially vulnerable to heritage language loss (Pew Research Center, 2012).

As demonstrated in this case, parents like Aimei consider heritage languages as essential to passing on their cultural heritage and building multigenerational ties. However, in DL spaces, these needs are often overlooked, whereas other non-heritage-related rationales are celebrated, such as future employment advancement and cognitive advantage (Cervantes-Soon et al.,

2021; Sun & Wang, 2021). Compared to other ethnic minority groups, Asian Americans are often depicted as model minorities, a stereotype that overlooks the heterogeneity of the population, ignores the structural racism they experience daily, and pits them against the struggles of other minoritized populations (Lee, 2001). As in this case, Chinese immigrant families are perceived as a high-achieving group without any needs in schools. Although they are minoritized in schools and DL spaces, and have every intention to preserve their children's heritage languages, their needs are seen as illegitimate. Parents such as Aimei are pitted against other minoritized families in the same district, even though the DL program prioritizes English-speaking parents' interests. Lack of emphasis on language minoritized children's needs in DL education can lead to the framing of DL programs as gifted or enrichment programs for privileged families.

To center the needs of immigrant families like Aimei's and interrogate the power in DL spaces, it is imperative to create spaces that critically listen to and highlight their voices outside the White gaze. These should be safe and encouraging spaces for parents like Aimei to work together with school administrators and other community members by engaging in critical dialogues that historicize the discrimination faced by Asian American communities, the high involvement of local Chinese immigrant communities in building a larger Spring Hill community, and the essential role that learning heritage languages plays in transmitting culture values and maintaining intergenerational ties for immigrant families. These voices and historicization should be critically listened to and incorporated throughout the DL program design and implementation. For example, rather than promoting the DL program using the neoliberal discourses that emphasize instrumental benefits, stakeholders in DL spaces should critically listen to and underscore the counter-stories of heritage language speaking families, by highlighting their needs, voices, and efforts in preserving their linguistic, cultural, and familial heritage inside and outside DL spaces, over other rationales.

This case reveals the importance of fostering critical consciousness among families, communities, and other stakeholders who are engaged in DL programs. It is crucial for Chinese immigrant parents to historicize the DL context and actively interrogate the power and politics in DL spaces that perpetuate the English hegemony and the model minority myths. Unpacking the power structure may allow them to further affirm their rights to their children's heritage language learning, and to detangle the hegemonic Whiteness that pits them against other marginalized communities. However, cultivating critical consciousness and promoting equity in DL programs are not solely the heritage language-speaking parents' responsibilities. Parents from the dominant community should acknowledge the linguistic rights of language-minoritized children, critically listen to all minoritized communities' voices, and "decenter themselves as the main beneficiaries" of DL programs (Palmer et al., 2019, p. 126). Other minoritized communities should interrogate the hegemonic Whiteness that perpetuates the model minority myth, and build solidarity with the Asian American communities, rather than treat them as the scapegoat (Chang, 1993). Aimei's empathy with the African American father shows that she is critically listening to the voices of other minoritized groups. Further, it reveals the necessity to critically listen to all minoritized groups' voices in DL spaces. Educators and policymakers should consciously center and critically listen to the experiences and counter-stories of heritage language-speaking communities and other minoritized communities in DL spaces, and actively challenge the discourse that frames DL programs as an enrichment program only. Researchers also have the responsibility to amplify the counter-stories of immigrant families, foster collective agency with families and stakeholders, and advocate for the cultivation of critical consciousness that makes DL spaces more socially transformative. We are all on a path towards critical consciousness that can be promoted or hindered by our environment. DL spaces should be (re)created so that critical consciousness is fostered, enacted, and celebrated.

Teaching Activities

1. Read the Linwood Chinese-English DL program's promotional materials (Figure 13.1). Analyze who are the targeted audiences of the text. How would you revise the text so that it can 1) further center the voices of Chinese immigrant families, 2) historicize the struggles, contributions, needs, and agency of immigrant communities, and 3) cultivate critical consciousness among all the stakeholders of the DL program?
2. Design an event that promotes dialogues about the inequity issues in DL programs among Chinese-as-heritage-language DL parents, English-speaking DL parents, and parents who oppose the DL programs. Discuss how to address the following questions in this event.

    - How would you facilitate the conversation that interrogates the power structure without targeting a minoritized group?

Why Mandarin?

Through our dual language program, students have access to a world-class education that prepares global citizens who are bilingual, biliterate, and bicultural—ready to thrive in a dynamic, competitive workforce.

Mandarin is the most widely spoken language in the world, with approximately 16% of the global population speaking Chinese.

Additionally, China is already the world's second biggest economy and one of the largest trading partners of the United States.

The study of Mandarin stimulates the mind and improves math and problem solving skills.

Figure 13.1 Linwood Chinese-English DL Program's Promotional Materials

- How would you engage in dialogues that historicize the racism against Asian American communities?
- How can you build solidarities among minoritized communities and support the dominant groups to be advocates and allies?
- How can you help stakeholders engage in critical listening?

References

Cervantes-Soon, C., Gambrell, J., Kasun, G. S., Sun, W., Freire, J. A., & Dorner, L. M. (2021). "Everybody wants a choice" in dual language education of el Nuevo Sur: Whiteness as the gloss for everybody in media discourses of multilingual education. *Journal of Language, Identity & Education, 20*(6), 394–410.

Chang, R. S. (1993). Toward an Asian American legal scholarship: Critical race theory, poststructuralism, and narrative space. *California Law Review, 19*, 1243–1323.

Lee, S. J. (2001). More than "model minorities" or "delinquents": A look at Hmong American high school students. *Harvard Educational Review, 71*(3), 505–528.

Li, G., & Wen, K. (2015). East Asian heritage language education for a plurilingual reality in the United States: Practices, potholes, and possibilities. *International Multilingual Research Journal, 9*(4), 274–290.

Liu, L. L., Benner, A. D., Lau, A. S., & Kim, S. Y. (2009). Mother-adolescent language proficiency and adolescent academic and emotional adjustment among Chinese American families. *Journal of Youth and Adolescence, 38*(4), 572–586.

Palmer, D. K., Cervantes-Soon, C., Dorner, L., & Heiman, D. (2019). Bilingualism, biliteracy, biculturalism, and critical consciousness for all: Proposing a fourth fundamental goal for two-way dual language education. *Theory into Practice, 58*(2), 121–133.

Pew Research Center. (2012). *The rise of Asian Americans*. http://assets.pewresearch.org/wp-content/uploads/sites/3/2013/04/Asian-Americans-new-full-report-04-2013.pdf

Sun, W., & Wang, X. (2021). A raciolinguistic analysis of the neoliberal promotion of dual language education in a new Latinx South state. *Discourse: Studies in the Cultural Politics of Education*. doi:10.1080/01596306.2021. Advance online publication.

14 Cultivating Critical Consciousness with Mothers of Bilingual Students

María de los Ángeles Osorio de la Rosa and Jody Slavick

Context

Easton City (all names are pseudonyms) is an industrial and residential community adjacent to a metropolitan city in the central western United States. The majority of the city's population self-identifies as Latinx[1] and speaks Spanish at home. In the Easton City School District (ESD), close to 90% of the students identify as Latinx, 63% report Spanish as being their primary language, and 45% are classified as English language learners. To serve its Spanish-speaking students, the district offered bilingual programming for over three decades, until the bilingual program suffered attacks in 2009 and 2017.

In 2009, district administrators eliminated the bilingual program due to pressures to increase student performance on the state's English standardized assessments. The new English-only language policy led to widespread discrimination of Latinx Spanish-speaking parents, teachers, and students, and resulted in an investigation by the Office for Civil Rights (OCR) (Romine, 2014). The OCR resolution agreement pushed the district to reinstate the bilingual program and repair its damaged relationship with the Spanish-speaking/bilingual community. Students and teachers were delighted to return to bilingual classrooms in 2015, but their joy was short-lived. In 2017, Superintendent Dr. Valera began dismantling the bilingual program once again, in the name of increasing English test scores.

Throughout the decade of turmoil, ESD bilingual education advocates fought back against discriminative and hurtful actions taken by district officials and pressured the district to fully support its students. This case study focuses on two Easton City mother advocates, Rocío and Lorena. It highlights the ways that the women's divergent lived experiences, cultural ways of knowing, motivations, and intuition interacted with the power exerted by ESD as the women developed their critical consciousness. The case narrative is followed by teaching notes to help schools transform their vision of "parent engagement" to one which cultivates critical consciousness for developing equitable collaborations within a community of solidarity.

DOI: 10.4324/9781003240594-18

Case Narrative

Rocío

Prior to establishing in the United States, Rocío del Valle completed three years of college education, which afforded her a good job opportunity in Mexico. After the birth of their first three children, Rocío and her husband (who held US legal resident status) wanted to provide their children with educational options that would allow them to become bilingual. Therefore, in the late 1990s (prior to Proposition 203) they moved to Arizona and enrolled their children in a transitional bilingual school. After three years and three more children, Rocío and her family moved to Easton City where all of her children continued their bilingual education. Rocío's six children were bilingual and embraced a bicultural identity, which had been facilitated by the family's ability to travel from the United States to Mexico.

When Rocío got to the United States, she drew on her intuition to support her children's schooling; however, her participation in a newcomers' group in Arizona "*en el salón 7*" was illuminating. Organized by a bilingual secretary, the group offered a welcoming space for newcomer mothers where they discussed school-based activities and how to participate in them. Early on, Rocío learned about the high esteem that literacy and math nights, parent-teacher conferences, coffee with the principal, advisory committees, and other parent groups had among educators. When Rocío moved to Easton City, Rocío was more conscious (albeit not critical) about actively participating in school-based activities, which was viewed favorably by educators. Rocío's experiences in ESD and AZ schools exemplify how educators in the two districts were satisfied as long as they saw "apparent involvement" because it involved non-disruptive presence, and it fit their expectations of how parental involvement should look (Fine, 1993).

Cultivating Rocío's Critical Consciousness

"*El salón 7*" marked the start of Rocío's journey towards harnessing her critical consciousness and spanned two decades after her family established in Easton City. There, she noticed the lack of a supportive mothering group. Nonetheless, Rocío, with her college education, accomplishments in Mexico, and her experiences in "*el salón 7*" in Arizona, adapted to support her children in their new context. In 2009, the district contracted a family education specialist, Mr. Eloy Pérez, originally from Mexico. Mr. Pérez's experiences with a host of family and societal ills "allowed [him] to relate with impacted populations" (Mr. Pérez's personal webpage). To him, "educating" culturally and linguistically diverse (CLD) families meant more than indoctrinating them in school-based activities. Rather, he cultivated families' power to grow their advocacy for change. During his tenure, Mr. Pérez engaged CLD parents in conversations about the 2009 elimination of bilingual education, and the poor communication and treatment of CLD students and families. By participating in these conversations, Rocío began to see how parents, both in ESD and her past school district in Arizona, were seen from a deficit view. Mr. Pérez cultivated parent leadership and advocated for parents to be recognized by district educators. Despite many accolades, Mr. Pérez was terminated in the spring of 2011, by the same superintendent who eliminated bilingual programming. Nevertheless, Mr. Pérez started a non-profit organization outside the district and continued his commitments to Easton parents.

Rocío and others followed him. Under his guidance, Rocío was part of the community advisory group that interviewed and hired Mr. Sedona as the new superintendent in 2014. The group insisted that Mr. Sedona reinstate bilingual programming and fulfill the district's OCR requirements. By then, half of Rocío's children had graduated from Easton schools, and she was doing all she could to ensure a decent and affirming bilingual education for the three that were still school-aged. Under Mr. Pérez's teachings and engagement of praxis (see the following), Rocío began to realize how her children were being robbed of opportunities by not being offered bilingual education. With Mr. Pérez's support, she became a *promotora* (a popular teacher to teach other parents), and in 2016 was invited to join a non-profit organization established in Easton City. These experiences furthered Rocío's critical consciousness journey by engaging her in social justice initiatives through a critical lens. Today, she continues her work as a *promotora* with a deep understanding of social, educational, and financial ills, which push immigrant, Spanish-speaking mothers to embrace English-only policies. With Mr. Pérez's commitment to develop parents' critical consciousness, mothers like Rocío were emboldened to reclaim a seat at the decision-making table, and act to reinstate bilingual education.

Lorena

Lorena Villa grew up in rural Mexico and by ninth grade, she sought employment to support her family. With her limited formal education, job opportunities were also limited in Mexico. At 19, Lorena embarked on the dangerous journey to the United States—with the shirt on her back and no papers—with hopes to better support her family. Years later, Lorena, her partner, and their three children moved to Easton City. Lorena's intuition provided the initial tools to support her children. For example, based on her own cultural understanding of schooling in Mexico, Lorena believed in the school's expertise to provide a quality education. She, like other immigrant parents without papers, didn't feel that she had a right to tell schools what she desired. While Lorena fully supported her children's education, she saw her job as making sure they were ready for school daily.

Lorena recounted how the school mostly reached out to parents about school activities via translated fliers; an impersonal approach which made it hard for Lorena to understand the importance the school placed on these activities. After all, Lorena remembered the relationship-building that happened between parents and teachers in Mexican schools, where teachers personally requested parents' presence and perspectives at meetings. Therefore, Lorena only attended events, like parent-teacher conferences and occasional math/literacy nights, when she was personally invited by her child's teacher. During meetings, she sat quietly to hear what the teachers had to say about her son. In spite of Lorena's wholehearted support, the school viewed her as needing to be more involved.

In 2015, the year that ESD reinstated bilingual education under the leadership of Mr. Sedona, Lorena enrolled her second child in the program. The bilingual teacher, Ms. Felicity, an avid social justice and bilingual education advocate, developed strong relationships with families, something Lorena had never experienced. Parent participation in activities such as math and literacy nights, parent-teacher conferences, and school plays increased, all because Ms. Felicity personally invited families to attend. Ms. Felicity also clearly explained to Lorena how Title I and Title VI schools are obliged to listen to parents when they feel strongly about a change. By learning about parents' rights, Lorena's perceptions about the unquestioned authority of educators began to change along with her critical consciousness. When the opportunity presented, Lorena vowed to participate towards change.

Cultivating Lorena's Critical Consciousness

In fall of 2016, the district hired a new superintendent, Dr. Valera, who started dismantling the bilingual program. Ms. Felicity shared with Lorena how detrimental this would be for the children. Lorena treasured the bilingual program, noting how her second child's bilingualism was developing more than her first, who was in English-only classrooms and was losing his Spanish abilities. Fueled by her desire to keep the bilingual program, Lorena joined every effort to fight for the program. While Lorena had never been invited to partake in school and district advisory meetings, with Ms. Felicity's support, she actively participated in meetings pertaining to bilingual education. During one meeting, the technical nature of the Spanish translation about bilingual programming made it impossible to understand the district's push to terminate it. When she tried to ask clarifying questions, she was dismissed by the presenter. At the end of the meeting, Lorena felt stunned and silenced. This meeting represented a critical moment in Lorena's cultivation of critical consciousness, because she saw how the poor communication and lack of clarity surrounding the matter marginalized mothers like her.

Encouraged by Ms. Felicity, Lorena began gauging other parents' knowledge about the bilingual program. This type of informal organizing allowed her to build relationships with other parents and advocates. On one occasion, she found a community organizer, Carolina, outside school handing out flyers for a meeting about the district's plan. She quickly partnered with Carolina, but after a few weeks of their partnership, Lorena realized that Carolina lacked strategy. Ultimately, she felt used by Carolina, who overly relied on Lorena's connection to other mothers. The last straw was when Carolina became angry that Lorena was trying to partner with other outside-the-district allies. Lorena not only felt disappointed in the community organizer but also in the tensions between parents, community, and ESD advocates.

Nevertheless, Lorena continued harnessing her critical consciousness by partnering with the district's teacher union (TU). The TU was working with a national network of professional organizers (offering leadership training and support) to overturn three other decisions made by Dr. Valera. Lorena brought in parents and, with guidance from professional organizers, began leading meetings with board members, teachers, and other families about bilingual programming and other matters. But Lorena did not feel connected to the TU: "I do not see any teachers talking to me directly. Like they do not make an effort to get to know [me]." Lorena felt once again disappointed that she was seen as the de facto parent leader tasked with the burden of bringing other parents into the efforts. In 2017 Lorena withdrew from the movement due to *activist burn-out* (Gorski & Erakat, 2019). Activist burn-out is characterized by the stress associated with organizing efforts that so heavily weigh "on activists' emotional or physical health that their abilities to remain effective and engaged in their activism are compromised" (p. 2). In short, this time period represented Lorena's fast-paced, challenging, and unpredictable uphill battle of cultivating and acting on her critical consciousness.

Lorena's cautionary tale is one to learn from. For Lorena, the months that she fought for bilingual programming demonstrated to her that no matter how much she tried, it would be impossible to get what her family wanted, spurring a sense of hopelessness in Lorena. Freire referred to hopelessness as people's inability to view their "limit situations as *possible* to supersede" (Darder, 2003, p. 23). To combat this type of despair, Freire encouraged educators to build communities of solidarity as a form of networking (Darder, 2003). Ms. Felicity's initial relationship-building with Lorena, including sharing key information and inviting her to participate in district meetings, was critical in cultivating Lorena's critical consciousness. However, as Lorena became more involved in other efforts, the lack of a close-knit community of solidarity did not sustain her. Building communities of solidarity is intentional work that takes time. Teachers can play a key role in fostering relationships with parents; however, organizations (i.e., teachers' unions, advisory committees, advocacy organizations, etc.) must also be intentional about developing these relationships. For these reasons, we highlight the importance of proactively involving parents as partners in decision-making at all stages and all levels to foster long-lasting relationships within a community of solidarity.

Teaching Notes

Historically, the schooling of CLD students was filled with injustices and poor accessibility to educational content for them and their families (Rodríguez, 2015). The Elementary and Secondary Education and the Civil Rights Acts tasked schools with creating parent involvement programs to afford low-income families opportunities to *participate* in the education of their children and to provide them with basic civil rights (Moreno, 2017). But these efforts continued to position families from a deficit perspective that resulted in families' unequal participation in their children's education. With the advent of No Child Left Behind, schools sharply focused on developing school-based family activities that support academic achievement and accountability. As illustrated by Lorena and Rocío's experiences, the hyper-focus in school-based activities marginalize underrepresented mothers who would most benefit from a solidarity approach to foster equitable collaborations. Most recently, the Every Student Succeeds Act (ESSA) highlights building a dual-capacity (parents and educators) for participation by incorporating parents' knowledge in parent involvement efforts. While English is valued over bilingualism in school oversight (de Jong, 2012) and supporting academic achievement and accountability still dominate the parent-involvement statutes, centering the knowledge of parents is a small window of opportunity to promote critical consciousness and foster a community of solidarity.

A community of solidarity is one that advances *conscientização*, critical consciousness, (Freire, 1970) and educational justice (Ishimaru, 2020) by fomenting praxis and centering CLD-families' values to build equitable partnerships. We define critical consciousness as one's ability to understand and take action against the influences that affect contradictions and oppressive elements in society. As a key element of critical consciousness, praxis involves cycles of reflection and action that result in individuals or communities becoming both critically aware and no longer permissive of their oppressive situations, while gaining new ways of knowing and being in the world (Darder, 2015). Much like the programs created by Mr. Pérez, educators and parents must come together as a community of solidarity and engage in dialogue to understand the historical, social, political, and economic influences affecting their experiences and to generate ideas on how to interact with, and thus transform their situations (Darder, 2015). We posit that educators and CLD parents coming together as a community of solidarity would foster practices that go beyond school-centric family engagement activities, resulting in a liberatory experience for students and families.

Research in the area of family and community engagement recommends the adoption and implementation of a four-part framework for co-designing equitable partnerships: 1) collaborate with diverse stakeholders for 2) identifying issues and 3) proposing solutions together, in an iterative manner, to 4) build stakeholders' capacities for "collectively imagining future possibilities, and . . . designing novel solutions for change" (Ishimaru, 2020, p. 129). Educators have historically focused on advocating and/or providing services *for* families. Instead, schools have the responsibility to enter into relationships with CLD families that are focused on cultivating advocacy and leadership so that "community members can create institutional and policy change on their own behalf" (Warren et al., 2011, p. 7). Therefore, a commitment to create equitable collaborations within a community of solidarity includes a willingness to cultivate CLD parents' leadership and agency.

The last ingredient for creating a community of solidarity includes an analysis of sources of distrust in three areas: relational, structural, and contextual (Schultz, 2019). The form most recognized is relational distrust, which identifies individuals and institutions as untrustworthy. However, examining and addressing the political and historical causes for distrust is also crucial in the process of changing praxis. Structural distrust is connected to local politics and consequential decision-making processes made by people in power positions. This is the type of distrust embedded in hierarchical structures with heavy top-down decision-making processes, like those in Easton, which silenced and dismissed mothers' and educators' voices. The third type of distrust is contextual distrust, which is situated in the sociocultural, historical, and political contexts of schools and communities and arises from local interactions that have persisted over time and that have been infected by power. Schultz (2019) warns: "Enduring relational distrust demands that the political and historical roots of the distrust are addressed if there is to be lasting change" (p. 4).

Educators, including administrative staff and family liaisons, must exercise their agency to build trust and create communities of solidarity that go beyond common parent-engagement approaches. Ishimaru (2020) comments that best-practice efforts to remove barriers to access school-based, accountability-driven activities do little "to disrupt the policies, institutional practices, and daily interactions that systematically structure marginalization and disengagement for [CLD] students, their families, and their communities" (p. 3). As illustrated in this case study, the school's efforts to remove barriers by sending translated communication flyers and hosting parent nights did little to support the marginalization of parents like Lorena and Rocío. Rather, it was the personal relationships initiated by Ms. Felicity and the community of solidarity fomented by Mr. Pérez that paved the way for Lorena and Rocío to grow and engage their critical consciousness.

Conclusion

The journey towards critical consciousness *for* change takes time, and is built on people's lived experiences and supported by relevant capacity building (Freire, 2011; Mapp & Kuttner, 2013). Lorena experienced a critical consciousness journey that was characterized by an intense learning process in a short period of time. Although her intuition and motivations positioned her as a leader, they were not enough to sustain her through the turbulence. Rocío's training with Mr. Pérez, when she learned about her rights and those of her children, went above and beyond the school-centric activities that positioned her as an empty vessel to be filled. Through Mr. Pérez's praxis, Rocío rejected the notion of being deficient, and embraced an active advocacy role which resulted in hiring a superintendent who restored bilingual programming in ESD.

Our purpose in writing this chapter was to show the potential and challenges of building critical consciousness through the eyes and experiences of two mothers. Despite the federal government's historical attempts to increase parental participation through legislation, parent engagement orientations and activities at schools today continue to overwhelmingly mirror neoliberal, market-driven logics (Schultz, 2019). We argue that uncritically promoting such values rather than fomenting a community of solidarity will result in a detriment to our public schools. Both Lorena and Rocío repeatedly attempted to insert their opinions about the importance of bilingual education, but instead of their opinions being valued, the district indoctrinated families in school-centric activities that ultimately disenfranchised, devalued, silenced, and generated distrust among them. We believe that if ESD had established a community of solidarity in which parents and educators had developed critical consciousness over time, then parents like Lorena and Rocío would have been more empowered to advance their opinions about the kind of education that they wanted for their children.

Teaching Activities

1. Developing a community of solidarity cannot happen without building *mutual trust* and understanding between educators and families. Understanding begins with teachers examining their own positionality and then learning about the lives of their students and families. Draft your own *story of self* in order to analyze your own positionality (for more, see Ganz, 2009).

    i. Address questions such as: What were your experiences with *learning* growing up (i.e., schooling, storytelling, chores, etc.)? (for more, see Moll et al., 1992). What were the obstacles that you and your caretakers faced in schooling? How were your caretakers involved in your education?

    ii. How do your experiences mirror or contrast the experiences of your students and families? Do you think all schooling should look like yours?

        b. Plan a series of *home visits*, which can strengthen home-school partnerships by building trust and respect over time. For further guidance, see Ginsberg (2007) and Johnson (2014).

   c. An essential component of critical praxis is to better understand the *historical economic, political, and social forces* that cause inequalities and exclusion (Darder, 2015). Consider what you learned through your story of self and home visits and what forces may be causing barriers and inequalities for your students and families.

2. Engaging and promoting critical consciousness in DLBE is collective work that requires the need for *connecting* parents, educators, and community advocates. Teachers can help facilitate these connections by *envisioning and developing a community of solidarity.*
   a. Engage in visioning exercises: What would a community of solidarity look and sound like? Who would be in the room and be talking? What would they be talking about and what action would they be taking? We suggest that teachers consider these questions individually and then with the larger group of advocates.
   b. Take stock of your school's/district's current approach to "parent engagement." What elements need to change in order to reflect your vision of a community of solidarity? (For more, see Ishimaru, 2014, 2020).
   c. As illustrated with Rocío and Lorena, parents come from different backgrounds in terms of privilege, power, and resources, and some may need more support to make connections and build community. Discuss ways that advocates at your school will become aware of the specific needs of parents from more marginalized backgrounds and support them in connecting with one another.

Note

1. We use the term Latinx in this paper to honor the preference of the mothers who are central to this chapter.

References

Darder, A. (2003). Teaching as an act of love: Reflections on Paulo Freire and his contributions to our lives and our work. In A. Darder, M. Baltodano, & R. D. Torres (Eds.), *The critical pedagogy reader* (pp. 497–510). Routledge.

Darder, A. (2015). *Freire and education.* Routledge.

de Jong, E. (2012). *Return to bilingual education. ¡Colorín Colorado! A bilingual site for educators and families of English language learners.* www.colorincolorado.org/article/return-bilingual-education

Fine, M. (1993). [Ap]parent involvement: Reflections on parents, power, and urban public schools. *Teachers College Record, 94*, 682–729.

Freire, P. (1970). *Pedagogy of the oppressed.* Continuum International Publishing Group.

Freire, P. (2011). *Pedagogía de la esperanza: un reencuentro con la pedagogía del oprimido, México: Siglo XXI*, 224p. ISBN: 987-607-03-0298-5

Ganz, M. (2009). *What is public narrative: Self, us & now (Public narrative worksheet)*. Working Paper. http://nrs.harvard.edu/urn-3:HUL.InstRepos:30760283

Ginsberg, M. B. (2007). Lessons from the kitchen table: Visiting with families in their homes. *Educational Leadership, 64*(6), 56–61. https://learningforward.org/wp-content/uploads/2007/12/lessons-from-the-kitchen-table.pdf

Gorski, P. C., & Erakat, N. (2019). Racism, whiteness, and burnout in antiracism movements: How white racial justice activists elevate burnout in racial justice activists of color in the United States. *Ethnicities, 19*(5), 784–808. https://doi.org/10.1177/1468796819833871

Ishimaru, A. M. (2014). Rewriting the rules of engagement: Elaborating a model of district-community collaboration. *Harvard Educational Review, 84*(2), 188–216. https://doi.org/10.17763/haer.84.2.r2007u165m8207j5

Ishimaru, A. M. (2020). *Just schools: Building equitable collaborations with families and communities*. Teachers College Press.

Johnson, E. J. (2014, March). From the classroom to the living room: Eroding academic inequities through home visits. *Journal of School Leadership, 21*, 357–385.

Mapp, K. L., & Kuttner, P. J. (2013). Partners in education: A dual capacity-building framework for family—school partnerships. *Sedl*, 1–30.

Moll, L. C., Amanti, C., Neff, D., & Gonzalez, N. (1992). Funds of knowledge for teaching: Using a qualitative approach to connect homes and classrooms. *Theory into Practice, 31*(2), 132–141. https://doi.org/10.1080/00405849209543534

Moreno, J. F. (2017). *The elusive quest for equality. 150 years of Chicano/Chicana education*. Harvard Education Publishing Review.

Rodríguez, M. S. (2015). *Rethinking the Chicano movement*. Routledge.

Romine, J. A. (2014). *OCR Complaint No. XX-XX-XXXX-X [Easton City School District]*. (Retrieval information not provided in order to protect anonymity).

Schultz, K. (2019). *Distrust and educational change: Overcoming barriers to just and lasting reform*. Harvard Education Press.

Warren, M. R., Mapp, K. L., & Community Organizing and School Reform Project. (2011). *A match on dry grass: Community organizing as a catalyst for school reform*. Oxford University Press.

15 When Life Gives You Lemons

Critically Conscious Family Engagement in a Virtual Dual Language Kindergarten Class During a Pandemic

Yalda M. Kaveh and Cory Buckband

Introduction

One of the most inspiring aspects of working with schools is meeting educators who have long engaged in the critical work that we, as educational researchers and scholars, often later come to label and theorize about. Nellie, a veteran kindergarten teacher in an urban two-way bilingual education program in Arizona, is one of those inspiring critically conscious educators. She was born and raised in small towns in Arizona. Having deep roots in her community for the past 27 years, Nellie engages in a critical pedagogy of love. During the COVID-19 pandemic, she navigated the sudden challenge of teaching online by partnering with the families and centering her pedagogy on their knowledge and experiences. Nellie's critically conscious pedagogy involved viewing families as experts, positioning parents and caregivers as "co-teachers," centering their lived experiences through multilingual family storytelling, and modeling the importance of community for children in early childhood education (ECE).

We define a "critically conscious dual-language teacher" as someone who *continuously* reflects on their practices and beliefs about racially and linguistically minoritized children and families and re-examines how they might mirror and perpetuate deficit-oriented narratives (Alfaro, 2019). Such a teacher builds on their critical reflection to empower children and families as agents of educational and social change. In dual language bilingual education (DLBE), critically conscious pedagogy promotes sociopolitical consciousness while supporting cultural competence, bilingualism/biliteracy, and academic achievement (Cervantes-Soon et al., 2017; Freire, J., 2020; Heiman & Yanes, 2018). For DLBE educators, the development of critical consciousness involves a few key actions (adapted from Palmer et al., 2019, p. 3):

- developing political and ideological clarity about the purpose of schooling

DOI: 10.4324/9781003240594-19

- interrogating the status quo
- disrupting deficit thinking about minoritized groups
- defining student achievement *outside* dominant political and societal narratives

In addition to these principles, major components of Nellie's critically conscious pedagogy included critical listening and *acompañamiento* (Heiman & Nuñez-Janes, 2021; Nancy, 2007). Informed by these ideas, we define "critically conscious family engagement" as a method of actively engaging racially and linguistically minoritized families as equitable partners and integrating their cultural and linguistic heritage as assets for building children's critical consciousness. In doing so, critically conscious family engagement challenges dominant deficit narratives about minoritized groups and refutes conventional modes of family involvement.

Context

This case study took place in a DLBE kindergarten classroom at a Title I K–8 urban public school in Arizona, United States. The school enrolls 90% Latinx, 6% Black, 3% White, and 1% Indigenous students. Nellie was the designated English teacher and worked with her teaching partner, Isabela, who taught Spanish. They shared a kindergarten cohort of 36 children. Each teacher had a homeroom, but they switched the groups between the morning and the afternoon.

Nellie's case is part of a larger study that uses critical ethnographic methods (Madison, 2020) to understand the experiences of the stakeholders, including children, parents/caregivers, teachers, and administrators in early grade levels in the DLBE program. Critical ethnography is a qualitative research approach that focuses on participants' viewpoints and experiences to interrogate inequities experienced by minoritized communities to foster social change (Palmer & Caldas, 2015).

Case Narrative

Since we began working with Nellie, we recognized her unwavering commitment to the school community she has worked with as an ECE teacher for the past 27 years. As we observed Nellie in her virtual classroom during the 2020–21 year, we were struck by the powerful ways she centered connections with families as they adjusted to the constant changes imposed by the pandemic. These practices were rooted in her strong convictions about the essential role of families in children's education. Nellie's pedagogy also displayed consciousness of socioeconomic realities shaping the lives of racially and linguistically minoritized families, particularly during the pandemic.

Viewing Families as Experts

Nellie believes in the importance of building strong relationships with families and valuing their expertise as their children's primary caregivers and "first teachers." Since the onset of the COVID-19 pandemic, she recognized the unique challenges facing families in her community, who were forced to reconcile schooling requirements with limited access to school supplies, technology, and the internet at home (Ladson-Billings, 2021). Thus, she valued their efforts and positioned them as competent in her classroom. Referring to the families in her class, Nellie said, "I completely believe in them, and I believe that whatever they are doing is what their children need . . . they know the needs of their children more than anybody else." She firmly believed whatever families did at home during the pandemic "was exactly what needed to be done at that time." This perspective positions families as valued, expert caregivers rather than those needing guidance and fixing by the schools (Ishimaru, 2019).

Positioning Parents and Caregivers as "Co-Teachers"

In addition to her ideological convictions, Nellie also adopted the term "co-teacher" and "co-maestros" to address parents, grandparents, adult caregivers, and adolescent siblings supporting children's schooling at home during the pandemic. This term reflects Nellie's positioning of families as agentive experts with an active role in children's education. Such framing contrasts traditional views on family involvement that place families, especially those from minoritized backgrounds, on the periphery. These practices demonstrate "*acompañamiento*" or solidarity: actions that support communities experiencing injustices through fellowship and relationship-building with them (Heiman & Nuñez-Janes, 2021).

Nellie chose the term "co-teachers" thoughtfully because the shift to online instruction necessitated engaging families equitably. She explained her thought process powerfully:

> I wanted them to see that there wasn't, like, a hierarchy. We're both at the same level because we have equal things to offer. They have just as many things to offer that I do. And being their first teachers, I wanted them to know that I validated their role, whatever they decided it was going to be. And, I at least wanted them to know that I saw them as the first teachers and the most important ones. The only difference between them and [me] was that I went to schooling for this, but that's such a minimal difference, you know, for what they've already offered to them and given to them and taught them.

Nellie's framing of parents/caregivers as "primary" and "the most important" teachers placed them as equal, fellow educators. To her, the institutional expertise as a certified ECE teacher did not overshadow families' vital role in educating their children.

Centering Minoritized Families During Instruction

Nellie's critically conscious family engagement practices occurred through both organic interactions and planned activities, demonstrating critical listening. Critical listening "embodies a relation of curiosity and attention, sharing, caring, reciprocity, and responsivity toward others," including educators, parents/caregivers, and children (Palmer et al., 2019, p. 12). These actions were represented in Nellie's organic engagement of bi/multilingual co-teachers, including addressing them in their heritage language(s) when possible. For example, Nellie's deep community knowledge allowed her to greet a student's grandmother, often present during online schooling, by name and ask her to share something in Diné with the class. The grandmother lovingly obliged, saying in Diné and then translating into English, "May God protect and bless you, my friend." Nellie responded with what we assumed was a Diné saying. The grandmother offered a kind correction to her pronunciation before heading to the kitchen.

Stemming from her belief in co-teachers as experts, Nellie also stepped back when necessary to allow them to support each other. For instance, one day, when some parents expressed difficulty signing onto an online assessment program, Nellie turned to the other co-teachers for help: "*Hay alguien que puede mostrar como hizo?* [Is there someone that can show how they did it?]" Instead of assuming the superior role, Nellie let families assist each other, fostering a sense of community among them. Two mothers volunteered to explain in English, and a third explained in Spanish. By the end, the co-teachers were collaborating and sharing experiences with the assessment program, with minimal mediation by Nellie. In this sense, Nellie refused to position parents as "helpers who need to be told what to do in someone else's kitchen" and instead allowed them to assist each other using their knowledge and resources (Ishimaru et al., 2019, p. 24).

In addition to daily engagement with families, Nellie planned activities to integrate their cultural and linguistic heritage. For example, during Hispanic Heritage Month and around Mexican Independence Day, she invited families to tell stories of Independence Day celebrations in their country or culture. As the co-teachers participated, she encouraged them to tell their stories in their heritage language(s). Nellie translated the stories shared in Spanish to English. She was particularly attentive to the co-teachers who were hesitant whether their upbringing was worth sharing. In one case, Nellie's follow-up questions on a mother's favorite folklore song from her childhood in Mexico led the mother to sing a beautiful rendition of the Spanish song for the class. Upon Nellie's probing, grounded in her loving and comforting presence, another mother opened up about her unique experience growing up with her father in Mexico and fishing for a very distinctive sea creature to earn a living. Nellie concluded the activity by emphasizing the importance of family stories: "It's really important, co-teachers, that we continue the line of storytelling at home. Books are made from, just, stories that are told at home. Children need that. That's their foundation."

Modeling the Importance of Community for Children

In addition to engaging families, Nellie organized lessons that emphasized the importance of community to the children. On a Friday morning in February before Valentine's Day, she delivered a lesson that modeled the importance of community. Instead of focusing on commercialized forms of celebrating this holiday, Nellie turned it into a lesson about the importance of showing love and kindness to one's community.

She introduced a book titled *Heartprints* and explained that similar to leaving a handprint after putting one's hand in the sand, one can leave a heartprint by acts of kindness. The story ended with, "How many heartprints will you leave today?" In collaboration with her partner teacher, who had joined this lesson with her class, Nellie encouraged the kindergarteners to make personal connections and think about how the story made them feel.

For the next activity, the class made heartprints by cutting construction paper into a heart shape and drawing an act of kindness they would do on Valentine's Day. Nellie shared the instructions in English and Spanish. She emphasized the importance of family and community:

> It is easy to be selfish, but you would make the world a better place if you think about yourself a tiny bit less and a little more about others. You need to be kind to people in your lives, and that is called "co.mmu. nity."

Nellie enunciated the word *community* and said, "That's a big word." She explained that a community could be bigger than one's family. She added the act of kindness would likely have to be limited to immediate family members the children were allowed to socialize with due to the pandemic. Still, Nellie found a way to bring the community into the conversation: "But you can also help pick up the trash from the street to make your neighborhood clean. That is helping your community."

Teaching Notes

What Does Critical Consciousness Look Like in ECE?

The concept of critical consciousness is founded upon the belief that the worldwide realities of inequity and oppression can be challenged and fundamentally reshaped by individuals with the capacity to critically reflect on their situation and its connections with those of others (Freire, P., 2000; Palmer et al., 2019). Evolving sociopolitical and economic realities always shape the lives of teachers and students, yet many are not "conscious" of the impact and their potential to transform these material and historical conditions (Bartolomé, 2004; Heiman, 2020). Educators who engage in critically conscious efforts demonstrate that they possess "the voice and courage to stand up against injustice and inequities" (Valenzuela, 2016, p. 196). Such educators problematize the deficit-oriented narratives that marginalize and stigmatize racially and linguistically minoritized students and families. In addition, these teachers "continually advocate, question, and contest issues of equity and access" in DLBE and the education system at large (Alfaro, 2019, p. 197).

While working with Nellie, we pondered how a pedagogy of "love and imagination" could be implemented in a DLBE kindergarten classroom (Heiman, 2020, p. 2). Like other researchers, we considered possible challenges for ECE educators, including restrictive curriculum and policy, perceived lack of children's background knowledge, questions of developmental maturity, and tensions with families (Husband, 2012; Quintero, 2003; Templeton, 2013). Culturally responsive and developmentally appropriate practices are essential when implementing critically conscious practices in ECE (Harlin & Souto-Manning, 2009; Matthews, 2010). Additionally, centering instruction on equitable and robust partnerships with families is foundational in doing this work in the early grades.

Equitable Family Engagement Starts with Transforming Power

Public education systems have historically applied deficit thinking towards racially and linguistically minoritized families and perceived them as disengaged and uninterested in their children's schooling (Valencia, 2010). On the contrary, racially and linguistically minoritized families play a vital role in advocating for their children's access to high-quality education (García & Kleifgen, 2018). Resources outside the formal schooling setting, such as rich linguistic exposure through storytelling and print and teaching morality and respect (Valdés, 1996), have come to be understood as "funds of knowledge" (Esteban-Guitart & Moll, 2014) from which parents and communities draw to contribute to their children's development. In order for schools to engage families equitably, schools should consider families' resources as legitimate contributors to children's structured school activities (Ishimaru, 2019). In fact, schools should start with the priorities, goals, and expertise of families and communities. Partnering with "deliberately silenced or preferably unheard" families is essential if schools intend to transform and redistribute power, rejecting the assumption that privileged parents/caregivers speak for all families or that only professional educators know what's best for the youth (Ishimaru, 2020). Nellie's case powerfully presented this redistribution of power through her belief in the families' primary role in children's development, her language use in addressing the families, and the practices positioning them as fellow educators.

Takeaway: Critically Conscious Pedagogy is Possible in ECE

Nellie's case demonstrates a radical sense of criticality and loving solidarity with her community. Her critical consciousness is reflected in her equitable and transformative family and community engagement, present in her beliefs and practices during in-person and virtual schooling. During virtual schooling, Nellie innovated her conventional strategies to equitably engage families and integrate their cultural and linguistic heritage into her instruction.

Her case shows that critically conscious pedagogy in ECE contexts may differ from those implemented in more advanced grades. Primarily, this work may involve building a "foundation of acceptance" within and among children regarding their cultural and linguistic heritage. This foundation is essential for developing critical consciousness throughout children's education. Additionally, Nellie's story has resounding implications for the power of critically conscious family engagement. By embracing parents/caregivers as "co-teachers" and fellow leaders, teachers can build new relationships that transform how families from racially and linguistically minoritized communities engage with schools. This form of family engagement also empowers children to view their families' and communities' funds of knowledge as assets. In this sense, "critically conscious family engagement" embodies a "counter-path" (Heiman & Yanes, 2018) that challenges the status quo and develops critical consciousness among children and their families.

Discussion Questions

1. Using Nellie's case narrative as an inspiration, what are additional ways critically conscious pedagogy can include families and communities?
2. How can Nellie's practices be adapted to promote equitable family engagement at the schoolwide level?
3. Reflecting on your own beliefs and practices, what lessons can you take away from Nellie's approach to critically conscious family engagement?
4. What are the differences in engaging families as "co-teachers" when children participate in online versus in-person schooling?

References

Alfaro, C. (2019). Preparing critically conscious dual-language teachers: Recognizing and interrupting dominant ideologies. *Theory into Practice*, *58*(2), 194–203.

Bartolomé, L. (2004). Critical pedagogy and teacher education: Radicalizing prospective teachers. *Teacher Education Quarterly*, *31*(1), 97–122.

Cervantes-Soon, C. G., Dorner, L., Palmer, D., Heiman, D., Schwerdtfeger, R., & Choi, J. (2017). Combating inequalities in two-way language immersion programs: Toward critical consciousness in bilingual education spaces. *Review of Research in Education, 41*(1), 403–427.

Esteban-Guitart, M., & Moll, L. C. (2014). Funds of identity: A new concept based on the funds of knowledge approach. *Culture & Psychology, 20*(1), 31–48.

Freire, J. A. (2020). Promoting sociopolitical consciousness and bicultural goals of dual language education: The transformational dual language educational framework. *Journal of Language, Identity & Education, 19*(1), 56–71.

Freire, P. (2000). *Pedagogy of the oppressed.* Continuum.

García, O., & Kleifgen, J. A. (2018). Family and community engagement. In *Educating emergent bilinguals: Policies, programs, and practices for English learners* (pp. 129–143). Teachers College Press.

Harlin, R., & Souto-Manning, M. (2009). Review of research: Educating Latino children: International perspectives and values in early education. *Childhood Education, 85*(3), 182–186.

Heiman, D. (2020). 'So is gentrification good or bad?' One teacher's implementation of the fourth goal in her TWBE classroom. *Anthropology & Education Quarterly*. https://doi.org/10.1111/aeq.12362.

Heiman, D., & Nuñez-Janes, M. (2021). "Research shows that I am here for them": Acompañamiento as language policy activism in times of TWBE gentrification. *Language Policy, 20*(3), 491–515.

Heiman, D., & Yanes, M. (2018). Centering the fourth pillar in times of TWBE gentrification: "Spanish, love, content, not in that order". *International Multilingual Research Journal, 12*(3), 173–187.

Husband, T. (2012). "I don't see color": Challenging assumptions about discussing race with young children. *Early Childhood Education Journal, 39*(6), 365–371.

Ishimaru, A. M. (2019). From family engagement to equitable collaboration. *Educational Policy, 33*(2), 350–385.

Ishimaru, A. M. (2020). *The prospects for just schools in the wake of COVID-19 responses* [Online blog post]. Teachers College Press.

Ishimaru, A. M., Lott II, J., Torres, K., & O'Reilly-Diaz, K. (2019). Families in the driver's seat: Catalyzing familial transformative agency for equitable collaboration. *Teachers College Record, 121*(11), 1–39.

Ladson-Billings, G. (2021). I'm here for the hard re-set: Post pandemic pedagogy to preserve our culture. *Equity & Excellence in Education, 54*(1), 68–78.

Madison, D. S. (2020). *Critical ethnography: Method, ethics, and performance.* Sage.

Matthews, L. A. (2010). *A case study examination of culturally relevant pedagogical practices for English-language learners in a pre-kindergarten classroom setting* [Dissertation]. Georgia State University.

Nancy, J. L. (2007). *Listening.* Fordham University Press.

Palmer, D. K., & Caldas, B. (2015). Critical ethnography. *Encyclopedia of language and education, 8*, 1–12.

Palmer, D. K., Cervantes-Soon, C., Dorner, L., & Heiman, D. (2019): Bilingualism, biliteracy, biculturalism, and critical consciousness for all: Proposing a fourth fundamental goal for two-way dual language education. *Theory Into Practice*, 1–13.

Quintero, E. (2003). Early childhood literacy: Creating a better world. *Journal of Early Childhood Teacher Education, 24*(3), 199–211.

Templeton, T. N. (2013). Teacher as researcher: Young children as forces of nature: Critical perspective in a preschool classroom. *Childhood Education, 89*(3), 185–187.

Valdés, G. (1996). *Con respeto: Bridging the distances between culturally diverse families and schools: An ethnographic portrait.* Teachers College Press.

Valencia, R. R. (2010). *Dismantling contemporary deficit thinking: Educational thought and practice*. Routledge.

Valenzuela, A. (Ed.). (2016). *Growing critically conscious teachers: A social justice curriculum for educators of Latino/a youth*. Teachers College Press.

16 Contextualizing Parent Activism in One of Milwaukee's Bilingual Public Schools

Luis "Tony" Báez and Andrew H. Hurie

Context

Throughout the 1960s and 70s, various Latina/o-led[1] social movements fought for and achieved substantial improvements in areas ranging from healthcare to farmworkers' labor conditions. In education, the Chicano and Puerto Rican movements further advanced calls for community control of schools, bilingual education, and greater representation in higher education. This era of civil rights struggles was a profound incubator of consciousness-raising about Latina/o community concerns that generated important social changes. It thus exemplifies our understanding of critical consciousness as multifaceted and messy awareness, reflection, and action (Heiman, et al., this volume).

Many of these struggles played out locally within the city of Milwaukee, Wisconsin, USA. Milwaukee Public Schools (MPS) was awarded pilot funding for a bilingual education program as part of the federal Bilingual Education Act (BEA) of 1968. On par with the initial design of the BEA, the program that began in Milwaukee in 1969 was limited in scope (Vargas-Harrison, 1995), consisting of bilingual "strands" at three schools. As the Latina/o community gained political organizing prowess, parent-led groups demanded a more robust program. In 1974, compelled by sophisticated Latina/o community activism, the Milwaukee school board of directors approved developmental bilingual education as official language policy. Crucially, the degree of community involvement did not stop there, because the parent-led City-Wide Bilingual Bicultural Advisory Committee (CWBBAC) became the official advisory board to MPS for issues related to bilingual-bicultural education (BBE), and protected the program during Milwaukee's drawn-out federal school desegregation case (Báez et al., 1980; Mercer, 2013).

A fundamental logic and goal of the Milwaukee BBE movement was to go beyond the civil rights "crumbs" that had been granted in the courts. Following reviews by the federal Office for Civil Rights, the "Lau Remedies" of 1975 required school districts to comply with the 1965 Civil Rights

DOI: 10.4324/9781003240594-20

Act (Báez et al., 1980). Many districts implemented transitional bilingual programs as a result. Rather than acquiesce, movement leaders in Milwaukee committed to the expansion of developmental BBE, working at local and state levels. Locally, the program grew to 19 schools by 1977. These schools included all Latinas/os who chose bilingual education, not just those identified as having limited English proficiency. The district's inclusive orientation to developmental BBE (now considered a form of dual language bilingual education, DLBE) continues as of this writing.

At the state level, the CWBBAC pushed legislators to pass the 1975 Bilingual Education Act (WI BEA), which also provided funding for BBE regardless of a student's English proficiency. At the time, the WI BEA was the only US legislation to do so (Peterson, 2017). Presently, however, the WI BEA only provides funding for students identified as English learners (ELs), yet MPS continues to provide funds for all students in DLBE programs (Beeman, 2014). Through the CWBBAC, parent and community influences were far-reaching, from teacher hiring to student assignment policies. The diligent organizing for BBE led by Latina/o communities in Milwaukee laid the foundation for a critical consciousness around the importance of sustaining heritage language and culture in education. More than fifty years after the launch of Milwaukee's BBE program, it is crucial to examine contemporary efforts to tap into and facilitate parent critical consciousness.

Case Narrative

At the current historical moment, neoliberalism—the philosophy that exalts economic logics, individualism, and the privatization of public goods and services—manifests in Milwaukee's education scene most notably through private school vouchers, public charters, and high-stakes accountability. For example, Milwaukee has the longest-running school voucher program in the nation. The city now enrolls the highest percentage of Latina/o students in private schools out of the 50 largest US metropolitan areas (Levine, 2016), with a comparable number of Latina/o students in charter schools. Contrary to the demands of the Latina/o-led BBE movement, the vast majority of charter and voucher schools offer only English-medium instruction (Peterson, 2017).

At the same time, the MPS board of directors has implemented a variety of policies to continue its support of DLBE, both ideologically and materially. For example, the board's 2014 Bilingual Resolution envisioned multilingual and multicultural education for all students

> by first establishing an English/Spanish and other languages bilingual and dual-language program in Milwaukee's near southside . . . and then, within a reasonable number of years, at the city-wide level until MPS becomes a school district in which students will graduate academically

well prepared in English, Spanish, and/or be conversant in another language.

(MPS, 2014)

Related school board measures in 2019 funded ethnic studies positions and created a bilingual education task force to financially support and accelerate the preparation of state-certified bilingual teachers for the full implementation of the Bilingual Resolution. Currently, there are over thirty schools with extensive DLBE programs out of 156 MPS schools, and immersion schools in German, French, Italian, and Spanish. Many of these schools are among the top-ranked bilingual schools in the state according to Wisconsin school accountability ratings. Amid this backdrop, Spanish-speaking parents at La Escuela Bilingüe Foster (EBF, a pseudonym, as are all names of individuals) have maintained an active Centro de Familias at the school that serves over 600 kindergarten-through-eighth-grade students, the vast majority of whom (97%) are officially identified as Latino/Hispanic.

EBF Parent Committee Development

In 1995, EBF began as a relatively small kindergarten-through-fifth-grade school on Milwaukee's near south side. It had a dual focus on DLBE and STEM education. In collaboration with Ms. Núñez, a Latina principal who was a leader of DLBE in the state, EBF's parent committee provided academic support for young readers. As parent committee member Sra. González explained, "*Nosotros le pusimos un carrito sanwichero . . . nos lo sacamos al pasillo y ahí les empezamos a enseñar, letra por letra, y de ahí a juntar palabras*" ["We got a sandwich cart together . . . we took it out into the hallway and there we began to teach them, letter by letter, and then to put words together."] Because of the school's academic success and culture, district officials decided to move EBF from its previous building and add a middle school with 100 new seats. After 15 years of relative stability, all members of the EBF community experienced growing pains in the new building, including parents. Weary of large schools, some parents enrolled their children elsewhere, although various families returned to EBF after experiencing unreceptive climates in other schools.

The Centro de Familias was a crucial component of EBF and its welcoming environment. Participation was voluntary for EBF families, and the group's composition was fluid, with about ten Spanish-speaking mothers forming its core. Parents served on teacher interview committees, spoke at school board meetings, and led presentations at the state DLBE conference. Through these activities, their understanding of the history, activism, and research supporting bilingual development and DLBE models greatly increased. For many, a critical language awareness replaced an angst about their children not learning English. Indeed, when a regional superintendent claimed that the school's test scores indicated a need for more

English-language instruction, Sra. González argued that the district should disaggregate the data to show the performance of long-term EBF students, not those who had recently arrived at the school. Partly because of parent activism, EBF was allowed by MPS to continue its DLBE program without altering its language allocation model.

EBF's parent coordinator, Sra. Ortiz, developed deep connections with community organizations. She arranged courses for parents to further develop their English skills, as well as learn about nutrition and sexuality. In addition, the parents themselves planned and delivered supplementary quarterly lessons for students, each connected to the parents' lived experiences and a school-wide theme. The parents also stretched themselves by learning a dance to the song "El Ahuelulco" which they performed at the school's end-of-year celebration to the joyful cheers of students and families in the audience.

Beyond these official activities, the parent committee designated one day a week as unstructured time to build community and exchange information. Over coffee, newer parents learned about the school, including ways to advocate for their children and engage in informal leadership (Green, 2017). For example, long-time committee member Sra. González shared her concerns about the high number of short-term substitute teachers after one teacher of record went on maternity leave. Another mother new to the parent committee also had concerns about the same classroom. After receiving a letter about her child's low academic performance, Sra. González approached the principal with the demand for a consistent substitute teacher: "*Yo fui a la dirección, le dije, '¿Para qué me mandaron esta carta? Porque el problema no es de mi hija. El problema es de ustedes, porque ustedes no buscan maestro para ese grado. Así que ¡órale!'*" ["I went to the school administration, I said, 'Why did you send me this letter? Because the problem is not my daughter. The problem is yours, because you aren't looking for a teacher for that grade. So get to it!'"] Recognizing the scope of the parents' concerns, Principal Núñez worked through district policies and practices to place a well-liked special education teacher as the long-term substitute. In this manner, members of the Centro de Familias engaged in informal leadership that brought about positive changes for their own children as well as other students at EBF. In doing so, they implicitly rejected neoliberal discourses of school improvement that frame parents as individual consumers in an educational marketplace.

Contemporary Challenges

Despite the accomplishments of the Centro de Familias, there were enduring challenges that EBF parents faced within the school, district, and region. Within the school, parent committee members assumed a leadership role because they understood that other families could not participate on the committee due to work and personal circumstances. Also, in spite of district-offered professional development, there were some teachers that did not consider their pedagogy in overtly political terms. While EBF teachers were deeply dedicated to their profession and embraced bilingual and multicultural education, not all went beyond this to explicitly interrogate power within the district's DLBE curriculum. This situation continues to be a challenge, and demonstrates that bilingual teachers—like all educators—benefit from ongoing opportunities to learn about multilingual and multicultural education (Beeman, 2014), as well as critical pedagogy.

At the district level, EBF's budget was affected by declining student enrollment throughout the district. While EBF had a positive school climate and robust student enrollment, non-bilingual schools in other parts of the district were closed due to population changes and a proliferation of charter and voucher schools. English-medium charter and voucher schools had even diverted some students from EBF, especially in the years immediately following EBF's move and expansion.

Outside the district, decades-long cuts in state aid constituted a major factor in the budget constraints that shaped schooling at EBF. The tight budget contributed to teachers' lack of planning time and students' large class sizes. Further, the geopolitical divisions that created the suburbs as white, middle-class enclaves continued despite the changing demographics of some suburban communities around Milwaukee. Elite suburbs with amply funded schools allowed for a handful of inter-district transfer students through a state policy that favored white and middle-class students. These multilayered issues functioned as constraints for the EBF parent committee and their efforts to enhance their children's bilingual schooling.

Teaching Notes

In this section, we provide readers with further historical context about the case, and connect these local issues to the broader scholarly literature.

Critical Consciousness is a Continual and Multifaceted Process

A key contribution of the mid-twentieth-century BBE movement has been to raise consciousness around language and culture in US schooling, and advocate for multiple forms of multilingual education. Specifically, the movement constituted a direct challenge to the hegemony of English (Macedo et al., 2003) in education. Ethnolinguistic communities fought for legislation that improved conditions for many.

Many models of bilingual education were implemented in multiple languages, forcing schools and states to respond to language-minoritized communities (Collier & Thomas, 2017). In the case of Milwaukee, the activism of Latina/o parents led to a developmental bilingual program that has succeeded in meeting the goals set by white-controlled institutions, despite the constant evolution of these goals. For example, Báez (2014) and Mendez (2012) demonstrate that EL-identified students, and particularly those in DLBE programs, tend to outperform non-ELs on state exams. Moreover, many leaders and administrators of DLBE programs have maintained their bilingualism and developed greater sociocultural competence. Further transformative possibilities emerge when parents and educators engage in the ongoing struggles to promote bilingualism and biculturalism, and resist standardized assessments promoted by white power structures. Sra. González and the EBF parent committee responded to neoliberal accountability pressures by drawing on their knowledge of language acquisition and collective agency to resist English hegemony. Again, in Milwaukee, resistance to English hegemony took place throughout the district, a scenario that differs from many other school districts and states.

Nonetheless, in some districts, a language-centered conceptualization of DLBE—exemplified by the shift in terminology from teaching *bilingual students* to teaching *dual languages* (García & Kleifgen, 2018)—may function to de-emphasize other demands of the BBE movement such as a transformation of the curriculum. In Milwaukee, vigilant community-led efforts like those of the CWBBAC generated bilingual curricula that centered community perspectives. At EBF, the parent committee delivered lessons by drawing on parents' funds of knowledge (González et al., 2005). These pedagogical interventions were a crucial aspect of parent activism because they prompted students and teachers to consider where the instructors were coming from and reconsider what identities and experiences constituted expert knowledge.

As evidenced by the Centro de Familias' efforts, sustaining the critical consciousness that emerged through the struggle to establish BBE is a continual and evolving process. In addition to language and curricular reforms, the pursuit of political and ideological clarity (Bartolomé, 2004) must form a central part of bilingual schooling, especially if parent activism is to be unleashed beyond the school building. These aspects of critical consciousness are crucial to transforming the enduring educational inequalities that continue to affect schools like EBF, which experience the incomplete and unequal schooling directed at minoritized groups in US society.

Remedies for Educational Inequalities are Often Ensnared in Whiteness

Whiteness—the dominative yet mutating social position and structure that violently places white tastes, ways of being and knowing, and cultural-historical traditions at the center and top of US and global society—has been a central organizing principle of US schooling (Leonardo, 2009; Urrieta, 2009). Crucially, communities of color have long waged sophisticated legal battles to combat the effects and root causes of whitestream schooling and racial segregation. For example, Mexican-origin communities in the US Southwest won key court decisions in *Alvarez v. Lemon Grove* (1931) and *Méndez v. Westminster* (1947), which then served as precedent for the well-known *Brown v. Board of Education* (1954). Some early bilingual education cases went beyond language to force districts to explore meaningful pedagogy and cultural competence—an aspect of critical consciousness (see Báez, 1995). Yet the 1974 *Lau v. Nichols* Supreme Court decision did not mandate these more transformative programs, and instead allowed transitional bilingual education approaches to proliferate and reinforce whitestream expectations of linguistic and cultural assimilation. Nonetheless, white racial domination is always incomplete, and important legal work continues to challenge it, as in the recent court case in New Mexico that considered how the lack of financial and cultural support affected the bilingual development and cultural engagement of Mexican-origin and Indigenous populations in the state (Sanchez & Blum-Martinez, 2019).

Despite their tenuous promise, legal remedies remain only one path for critically conscious action. The end of *de jure* segregation in US schools through supposed race-neutral rights did not shield against the resegregation of schools over the last five decades (Wells et al., 2019). Given these current constraints, activism is needed in multiple arenas, all of which can benefit from parent and community leadership. Within the case of Milwaukee, the MPS board's establishment of developmental BBE policy and most of the program's growth happened before important rulings in the federal court's desegregation case. It was the consistency and clarity of the CWBBAC's vigilant strategies that protected and expanded the program during the multiple decisions in the federal litigation challenging the district's intentional segregation of Black students (see Mercer, 2013). Prompted by Latina/o parent and community activism, the MPS board ruled that both desegregation and bilingual education were compatible since they each sought equal educational opportunities for historically marginalized students (Báez et al., 1980). Collaborative work between Black community representatives and the CWBBAC therefore confronted enduring inequalities, and engaged in a long-term effort to mobilize informal leadership and grassroots activism in support of desegregation and bilingual education.

While the best ways to remedy the underlying causes of racial and economic segregation remain contested, it is clear that the whitestream neoliberal approaches of moving student bodies and promoting individual choice have left unaddressed minoritized communities' demands for material redistribution and equitable education funding. The structural constraints and potentials of DLBE programs pose implications for the cultivation of critical consciousness and parent activism. The final section of this chapter outlines teaching activities that invite participants to become aware of and work toward minoritized-community priorities.

Teaching Activities

School-Community Outreach: Identify Informal Leaders

In order to tap into and facilitate parent critical consciousness, it is necessary to identify informal leaders throughout the school-community, those people with the authority of an organizer. Consider these questions, adapted from Green (2017):

- When this community has had a problem in the past, what person(s) has been involved in working to solve it?
- Whom do people in this neighborhood go to for help or advice?
- Whom do children go to for help or advice?
- Who gets things done in the community?

Once you identify informal community leaders, discuss the following questions with them:

- In your opinion, what are the most pressing issues facing our school-community?
- How do language and culture influence this issue?
- What factors beyond language and culture contribute to this issue?
- Are there organizations and resources outside the school that could help improve this issue?

Op-Ed Column: Historicizing Your School-Community

Because historicizing schools is an important component of developing critical consciousness (Palmer et al., 2019), individuals and organizations should investigate the history of the community and the region where you teach or where your children attend school. In many contexts, suburbanization processes in the twentieth century continue to affect school-communities across urban, suburban, and rural spaces.

Write a synthesis of your learning, and submit your writing to the op-ed column of your local community-based newspaper. Alternately, record a short video and upload it to official or unofficial locally based social media sites (e.g., parent-led WhatsApp chats, Facebook groups, etc.). Sharing your analysis in these forms can encourage a broader critical engagement with the historical and contemporary conditions of racial, economic, and linguistic oppression that continue to structure schooling for language-minoritized students.

Note

1. As educators engaged in our communities, we believe that our use of language must be inclusive and diverse because it forms a part of greater struggles against economic inequalities, racism, xenophobia, heteropatriarchy, and colonialism. For that reason, we use the term *Latina/o* in this chapter as one way to refer to people of Latin American descent, in recognition of different linguistic debates going on across the Americas.

References

Báez, L. A. (1995). *From transformative school goals to assimilationist and remedial bilingual education: A critical review of key precedent-setting Hispanic bilingual litigation decided by federal courts between 1974 and 1983* [Doctoral Dissertation]. University of Wisconsin-Milwaukee.

Báez, L. A. (2014, June). *Analysis of WKCE scores and ELLs in MPS for 2011–12*. Milwaukee Public School Board Proceedings on Resolution on Bilingualism.

Báez, T., Fernández, R. R., & Guskin, J. T. (1980). *Desegregation and Hispanic students: A community perspective*. National Clearinghouse for Bilingual Education.

Bartolomé, L. I. (2004). Critical pedagogy and teacher education: Radicalizing prospective teachers. *Teacher education quarterly, 31*(1), 97–122.

Beeman, K. (2014). *Milwaukee public schools bilingual program review*. Milwaukee Public Schools Department of Bilingual Multicultural Education.

Collier, V. P., & Thomas, W. P. (2017). Validating the power of bilingual schooling: Thirty-two years of large-scale, longitudinal research. *Annual Review of Applied Linguistics, 37*, 203–217.

García, O., & Kleifgen, J. A. (2018). *Educating emergent bilinguals: Policies, programs, and practices for English learners*. Teachers College Press.

González, N., Moll, L. C., & Amanti, C. (Eds.). (2005). *Funds of knowledge: Theorizing practices in households, communities, and classrooms*. Routledge.

Green, T. L. (2017). Community-based equity audits: A practical approach for educational leaders to support equitable community-school improvements. *Educational Administration Quarterly, 53*(1), 3–39.

Leonardo, Z. (2009). *Race, whiteness, and education*. Routledge.

Levine, M. V. (2016). *Latino Milwaukee: A statistical portrait*. Center for Economic Development Publications. https://dc.uwm.edu/cgi/viewcontent.cgi?article=1004&context=ced_pubs

Macedo, D., Dendrinos, B., & Gounari, P. (2003). *The hegemony of English*. Routledge.

Mendez, E. (2012, February 20). Special report: Latino English language learners outperform non-ELL peers. *Milwaukee Neighborhood News Service*. https://milwaukeenns.org/2012/02/20/3224/

Mercer, L. (2013). *A necessary safeguard: The Latino strategy to create and expand bilingual bicultural education in Milwaukee, 1969–1979* [Unpublished manuscript]. History Department, University of Wisconsin-Milwaukee.

Milwaukee Public Schools (MPS). (2014, June 19). *Resolution 1415R-003 to establish the equivalent of a region that promotes bilingualism*. https://mps.milwaukee.k12.wi.us/MPS-English/CAO/C-I/Bilingual/June2014ProceedingsoftheMBSD.pdf

Palmer, D. K., Cervantes-Soon, C., Dorner, L., & Heiman, D. (2019). Bilingualism, biliteracy, biculturalism, and critical consciousness for all: Proposing a fourth fundamental goal for two-way dual language education. *Theory Into Practice, 58*(2), 121–133.

Peterson, B. (2017). The struggle for bilingual education: An interview with bilingual education advocate Tony Baez. In E. Barbian, G. C. Gonzales, & P. Mejía (Eds.), *Rethinking bilingual education: Welcoming home languages in our classrooms* (pp. 274–279). Rethinking Schools.

Sanchez, P., & Blum-Martinez, R. (2019). A watershed moment in the education of American Indians: A judicial strategy to mandate the state of New Mexico to meet the unique cultural and linguistic needs of American Indians in New Mexico public schools. *American University Journal of Gender, Social Policy & Law, 27*(3), 317–355.

Urrieta, Jr. L. (2009). *Working from within: Chicana and Chicano activist educators in whitestream schools*. University of Arizona Press.

Vargas-Harrison, J. A. (1995). *A history of Hispanic bilingual education in Milwaukee's public schools: People, policies, and programs, 1969–1988* [Doctoral dissertation]. University of Wisconsin-Milwaukee.

Wells, A. S., Keener, A., Cabral, L., & Cordova-Cobo, D. (2019). The more things change, the more they stay the same: The resegregation of public schools via charter school reform. *Peabody Journal of Education, 94*(5), 471–492.

17 Relational Pedagogies and the Building of a Social Architecture of Authentic *Cariño* in the Teaching of Healing Practices at Academia Cuauhtli

Christopher Milk Bonilla and Angela Valenzuela

Context

On a cold night in February 2013, Nuestro Grupo met to discuss the paucity of local DLBE curricula that took children's language and cultural heritage into account. Nuestro Grupo is a Latinx, community-based organization in Austin, Texas that includes university faculty and students, low-income Latinx families, community members, dual language/bilingual education (DLBE) teachers, and education advocates. This paucity of culturally relevant and locally designed DLBE curricula was not surprising, since research has long established that low-income, Latinx DLBE schools had long been entrenched with deficit ideologies when it came to home-school relationships and curriculum (Valenzuela, 1999; Darder, 2012). Such harmful ideologies assume that the people they are serving lack either the intelligence or knowledge to succeed. Hence, when teachers work in low-income schools, they often approach the relationship with their students and their families as having little of any value to inform the curriculum or the instructional process. After discussing these issues for over three hours, Nuestro Grupo decided to found their own bilingual after-school program that would be premised on asset-based approaches to Latinx knowledge, with a positive view of the knowledge that students and their families bring to school. Currently in its eighth year of operation, the program became a Saturday school known as Academia Cuauhtli (AC), that runs from October to April.

AC boasts a Nuestro Grupo–Austin Independent School District (AISD)–City of Austin partnership whose aim is to provide bilingual ethnic studies to low-income, Latinx fourth- and fifth-grade students. AISD provides the DLBE students and teachers. The City of Austin provides the physical location at a downtown river-front community arts institution. Nuestro Grupo provides logistical support to AC, co-constructs curriculum, and offers professional development opportunities for AISD bilingually certified teachers.

Since part of the aim is to provide transformational professional development for DLBE teachers that work in low-income schools, the program

DOI: 10.4324/9781003240594-21

raises their critical consciousness by challenging implicit biases that inform deficit ideologies. To do this, we intentionally build spaces for teachers and families to collaborate within asset-based frameworks that build curricula based on family knowledge. In what we refer to as a social architecture of "authentic *cariño*," our practice is centered on trust-building, collaborative relationships in which teachers and families can engage critically in curriculum construction. By engaging in these spaces of critical consciousness, we have found that teachers are able to disavow deficit notions and instead engage with families in a constructive manner by building on their knowledge, values, and expressed wishes and desires.

Curandera *Lesson Case Study*

In the following case study, we trace the planning and implementation of a *plantas medicinales* (medicinal plants) unit in 2019. We highlight how familial home funds of knowledge and Indigenous epistemologies were integrated into our curriculum through the relationships we built, i.e. our social architecture. We highlight our use of two relational strategies—*pláticas* and *convivios*—to examine how a *cariño*-based social architecture builds on everyone's knowledge to support a holistic approach to student learning. *Convivios* are social events which intentionally create space for sharing of knowledge. *Pláticas* are meetings which intentionally create the space for relationship building. Both of these forms of *cariño*-based social architecture integrate social relationship building with social knowledge construction that both fosters and enacts critical consciousness.

Our curricular planning for the *plantas medicinales* unit can be traced back to the *convivios* we had the spring of 2019. During the graduation *convivio* of our 2018–2019 cohort, teachers asked families what they had enjoyed most about the previous year. Multiple families discussed how they appreciated the fact that teachers mentioned the use of herbs for healing during one of the lessons. Specifically, they wanted to pass on this knowledge to their children, but the children often did not take this knowledge seriously. Teachers responded that they had also enjoyed these conversations with the students and would explore how to continue this topic.

Soon after the graduation, we sponsored a *temazcal* for the teachers as a healing *convivio*. A *temazcal* is a healing sweat bath ritual performed by our *calpulli* community partners. A *calpulli* is a community that shares *Mexica* Indigenous knowledges by practicing and sharing this knowledge through community events, like *temazcales*. As part of this process, teachers were introduced to the healing herbs used in the *temazcal* and this once again brought up the idea of the medicinal herb lesson and its importance in teaching the students to heal themselves. During this conversation, teachers committed to doing a medicinal herb unit the following fall. During *convivios*, we found that teachers were able to connect with a broader range of knowledge, including with families and the *calpulli*, because they were in comfortable, relational spaces that allowed them to make connections they might not make in more formal schooling environments.

That same summer, we sponsored a series of curriculum *pláticas* during which we worked with teachers to construct the curriculum for the fall. We began the curriculum writing by asking the teachers what they knew about Indigenous healing practices and how they could turn that knowledge into an AC unit. At first, teachers shared how difficult it was to have these discussions with their students in their DLBE school because they always felt pressured to teach the standardized curriculum. But as teachers warmed up to each other, they started to share the different ways they included Indigenous knowledges in the classroom, from legends to history. Specifically, they shared how excited they had been to research this topic because it was something that had always sparked their interest but never had time to implement.

Teachers also shared how important *curandera* knowledge was for them. *Curanderas* are Mexican healers who use Indigenous, local knowledge as part of their healing practices. The teachers shared stories about their own experiences with *curanderas*, how *curanderas* had taught them to heal themselves, and the importance this knowledge played in their lives. Based on this discussion, they decided to focus one of their lessons in the unit on *curanderas* as sources of Indigenous knowledges. By sharing family stories and personal experiences in *pláticas*, teachers were able to interrogate power and critique how schooling policies negatively impacted their students and what they could do to counteract these policies, like create curricula which affirmed Indigenous knowledges.

Before teachers taught the *plantas medicinales* unit, they shared the unit with families in a family *plática*. They asked families to share their experiences with Indigenous healing and what they wanted to share with the children. In this way, families engaged in self-historicizing, allowing ancestral knowledge and stories to come to the surface. Some mothers shared their knowledge about the uses of herbs in their daily practice—and how their own mothers, fathers, and *curanderas* had taught them this knowledge throughout their lives. Other mothers said they knew little about the topic, but felt it was an important part of their culture and they did not want their children to lose their culture. The teachers then invited families to share their knowledge with the students during the lesson. By focusing on building understanding through caring and critical relationships with families in *convivios* and *pláticas*, families felt more comfortable sharing their knowledge and opinions both with teachers and with students. Simultaneously, teachers learned how to make explicit sociocultural connections between academic social studies content, Indigenous epistemologies, and familial home funds of knowledge.

The *curandera* lesson exemplifies many of the pedagogical practices found in each lesson. The third and final lesson of the *plantas medicinales* unit was on how families use *curandera* knowledge. The lesson was conducted in a circle with about eight children and a couple of family members with *ruda* (rue plant) and *copal* on a table in the center of the circle. The teacher asked the students if they knew what the *ruda* and *copal* were. *Copal* is the resin of the copal tree, which is burned as incense in healing ceremonies. One child said she thought that she had smelled *copal* at church. At this, one of the mothers told her child that of course she knew what both were because they used *ruda* to get a *limpia*, or cleansing, from negative energy. At this, several other children raised their hands and said that they knew what a *limpia* was and discussed either being cleansed with *ruda* or having seen someone being cleansed with it. The teacher then showed a quick video of a *curandera* teaching children the importance of *ruda*. She then demonstrated how to conduct a *limpia* with one of the children. The families and teachers then conducted *limpias* on all the children after lighting the *copal*. When the children were asked to describe what they had learned, one child noted, "*Nuestras mamás nos dan limpias para cuidarnos . . . Esto aprendieron de sus mamás* [Our mothers cleanse us to take care of us . . . They learned this from their mothers]." By participating in lessons, family members helped to make more explicit connections between familial knowledge and the content while contributing themselves to the caring social architecture of the school.

After the lesson, the teachers asked a few families to stay as part of their after-lesson reflective *plática*. During reflection, teachers took turns expressing one thing they liked and one thing they needed to improve. As was often the case in familial reflective *platicas*, the three invited mothers expressed great emotion and excitement about the lesson and spoke at great length about what the experience meant to them. For instance, one mother spoke about how important it was that her daughter understand the wisdom of the knowledge that came from Mexico, "*Por primera vez pude compartir con mi hija la importancia de nuestro conocimiento . . . nunca he podido hacer esto . . . y me comprendió* [For the first time I could share with my daughter about the importance of our knowledge . . . I have never been able to do this . . . and she understood]." Teachers were just as enthusiastic, discussing how meaningful and important it was both to have the mothers present and to make the links between the Indigenous roots of this knowledge and the fact that parents practiced it at home. Parents underscored how valuable it was for their children's schools to value this knowledge because they found it so difficult to discuss it with their children in the United States.

Using practices like *convivios* and *pláticas*, AC centers critical relationship building to construct a social architecture of caring between students, families, and teachers that fosters a critical consciousness that decolonizes knowledge content and learning processes. Within this architecture, teachers and families critically examine their curriculum and teaching to provide an enriching bicultural educational experience for DLBE students, one constructed in *cariño*.

Teaching Notes

In this case study, we use an Indigenous unit we taught at AC to detail how we create a social architecture of *cariño* within teacher-family relationships. We have found that by being intentional in how we build a relational, social architecture premised on authentic *cariño*, we empower our teachers to critically engage with families in the co-construction of knowledge.

Building a Social Architecture of Authentic Cariño

DLBE programs have struggled to provide asset-based approaches with working-class, Latinx home-school relationships (Pacheco & Hamilton, 2020). Accordingly, we draw on the work of Curry (2016) and Valenzuela (1999) to critically examine how children should be cared for in their schools. Curry expands on Valenzuela's (1999) and Noddings's (1984) concept of "authentic caring," to describe key components of familial, intellectual, and critical care that build a social architecture of relationships between families and teachers. An architecture of authentic *cariño* is a critical infrastructure of caring, wherein caring relationships between teachers and families work in partnership to provide children with a culturally revitalizing environment to counter oppressive structures in schools and society.

The AC partnership enables this architecture by having teachers build relationships with families both outside and inside the classroom. To do this, we privilege two pedagogical practices that frame our teacher-family relationships: *convivios* (Trinidad-Galvan, 2010) and *pláticas* (Guajardo & Guajardo, 2013; Rubio et al., 2020). The key components are a combination of relationship building and collaborative knowledge building. This allows both teachers and families to feel more comfortable sharing personal accounts about how they experience inequities in their lives and why this knowledge is necessary for their children.

In terms of curriculum development, this social architecture allows us to center familial knowledge while still critiquing the content we want to explore with the students. Using the more relationship-building-focused *convivios*, we partner with families to get their feedback on which topics we should consider teaching the students. We use the more knowledge-construction-focused *pláticas* to discuss the best ways to include home funds of knowledge (Valenzuela, 2016) within the curriculum. We also ask families to be part of the lessons themselves so that they become integral to their children's knowledge development and exploration. Building a social architecture is as much about building asset-based knowledge as it is about encouraging critical dialogue about education and schooling, generally.

Authentic Cariño *and Critical Examinations of Indigenous Knowledges*

In order to challenge deficit ideologies of home-school relationships and Indigenous Latinx identities, centering authentic *cariño* is central to our practice. By creating time to center and integrate the three distinct perspectives of familial, critical, and intellectual notions of care, we uplift students' home knowledge and promote a more holistic approach to learning.

This can be examined during the Indigenous unit. Initially, the unit was discussed in *convivios* because families wanted to discuss family medicinal healing as passing on familial perspectives of care. In *pláticas*, teachers recognized this as something that could be integrated into culturally relevant forms of intellectual care in social studies and language arts school curricula. For both families and teachers, this knowledge supported the kind of care that they wanted to engender for the students from their perspective.

Integrating critical care into the curricula, however, required more in-depth dialogue between teachers and families. One of the main challenges when discussing Latinx indigeneity in the United States has been the erasure of Indigenous identity and knowledge by all colonial powers, including the United States and Mexican educational systems (Urrieta & Calderón, 2019). This has resulted in a shaming of the familial practices, knowledge, and senses of belonging that families want to sustain. For instance, familial uses of herbs are often seen as less effective than Western notions of medicine. This was initially reflected in difficulties that both teachers and families had in impressing upon their children the importance of herbs in healing.

Thus, during *pláticas* we focused not only on what we wanted to explore with the children, but on interrogating power by discussing how this knowledge has been framed by both society and educators in the past. Families and teachers shared personal experiences of how their own relatives and former teachers devalued their own parents' healing practices, but then learned that these same healing practices were celebrated by holistic doctors. Taking this into consideration, the unit came to be about the healing herbs, those who continue to practice this knowledge like *curanderas*, and the importance of this Indigenous healing knowledge to our families. In this way, the unit integrated critical, familial, and intellectual notions of care so that students were enveloped by a social architecture that took care of them from multiple perspectives and fostered their critical consciousness.

Teaching Activities

Relationship-Building Activities

1. Family partnership role-plays—We practiced building family-teacher partnerships by role-playing how they can use *pláticas* to build common goals with families (especially during family conferences). During a faculty meeting/class, we would present the goals of *pláticas* to understand the internal motivations of families and then model a family *plática* with a teacher volunteer, providing three questions (see the following). We would then ask teachers to role-play these *pláticas*, taking turns being a family member. These questions are only meant as a beginning frame.

We encouraged the teachers to be flexible and use their own approaches and styles for building family-centered partnerships.

1. What are your hopes and dreams for your child?
2. What are your concerns about this grade level? (We generally found this question came up naturally after the first question. We would also model praising three student's strengths before sharing any concerns we may have about students.)
3. How can we work together as partners to reach our shared goals?

2. Indigenous heritage family questions—Teachers shared questions which helped them promote conversations with families in which they discussed family perspectives about Indigenous heritage.

    1. We are learning about the Indigenous heritage in Mexican/Latinx cultural traditions, cultures, and history. We are asking families to share with their own children their thoughts about Latinx Indigenous heritage.

        i. In what ways is Indigenous heritage important to you and your family?
        ii. We will discuss the importance of Indigenous knowledges in what we eat and how we take care of ourselves (for instance, herbal teas). What is important for you and your family that we discuss?
        iii. We will discuss the importance of Indigenous knowledges in how we take care of each other and the Earth (for instance, water conservation). What is important for you and your family that we discuss?

References

Curry, M. (2016). Will you stand for me? Authentic carino and transformative rites of passage in an urban high school. *American Education Research Journal, 53*(4), 883–918.

Darder, A. (2012). *Culture and power in the classroom: Educational foundations for the schooling of bicultural students* (The 20th anniversary ed.). Paradigm Publishers.

Guajardo, F., & Guajardo, M. (2013). The power of platica. *Reflections: A Journal of Public Rhetoric, Civic Writing and Service Learning, 13*(1), 159–165.

Noddings, N. (1984). *Caring: A relational approach to ethics and moral education*. Universtiy of California Press.

Pacheco, M., & Hamilton, C. (2020). Bilanguaging love: Latina/o/x bilingual students' subjectivities and sensitivities in dual language immersion contexts. *TESOL Quarterly, 54*(3).

Rubio, B., Milk Bonilla, C., & Bell, R. (2020). Decolonial Latinx urban educational leadership development through a community-based partnership. In R. Guillame, N. W. Arnold, A. F. Asanloo, & C. M. Grants (Eds.), *Handbook of urban educational leadership* (2nd ed.). Roman and Littlefield.

Trinidad-Galvan, R. (2010). Calming the spirit and ensuring super-vivencia: Rural Mexican women-centred teaching and learning spaces. *Ethnography and Education, 5*(3), 309–323.

Urrieta Jr, L., & Calderón, D. (2019). Critical Latinx indigeneities: Unpacking indigeneity from within and outside of Latinized entanglements. *Association of Mexican American Educators Journal, 13*(2), 145–174.

Valenzuela, A. (1999). *Subtractive schooling: U.S.-Mexican youth and the politics of caring.* State University of New York Press.

Valenzuela, A. (2016). *Growing critically conscious teachers: A social justice curriculum for educators of Latino/a youth.* Teachers College Press.

Section IV

Teaching, Teacher Learning, and Critical Consciousness

18 Black Liberation in Bilingual Education

A Case for Black Freedom Dreaming

Brittany L. Frieson and Vivian E. Presiado

Context

Over the past few decades, student demographics in US schools have shifted to communities of color being the majority of students enrolled in public school systems across the nation. On the heels of a changing linguistic landscape within US contexts, classrooms have also experienced shifting environments with the increased demand for dual language bilingual education (DLBE). The goals of DLBE programs prioritize the development of students' bilingualism and biliteracy and foster academic achievement and cross-cultural competency. Although DLBE program goals appear to advocate for linguistically minoritized children, the linguistic and academic needs of Black American children are not consistently met (Valdés, 2018).

Black American students who speak Black language are often homogenized with Anglo, White mainstream English (WME) speakers with the categorization of "English speakers." The challenge with Black language being reduced to WME in DLBE programs is the erasure of Black language, similar to the stigmatization that Black language receives in academic spaces (Frieson, 2021). Thus, DLBE programs are structurally positioned as a space for the possible continuation of linguistic trauma and violence. Regardless of the minimal support that Black American children experience from DLBE programs, Black children often demonstrate linguistic flexibility to advocate for their linguistic rights (Frieson, 2021). However, recent developments in bilingual education critical scholarship have advocated for the centering of critical consciousness that is praxis-oriented in nature which would prioritize the linguistic genius of Black children. This hypothetical case demonstrated how Jewell, a Black American girl, and her elementary DLBE teachers enacted critical consciousness by the co-creation of spaces where she experienced Black liberation by going beyond linguistic boundaries and encouraging Black freedom dreaming (Kelley, 2002). Although this case study is imagined, it is grounded in data collected from previous research, as well as our own experiences as students and teachers in language education programs. Specifically this case provides starting points for bilingual teachers on how to leverage the linguistic brilliance of Black American

DOI: 10.4324/9781003240594-23

children, their families, and communities. In the case narrative that follows, we will demonstrate how critical consciousness is achieved through critical listening, interrogating power, critical reflective practice, and taking action *with* Black freedom dreaming in DLBE spaces.

Introducing Jewell and Her Teachers

Jewell, a fifth-grade Black American girl, is finishing up her last year in the Spanish/English DLBE strand program at Parks Elementary. She has always enjoyed the DLBE strand program because she has had many teachers who built upon her full linguistic repertoire as a Black language speaker and prioritized it as a part of their instruction. Something that Jewell loved most about her former teachers in K–4th grade is that although Black language was not a targeted instructional language, it was a part of the multilingual ecology of her classes. Her teachers ensured that the DLBE program was a space where Jewell could leverage all of her linguistic tools and not just the ones that the DLBE strand program endorsed.

Jewell's new fifth-grade teacher, Maestra Lilly, had just transferred from another school district where the student demographics were drastically different from Park Elementary, where the majority of students in the DLBE program are Latinx and Black American. As Jewell grew accustomed to Maestra Lilly, she noticed that her linguistic repertoire was not being centered and drawn upon as a linguistic strength as it previously had been. For example, when Jewell and her friends were using Black language in the classroom, Maestra Lilly would translate their words to WME, which often missed the point of many of their conversations. Her lack of linguistic and cultural responsiveness left Jewell feeling uneasy and like her discursive practices didn't matter at school as much as they had before until she overheard Maestra Lilly and Maestra Santos, her third-grade teacher, engaged in a conversation. Maestra Lilly explained that she was at a loss for how to navigate the new linguistic landscape of her classroom since her previous school did not have Black language speakers and unfortunately her teacher preparation program did not account for Black American children participating in DLBE programs. She further explained that she wanted to center the literacies, voices, and soundscapes of children like Jewell in her classroom but wasn't knowledgeable on where to start. Maestra Santos shared some teaching ideas that she previously incorporated in her classroom, while Jewell started reflecting on her previous experiences.

Case Narrative

Braiding Hair in Literacy

While Maestra Lilly and Maestra Santos were engaged in a conversation, Jewell began quietly recounting memories to herself. The first snapshot that Jewell recounted was from her first year in the DLBE program when her kindergarten teacher was a Chicana. She recalled the beginning of the school year when families were invited to spend time in the classroom during storytelling time. Jewell's grandmother and community hairdresser visited to share stories as Jewell's grandmother braided Jewell's hair and the community hairdresser braided the teacher's hair. The teacher read pages from *I Love My Hair* (1998) by Natasha A. Tarpley as the hairdresser styled the teacher's hair. Jewell listened as the community hairdresser, Ms. Shante, described the steps for how to braid hair; however, her classmates and teacher were interested in learning more about her grandma and Ms. Shante. They and other Black language speakers discussed family rituals and memories, and even her teacher shared stories about growing up. Jewell smiled when Angelica, now Jewell's best friend in fifth grade, shared that her *abuela* (grandmother) would also do *trenzas* (braids) in her hair. A few weeks later Angelica's grandmother visited the classroom to braid Angelica's hair and also shared life stories and family wisdom. As a fifth grader, Jewell still remembered when classmates excitedly showed her that they chose to write about her grandmother and Ms. Shante's visit. The events led to conversations about how boys can get their hair braided too, and an area of the room naturally evolved into a beauty/barbershop, where the teacher added props and materials for students. Jewell recalled making magazines for the beauty salon and a list of products needed, as she took on the role of "boss" to help organize the space with classmates.

Takin' it to Church: Honoring Literacies

In first grade, Jewel remembers her teacher, a Chicana, asking the class about family events. Jewell's first grade teacher was known to go out into the community to spend time with students at public events and to learn from the community. Jewell was ecstatic when her teacher visited her church to see Jewell perform a praise dance with the praise team. As soon as her teacher walked in, the pastor approached her teacher and had her sit in the front row so he could present her to the congregation. Jewell remembers her teacher looking overwhelmed with church members approaching to welcome her, but Jewell also saw her excitement and appreciation as her teacher learned about her church. Later that week, her teacher had her perform the dance for the class and she was able to write about it in her class journal. Angelica also shared how dances would be included at her Roman Catholic Church on the day of La Virgen de Guadalupe. It was the year that Jewell also noticed that Angelica was picking up on Black language, with Angelica often saying, "Let me cut off them lights *para la maestra*."

"Time is Money" in Mathematics

Another snapshot that Jewell recounted was in third grade with her teacher, Maestra Santos, who identified as Afro-Latinx. Third grade continues to remain one of her favorite grade levels since her teacher could relate to similar lived experiences, such as spending Saturdays "in the chair" at the salon and barber, kickbacks with family and friends who lived in the neighborhood, and heart-to-heart conversations with the aunties at the kitchen table. Another element that was special about Maestra Santos is that she incorporated these shared experiences into the curriculum. For example, during a unit on time, Maestra Santos instructed the class to interview a community barber or stylist. Angelica decided to go with Jewell and her grandma to interview Mr. Ceddy, the neighborhood barber. Jewell and Angelica made a list of questions that they wanted to ask him beforehand because as Mr. Ceddy always said, "Time is money," and the last thing the girls wanted to do was waste his time by not being "on point." During the interview, Jewell and Angelica asked Mr. Ceddy questions about estimating time for walk-ins since his shop took both appointments and walk-ins because they never wanted to turn people away who wanted a fresh cut. He explained his process such as knowing that it took him about 15–20 minutes per cut and how he strategically placed two 10-minute intervals in his schedule during each hour to accommodate one walk-in per hour. Mr. Ceddy also emphasized that his system for estimating time was never perfect, but it served him and his clients well. Therefore, his clients understood if the wait was a little longer or shorter, which was the purpose of an estimate.

The interview with Mr. Ceddy provided clarity on the concept of time estimation for Jewell and Angelica, and made it "come to life" as they visualized how time estimation was useful. In addition, the girls also learned how practical the mathematical concept of fractions was in barbershops. Part of the assignment was to interview the barber about time, but Mr. Ceddy also invited Jewell and Angelica to take a short video when one of his walk-in clients requested a high top fade with a star design tapering off in the back. Mr. Ceddy discussed his process of using fractions to estimate where to start the fade and how to taper off with the design. He further explained how he visualizes a sketch of the design on the client's head and uses estimation to get it just right. This example is just one of many that Maestra Santos used to demonstrate how to provide space for her students' collective freedom dreaming. Instead of utilizing mandated curriculum as a starting point for teaching, which was often crippling for students' creativity, she prioritized their life experiences, their voices, and their community as valuable learning vantage points.

Identity in Social Studies

Now as a fifth grader, Jewell recalled the beginning of fourth grade when her teacher, Maestra Flores, a White woman, asked the class to work on an "All About Me" project. The project started with reflecting on the question, "*¿Quién soy?*/Who am I?" Jewell and her classmates were able to use multiple ways of representing who they were. Jewell recalls recording an interview on her phone with her mom and grandma sharing family history. During the interview, Jewell learned she had Native American descent in her family as well as how her family had migrated to the area many years ago. Jewell also heard about how her mom decided to enroll her in the DLBE program. There were many moments of reflection that year, conversations that got Jewell thinking about the different ways she speaks and exists. Jewell and her class were able to talk about power, what it means, who has it, and most importantly how power and genius have been a part of students' lives for generations.

Black Freedom Dreaming en Comunidad

After much reflective practice and guidance from colleagues like Maestra Santos at the beginning of the chapter, Maestra Lilly understood how her pedagogical practices provided minimal support for leveraging Jewell's linguistic brilliance. Once Maestra Lilly acknowledged how program structure and the linguistic landscape was excluding Jewell's linguistic repertoire and knowledge, she took action by inviting Jewell and a few of her classmates to plan a thematic unit *en comunidad*. Focused on the collective rebuilding of their classroom ecology with the voices and experiences of Jewell and her peers, Maestra Lilly recognized the linguistic injustice in her classroom, and co-constructed a thematic unit with her students. By positioning Jewell and other Black American and Latinx children as experts of their own learning, Maestra Lilly encouraged them to freedom dream alongside her, recognizing their full humanity and the pedagogical possibilities that exist beyond sanctioned curriculum in DLBE spaces (Love, 2019).

Jewell, her peers, and Maestra Lilly created an interdisciplinary thematic unit that centered on the history of family reunions in Black and Latinx communities. The activities within the unit consisted of students creating intergenerational digital stories with their families about their own family reunions, researching the history and significance of family reunions across cultures, and sharing their findings with the class. In addition, students lead critical conversations with each other about their thoughts of incorporating family reunions amongst their fifth grade DLBE classes as a graduation tradition and wrote persuasive speeches using their entire linguistic repertoires about the benefits of recreating community within the DLBE classes through fifth grade family reunions. The central idea would be to invite previous fifth graders back to engage in dialogue with the current graduating fifth grade class about the importance of *comunidad* and freedom dreaming. Not only is the thematic unit rooted in freedom dreaming, but it also demonstrates sustainability of the freedom dreaming movement by inviting previous DLBE students back to uplift the essence of Black liberation in DLBE spaces.

Teaching Notes

Narrow visions of the "norm" in educational spaces is a stifling space for children's diverse ways of being with "children being condemned to be invisible within the scope of an extremely narrow curricular lens" (Genishi & Dyson, 2009, p. 10). In specifically centering Black American children's experiences in DLBE programs we see how grouping Black language speakers with "dominant English speakers" may indirectly exclude and target Black language speakers, since their language is corrected or excluded in official classroom spaces. When approaching schooling from a freedom dreaming perspective, it is critical to understand that "the essence of anti-Blackness in education policy" is that "the Black is constructed as always already problem – as nonhuman; inherently uneducable, or at very least, unworthy of education; and even in a multiracial society, always a threat to what Sexton (2008, p. 13) described as 'everything else'" (Dumas, 2016, p. 16). This realization leads to an unearthing of a social and personal history, an archeology of the self, which is crucial to engaging in humanizing work (Sealey-Ruiz, 2018). Jewell's kindergarten teacher engaged in personal exploration with the class when reflecting on her own familial experiences, the hope being that a deeper exploration of the self continued *en comunidad* with her students.

It is crucial that teachers "take a seat and sit a spell" and become learners in students' communities by exploring knowledge that goes beyond those that are sanctioned by schooling. We saw this with Jewell's first grade teacher who engaged in critical listening by participating in students' family and community practices, which is an essential component of critical consciousness. Jewell's first grade teacher also incorporated what she learned about Jewell into the classroom by having Jewell teach her practices to peers. Jewell's fourth grade teacher extended the conversation by creating a critical space, much in the spirit of April Baker-Bell (2020) and Muhammad (2020); students were able to engage in interrogating relationships between power and race through their own histories. The multimodal ways of exploring the self also lend to a space that decenters White mainstream practices, as we saw when Jewell recalled her fourth grade teacher encouraging the use of music, dance, technology, poetry, and artifacts to "read and write." Although there are shared experiences among Black children participating in bilingual programs as Black language speakers, the ways that knowledges and signs are "produced, and shaped, and constituted distinctly in different modes" (Kress, 2011, p. 242) are critical. When teachers realize their agency in their roles as policymakers in the classrooms, moving policy to practice, they find spaces to disrupt the norms of Whiteness.

Teachers entering a space as learners allows for a learning environment that is truly equity-oriented, social justice-minded, and critical for all stakeholders, most importantly educators and students. White, monolingual, cisgender women make up the majority of the teaching force, while DLBE spaces have also seen an influx in White cis-gender women as DLBE teachers. Murillo (2010) demonstrated how the cycle of hegemonic Whiteness continues to reproduce itself even among well-intentioned Latinx teachers who make choices based on their own linguistic suffering. Therefore, disruption must occur at various levels, starting with the policy makers in the classroom, the teachers. Exploration is at the core of Black liberation. Ideally, this would occur during teacher preparation programs, in which pre-service teachers could explore how their identity and pedagogical choices can make an impact and most importantly disrupt White norms (Bertrand & Porcher, 2020). Reflection must remain a permanent practice for educators in order to engage in Black freedom dreaming. Jewell's teachers put themselves at risk on a personal and professional level by engaging in discomfort and pushing back against norms. Those instances became key events for Jewell because centering her voice in classroom spaces aided in Jewell's success by "leaving every day with her darkness intact . . . loving her Blackness as an act of political resistance" (Love, 2019, p. 52).

Teaching Activities

1. Engage in an exploration of the self. Questions to consider during reflection: Who am I? Who are my students? What is Black language and do any of my students speak Black language? How can I learn about my students and their communities? How do I define literacy and how are they related to language practices? What are multimodal ways of drawing from language and literacy practices?
2. Look back at Jewell's memories. What literacy practices are being highlighted? How is the exploration of family, community, and identity tied to reading, writing, and other disciplines? How did the teachers address learning goals during each memory?

Recommendations to accompany this reflection: *En communidad: Lessons for centering the voices and experiences of bilingual Latinx students* by Carla España and Luz Yadira Herrera (see chapter 24) and *Cultivating Genius* by Gholdy Muhammad.

References

Baker-Bell, A. (2020). Dismantling anti-black linguistic racism in English language arts classrooms: Toward an anti-racist black language pedagogy. *Theory into Practice*, *59*(1), 8–21. doi:10.1080/00405841.2019.1665415

Bertrand, S. K., & Porcher, K. (2020). Teacher educators as disruptors redesigning courses in teacher preparation programs to prepare white preservice teachers. *Journal of Culture and Values in Education*, *3*(1), 72–88.

Dumas, M. (2016). Against the dark: Antiblackness in education policy and discourse. *Theory into Practice*, *55*(1), 11–19. http://dx.doi.org/10.1080/00405841.2016.1116852

Frieson, B. L. (2021). Remixin' and flowin' in centros: Exploring the biliteracy practices of Black language speakers in an elementary two-way immersion bilingual program. *Race Ethnicity and Education*, 1–21. https://doi.org/10.1080/13613324.2021.1890568

Genishi, C., & Dyson, A. H. (2009). *Children, language, and literacy: Diverse learners in diverse times*. Teachers College Press.

Kelley, R. D. G. (2002). *Freedom dreams: The black radical imagination*. Beacon Press.

Kress, G. (2011). 'Partnerships in research': Multimodality and ethnography. *Qualitative Research*, *11*(3), 239–260.

Love, B. L. (2019). *We want to do more than survive: Abolitionist teaching and the pursuit of educational freedom*. Beacon Press.

Muhammad, G. (2020). *Cultivating genius: An equity framework for culturally and historically responsive literacy*. Scholastic Inc.

Murillo, L. A. (2010). *Local literacies as counter-hegemonic practices: Deconstructing anti-Spanish ideologies in the Rio Grande Valley*. In the 59th yearbook of the National Reading Conference (pp. 276–288).

Sealey-Ruiz, Y. (2018, January 5). Yolanda Sealey-Ruiz: The archaeology of the self [Video]. Vimeo. https://vimeo.com/299137829

Sexton, J. (2008). *Amalgamation schemes: Antiblackness and the critique of multiracialism*. University of Minnesota.

Tarpley, N. (1998). *I love my hair!* Little, Brown.

Valdés, G. (2018). Analyzing the curricularization of language in two-way immersion education: Restating two cautionary notes. *Bilingual Research Journal*, *41*(4), 388–412. https://doi.org/10.1080/15235882.2018.1539886

19 *Intentando Incluir a Todes*

A First Grade Team's Gender-Inclusive Pedagogies

Caitlín Dougherty, Deborah Palmer, Stacie Aldana, and Mary Gilreath

Context

The week before school opened in August 2019, teachers at Mountain View Elementary (MVE) were back in the building preparing for the year to come. Gathered together for a staff meeting, teachers sat in grade-level clusters, engaged in animated bilingual conversations after a summer apart. Deb sat at a table with the second-grade team. The previous school year she had spoken with the principal about conducting classroom research and directing professional development sessions for the whole staff around language ideologies and critical consciousness in dual language bilingual education. This was her first opportunity to attend a meeting with the full faculty. A White cis-gendered woman and elective bilingual, Deb has been invested in the struggle for justice for bilingual learners and their teachers for nearly three decades—first as a teacher, then as a researcher and teacher educator.

This year, a day had been dedicated to the group A Queer Endeavor (AQE http://aqueerendeavor.org/), a local organization that works to create safe and supportive schools for LGBTQ+ students. The previous year, a transgender[1] student, Lexi[2], had transferred to MVE, a 50/50 two-way bilingual school (TWBE), (in part) because of its reputation as welcoming for the LGBTQ+ community. The issue of how to incorporate gender-inclusive language in a bilingual context arose in response to Lexi's identity. Teachers agreed to use they/them/their pronouns in English, but the decision over what to do in Spanish was more contentious.

Acknowledging their limited knowledge of gender-inclusive Spanish, the AQE facilitators showed a video (TKM, 2018) of an Argentine girl explaining why she uses the gender inclusive term "*todes*." While some teachers accepted the use of "e" endings (e.g., *elle*, *amigue*), many of the Spanish-side teachers resisted. Some expressed frustration over English-speakers dictating changes to their language, others suggested that gender and sexuality should be addressed at home, and many argued that the Latine[3] community at MVE faced more pressing issues such as racism, poverty, or the impact of immigration policies. These teachers objected to what they saw as further evidence of the subordination of their language and community.

DOI: 10.4324/9781003240594-24

The staff at MVE frequently discuss issues of social justice and equity, and this meeting proved no different. As a 50/50 TWBE school, MVE aims for equal enrollment of English-dominant and Spanish-dominant students. Each grade is split into an English side and a Spanish side with teachers responsible for instruction in one language only. While student and teacher language practices often defy this binary categorization, the labels echo racial, cultural, and economic divisions within the student body and the community at large. In MVE's school district, 80% of the population identifies as White (non-Hispanic/Latine); only 10% identifies as Hispanic/Latine. MVE is a Title I school and, in general, Spanish-dominant students come from Latine families with lower socio-economic status and English-dominant students come from White or biracial families with higher socio-economic status.

As the discussion grew more heated, Stacie, a US-born bilingual Latina and the Spanish-side teacher slated to teach Lexi, defended the changes. In response, the other first-grade Spanish-side teacher, a native of South America, dismissed her opinion: "It's different for you. You're from here." The next day when Deb asked about this incident in an interview, Stacie exclaimed, "Oh my god, I was so mad yesterday! I thought, are you minimizing me? I'm diminished because my Spanish is from the United States?" She continued to express incredulity over her colleagues' reasons for resisting the shift in Spanish:

> We're seeing all these bad things happening, like the shooting in El Paso. Last night 680 people got deported in Mississippi. Of course, we don't want that to happen! You want change to happen, to help all these people . . . it's the same thing for the LGBTQ+ community. They also need advocacy. We're talking about the same thing, how people are not treated equally.

Stacie's frustration stemmed from an awareness of the intersectional nature of oppression and the need for solidarity when working toward social justice.

Case Narrative

Back in the classroom later that week, Stacie and Mary, her White English-side co-teacher, began planning in earnest to welcome Lexi. While they recognized the severity of the issues facing Latine communities, they did not see LGBTQ+ issues as separate. Rather, they speculated that by questioning dominant discourses that centered cis-gender and heteronormative stories, or queering their classrooms, all first graders, including those from Latine Spanish-speaking families, would be better supported and feel included. They each drew on their own experiences of marginalization in schools to ground their approach toward creating inclusive classrooms that considered students' multiple and intersecting identities. Mary is a lesbian; her experiences as a student in Georgia and a teacher in Massachusetts pushed her to advocate for safe and supportive schools for the LGBTQ+ community. Stacie's experiences as a bilingual Mexican American student in English-only schools in Arizona motivated her to become a bilingual teacher and advocate for EB students.

Despite feeling discomfort over the probability of making mistakes, their respective experiences shaped how they understood the need for change:

Mary: I felt a real responsibility to Lexi. Is using non-binary language something that I was comfortable with? Honestly, no. I hadn't used 'they, them and their' a lot so I was sure I was going to make mistakes. But when you have a kid in front of you that's choosing your school because they feel like it's going to be a safe place—I wasn't going to debate trying to meet this kid's needs, of course I would. Would it be a learning curve for us? Absolutely.

Stacie: I agree! At first I also had been worried about not knowing what to do, but eventually I became excited. Now I love to share articles I find about gender and language! When I reflect on some of my colleagues' resistance, I think about how language is very fluid; it changes all the time. So why are we going to keep Spanish how it is? This is how it's always going to be? It just doesn't make sense to me. You weren't born speaking Spanish. You acquired it. So why can't you acquire a few more vocabulary words that are going to make someone feel better?

A willingness to experience discomfort and embrace learning like Stacie and Mary describe is a crucial part of the work of developing critical consciousness.

Introducing Inclusive Language

Mary's and Stacie's collaborative efforts included changing their speech, the language of lessons and home-school communication, and strategically incorporating children's literature. When speaking to groups of students, Stacie would say "*estudiantes*" or "*todes*" and Mary would say "friends." When referring to Lexi in Spanish they used the pronoun "*elle*" and in English "they." Students and families took the changes in stride; the gender-inclusive language in bilingual newsletters home was received without question, and students readily accepted the shift in language, even correcting Stacie and Mary when they said "*todos*" or "she." Having recognized the "learning curve" of adopting new language practices, Stacie and Mary embraced these instances as opportunities for students to teach them.

They made anchor charts that reinforced the pronouns they were teaching in their classrooms. Mary's anchor chart included the statement, "Language can change to include everyone!" along with the words "Latinx" and "*amig@*" to demonstrate inclusive language in Spanish. Next door, Stacie's anchor chart, in addition to "*él, ella, elle*," included a section for "*palabras que incluyan*" such as "*todes*," "*niñes*," and "*amigues*." When teaching a lesson on determiners, Stacie added a third category beyond masculine/feminine. For direct articles, she introduced "*le/les*" for nouns i.e., "*le amigue*," "*le doctore*," and "*les maestres*." She emphasized that non-binary nouns were for people who did not identify as male or female but objects like "*la mesa*" would not change.

Transgressing Gender and Language Norms Through Literature

The teachers introduced the idea of non-binary pronouns at the beginning of the year through the book *They, She, He, Me: Free to Be!* (Gonzalez & Matthew, 2017); Stacie translated it into Spanish. Afterward students created bilingual books using their preferred pronouns. Initially a few students used "*elle/they*," but as the school year progressed only Lexi continued to do so.

Other books read by Stacie and Mary that questioned cis-gender heteronormativity included *They Call Me Mix/Me Llaman Maestre* (Rivas, 2018) and *Worm Loves Worm* (Austrian, 2016).

Additionally, Mary worked to create a classroom where students felt comfortable speaking both English and Spanish, challenging English dominance at the school and in society. During a read-aloud of *Worm Loves Worm*, Mary encouraged translanguaging, weaving in a student's questions and comments in Spanish, supporting her bilingual participation, and ensuring her comprehension.

Sharing Our Collaborative Efforts

On a chilly Saturday morning in February, Stacie and Mary met with Caitie at a cafe to plan an upcoming conference presentation. Caitie joined the project in August as a doctoral student researcher. A cis-gendered White woman and elective bilingual, she had previously taught at a TWBE middle school in Maryland where she had grappled with how best to support her queer students of color. A participant observer in Stacie's and Mary's classrooms, she was impressed at their care, criticality, and collaboration, and so encouraged them to co-present with her at a local conference for bilingual educators (Co-CABE). Over coffee and bagels, they updated her on their attempts to bring inclusive language to the broader school community. Some reports were positive. A fifth grade Spanish-side teacher had expressed interest and a willingness to learn from them, and their principal had addressed the faculty as "*maestros, maestras, y maestres*" over the loudspeaker. Other anecdotes touched on the complicated power dynamics at the school. Stacie shared how she'd asked Mary to forward an article to the faculty instead of her, feeling that Mary, as a White veteran teacher, had more "clout" on campus. Also, in response to the principal's use of "*maestres*," a Spanish-side teacher had emailed other Spanish-side teachers (notably not Stacie) to convey his outrage. While their classroom community had embraced the language changes, the topic continued to be controversial for some colleagues, so Stacie and Mary were nervous about sharing outside their school.

Though anxious at the possibility of resistance, the team combined forces to create a presentation that touched on the intersectional nature of this work and the practical application. They began by describing their various identities and acknowledging how these have shaped their experiences. Next, they addressed the transformation of their languaging and teaching and how the teachers considered racism, English hegemony, heteronormativity, and other oppressive systems in the process. They gave examples of how that transformation took place in their classrooms, showcasing student work and sharing resources. The day of the conference, they smiled widely as they greeted attendees, recognizing colleagues' friendly faces in the crowd. The session was well attended; the audience was lively and asked many questions. The experience underscored that when teachers want to do their best for their students, they are willing to learn more to accomplish this goal.

Teaching Notes

Stacie and Mary worked together to create more gender-inclusive classrooms; this work involved a praxis cycle of reflection/action and engaging in a range of actions: critically listening to Lexi and to Lexi's family, experiencing the discomfort of the unknown, interrogating colleagues' oppositional comments and attitudes, shifting their curriculum and pedagogies, and sharing their experience with their community at large. Researchers have shown that trans and gender-creative students like Lexi report less victimization at school when they can identify one or more teachers or staff members who publicly support them and speak out against oppressive practices, and that White students report feeling more supported than BIPOC students and English learner-designated students (Kosciw et al., 2018). Taken together, this suggests that teachers who seek to be LGBTQ+-inclusive must not only rethink dominant belief systems about gender and sexuality but also consider other systems that contribute to privilege and oppression (Meyer et al., 2015) and connect their shifting beliefs to practice, because "embodying GSD-inclusive praxis involves disrupting normativity across several domains [of schooling], including the personal, pedagogical, curricular, social, and institutional" (Staley & Leonardi, 2019, p. 30). Carol Brochin (2019), a queer, Chicana, bilingual teacher educator, cautions that unless LGBTQ+ content and perspectives are incorporated into bilingual teacher education, teachers may be encouraged "to become advocates for some marginalized groups while inadvertently silencing others" (p. 82).

Stacie and Mary deliberately employed critical and intersectional perspectives as they worked to queer their classrooms. Intersectionality, a foundational tenet of critical race theory rooted in Black feminist thought (Crenshaw, 1990; Collins & Bilge, 2020), acknowledges that individuals hold multiple identities and that institutions like schools marginalize individuals whose identities differ from dominant ones. Considering the multiple matrices of power within their context, Stacie and Mary labored to create classrooms that were inclusive for all their students and families. In the process, they embraced their status as learners, the partiality of their perspectives, and the uncertainty inherent in anti-oppressive teaching (Kumashiro, 2002). Teachers' identities, their linguistic backgrounds, their educational histories, and their ideologies all shape their teaching practices; without developing critical consciousness they run the risk of perpetuating oppressive conditions in their classrooms. As Cervantes-Soon and others (2017) explain, critical consciousness entails "overcoming pervasive myths through an understanding of the role of power in the formation of oppressive conditions" (p. 419). Stacie and Mary show that the questioning process inherent in queering classrooms (Kumashiro, 2002; Staley & Leonardi, 2019) resonates with the process of developing critical consciousness; in both, teachers challenge norms and dominant narratives and attend to the role of power in their schools.

As schools become increasingly the target for anti-trans and anti-gay legislation and policies prohibiting critical race theory, combined with the gentrification of bilingual education (Valdez et al., 2016; Flores & García, 2017), we see a pressing need to consider intersectionality as we work toward inclusive TWBE. As Lexi shows us, children from a very young age are aware of who they are, and following Stacie and Mary's lead, teachers must sometimes go beyond our comfort zones to consider what inclusion looks and sounds like in our classrooms.

Teaching Activities

Activity A: Children's Literature and Queering Classrooms

Teachers often use picture books in their efforts to "queer classrooms"; i.e., introduce students to LGBTQ+ topics and question "pervasive myths" about gender, sexuality, and language. Of the three picture books mentioned in this chapter, *He, She, They, Me: Free to Be* and *They Call Me Mix/Me Llaman Maestre* challenge cis-gender norms and *Worm Loves Worm* encourages readers to question their assumptions about love and relationships.

Discussion Questions

1. In your own classroom, how do you engage with ideas about cis-gendered heteronormativity, or the privileging of relationships between a man and a woman?

2. Examine the books in your classroom; how do they portray gender and sexuality?
3. Stacie translated English books into Spanish. Mary translanguaged during read-alouds. Students wrote bilingual books using their preferred pronoun. How could you support students' emerging biliteracy while queering your classroom?
4. How could you address the tension between teaching grammatical structures and rules while simultaneously questioning language norms and showing how languages change?

Activity B: Identity Inquiry

Stacie's and Mary's experiences of marginalization in schools, as a bilingual Latina and as a lesbian respectively, influenced their intersectional stances toward inclusivity.

- Consider your experiences in schools—as a student, a teacher, a parent (if applicable).
- What aspects of your identity have been accepted, questioned, critiqued, or celebrated, and why? How did you feel/react in response to these experiences of affirmation or marginalization?

Discussion Questions

1. As society changes, how should teachers respond to the increasing presence of diverse students and families in their schools, whether they be culturally and linguistically diverse (CLD), queer, or gender-nonconforming?
2. How are these responses tied to broader movements that seek to disrupt oppressive systems?
3. How might you draw on your own experiences with marginalization to connect with other teachers in solidarity, "looking to the margins" to create anti-oppressive classrooms?

Teaching Activity C: Role Play

Imagine you are Stacie or Mary and it is several months into the school year. You are chatting with the other Spanish-side first grade teacher, Nadia, on the playground. She is telling you she saw Lexi and their family over the weekend—but as she talks she continually misgenders Lexi, saying "she" and "her". Nadia is from South America, emigrated to the US after college, and was one of the teachers to express disapproval of the switch to "*todes*" in Spanish. Use the following questions to consider how you might respond.

Discussion Questions

1. How can/should teachers engage with colleagues and their community about their efforts to create inclusive classrooms?
2. How might an intersectional perspective serve you as you navigate disagreements with colleagues or community members?
3. What do you think about Nadia's concerns that there are more pressing issues than LGBTQ+ inclusion for Latine families? How about her concern that parents might prefer to discuss gender identity and sexuality at home?

Notes

1. Rands (2009) defines transgender as "those who transgress societal gender norms" (p. 419) extending beyond male and female to include non-binary individuals.
2. Names throughout (except authors) are pseudonyms.
3. Stacie and Mary chose the gender-neutral "e" ending over the more well-known "x" ending because of the existence of "e" ending nouns in Spanish (i.e., *presidente*, *gente*) and its easier pronounceability. "Latine" is pronounced /lə-*teen*-ay/ according to Spanish phonetic conventions.

References

Austrian, J. J. (2016). *Worm Loves Worm*. Balzer + Bray.

Brochin, C. (2019). Queering bilingual teaching in elementary schools and in bilingual teacher education. *Theory into Practice*, *58*(1), 80–88.

Cervantes-Soon, C. G., Dorner, L., Palmer, D., Heiman, D., Schwerdtfeger, R., & Choi, J. (2017). Combating inequalities in two-way language immersion programs: Toward critical consciousness in bilingual education spaces. *Review of Research in Education*, *41*(1), 403–427.

Collins, P. H., & Bilge, S. (2020). *Intersectionality*. John Wiley & Sons.

Crenshaw, K. (1990). Mapping the margins: Intersectionality, identity politics, and violence against women of color. *Stanford Law Review*, *43*, 1241.

Flores, N., & García, O. (2017). A critical review of bilingual education in the United States: From basements and pride to boutiques and profit. *Annual Review of Applied Linguistics*, *37*, 14–29.

Gonzalez, M., & Matthew, S. G. (2017). *They she he me: Free to be!* Reflection Press.

Kosciw, J. G., Greytak, E. A., Zongrone, A. D., Clark, C. M., & Truong, N. L. (2018). *The 2017 national school climate survey: The experiences of lesbian, gay, bisexual, transgender, and queer youth in our nation's schools*. GLSEN.

Kumashiro, K. K. (2002). *Troubling education: Queer activism and anti-oppressive pedagogy*. Psychology Press.

Meyer, E. J., Taylor, C., & Peter, T. (2015). Perspectives on gender and sexual diversity (GSD)-inclusive education: Comparisons between gay/lesbian/bisexual and straight educators. *Sex Education*, *15*(3), 221–234.

Rands, K. E. (2009). Considering transgender people in education: A gender-complex approach. *Journal of Teacher Education*, *60*(4), 419–431.

Rivas, L. (2018). *They call me mix/Me llaman maestre*. Lourdes Rivas.

Staley, S., & Leonardi, B. (2019). Complicating what we know: Focusing on educators' processes of becoming gender and sexual diversity inclusive. *Theory into Practice, 58*(1), 29–38.

TKM. (2018, June 1). *Niña defiende El Lenguaje de Género*. Facebook. Retrieved January 25, 2022, from www.facebook.com/watch/?v=10156447921604722

Valdez, V. E., Freire, J. A., & Delavan, W. G. (2016). The gentrification of dual language education. *Urban Review, 48*, 601–627.

20 English-only as a Magic Pill? Dispelling the Myths About Disability and Dual Language Bilingual Education

Steve Daniel Przymus

Context

The context of this fictional case study, based on the author's experience working with multidisciplinary teams' decisions regarding language and disability, is Corazón Elementary School, a pre-K through 5th grade campus in the large north Texas Independent School District (NTISD). Of Corazón's 787 students, 84% are Latinx and 52% are classified as English learners (henceforth *active bilingual learners/users of English* [ABLE] students, Przymus et al., 2022). Corazón's ABLE students are placed in dual language enrichment (DLE) classrooms, a one-way dual language bilingual education (DLBE) program, that is also the primary source of English as a second language (ESL) services at Corazón. Removal from these classrooms requires parents to complete denial of ESL services documentation.

Corazón's teachers, service providers, and administrators struggle with understanding the intersection of language (bilingualism) and disability and are often faced with difficult placement, assessment, and instructional decisions for exceptional ABLE students. With a lack of professional development on the holistic nature of bilingualism, most fall back on deficit ideologies regarding who is able to be bilingual. The development of teacher and student critical consciousness is needed to address the historical narratives of bilingualism and disability in schools and to raise the awareness of the structural oppression that keeps dually identified students from reaping the social, emotional, and educational benefits of life-long bilingualism. In committing to critical consciousness, educators seek to engage in dialogue and advocacy to perceive and act on social, political, and economic inequities present in society (Broughton et al., 2022; Palmer et al., 2019). This chapter details the holistic nature of bilingualism, provides a critical consciousness decision-making model, and relates a fictional case narrative, including the Language Proficiency Assessment Committee (LPAC) coordinator, a DLBE teacher, and a speech language pathologist (SLP). Within the narrative, we observe the emerging development of greater critical consciousness awareness, reflection, and action among the participants.

DOI: 10.4324/9781003240594-25

Case Narrative

Thursday, November 5, 2020

RE: G.M.

Sanchez, Graciela (2nd Grade, Dual Language Teacher)

Thu 11/5/2020 12:04 p.m.

To: Mills, Amy (LPAC Coordinator)

Hello,

I spoke with Gael's mom this morning and she would like to switch him to a regular program classroom. He struggles to read in both Spanish and English, and hardly speaks Spanish. I explained to her that continued Spanish use at school and maybe at home might be confusing him, especially considering he has a learning disability in reading and writing. I've already arranged for Gael's mom to sign the denial paperwork. Let me know when we can make the switch. I would hate for him to be wasting his time in my class when he can be more successful in an all-English class.

Thank you!

RE: G.M.

Mills, Amy (LPAC Coordinator)

Thu 11/5/2020 3:34 p.m.

To: Sanchez, Graciela (2nd Grade, Dual Language Teacher)

Hi Graciela, Thanks for reaching out to me about this. I'm glad that you have good communication with Gael's mom, but decisions like this (removal from DLE) really should be discussed first in a team, including his special education case manager (Sandra Pantoja, speech language pathologist). Parent denials should only ever be initiated by the parent. Then, the LPAC, in collaboration with the ARD[1]/IEP team, would counsel the parent on the denial of ESL services.

I have asked Sandra to meet with us tomorrow morning (7:30) in your room. See you tomorrow.

Friday, November 6, 2020, 7:30 a.m.
Room #823, Graciela Sanchez's 2nd Grade Dual Language Classroom

Welcoming Sandra Pantoja (speech language pathologist) and Amy Mills (LPAC coordinator) to her room, Graciela begins, "Good morning Sandra, hi Amy, come on in!"

"Hi Graciela!," responds Sandra, and after settling into small seats around Graciela's teacher table, she begins the meeting. "Amy has asked me to visit with you today about Gael. I started seeing him for speech fluency and articulation in kindergarten and he was just tested and qualified for a specific learning disability (SLD) in reading and writing, this fall. After hearing of your concerns, a couple of things came to mind. First, due to his SLD in reading, if moved to an all-English classroom, his disability won't go away, he'll still struggle to read and will need to receive the same accommodations, outlined in his IEP. The big difference is that in all-English instruction, he will require a new accommodation. Do you know what that new accommodation will be?"

After thinking through what would change for Gael in all English instruction, Graciela responds, "Maybe . . . home language supports in Spanish?"

"That's exactly right!" replies Sandra. "By default he currently gets that in DLE and that's one reason, but not actually the biggest one, that we need to think of before moving him out of DLE."

Intrigued, Amy asks, "Sandra, what's the biggest reason to keep ABLE kids with disabilities in DLE?"

"Well," responds Sandra, "Gael has been with the same group of friends for over three years. I have witnessed how moving kids out of their peer network has resulted in an identity of shame, failure, and embarrassment at school. Removing them from bilingual education can result in them not developing and sustaining their bilingualism, which can also act to sever intimate relationships in their churches, with neighbors, cousins, and most importantly, with monolingual Spanish-speaking parents."

As students start coming into the classroom, Graciela says, "I get all of this, and maybe moving him to all-English is not the 'magic pill' that I thought it was, but what should I do?" Wanting to continue the conversation, but not in front of the kids, Graciela asks that they briefly go into the hall, and then continues, "I mean, Gael can't even spit out a complete sentence in Spanish!"

Nodding understandingly, Sandra begins, "Graciela, I know you are required to follow a strict language separation for DLE curriculum, but I don't in speech with Gael. And frankly I'm surprised by what you just said about Gael. I do think it's clear that Gael has low self-esteem about his expressive Spanish, but I know from years of working with him that his receptive Spanish skills are quite good and when allowed to translanguage, he often produces full sentences in Spanish. I actually brought with me today a sample language transcript of the last time Gael re-told a story for me in speech. Using the picture book *Frog, Where Are You?* by Mercer Mayer (1969), I bilingually told the story and asked Gael to retell the story, using whatever language he needed. Here is part of his transcribed oral language sample." Sandra shows Graciela and Amy Table 20.1.

Sandra continues, "He clearly makes errors, and we work on those in speech. However, this demonstrates two things. First, he produces more

Table 20.1 Gael's Retell of *Frog, Where Are You?*

And the bee *stá nojado*	and *ya salió una* moose
Y the puppy *corrió*	no, it's a deer
una niño ya cayó	and the puppy y la niño *cayeron*
ya cayó in the grass	*pero, sapo no están*
después, the boy climb the *roca*	he can't find it
y say *sapo*, where are you?	

overall language when not restricted to just Spanish or English, and second he exhibits more content knowledge with storytelling. I have worked with other teachers to create content-based stories to have students retell, and I would love to try this with you and Gael."

Clearly intrigued, Graciela starts, "You've given me a lot to think about, but I'm going to need help . . . especially with developing and administering content-based story retells. I'm going to talk to the other DLE teachers, who have struggled with similar students. Could you meet with us next week to talk about this?"

"Absolutely!" responds Sandra. "How about Wednesday after school?"

Amy jumps in, "Thanks Sandra. I plan to attend on Wednesday, also!"

Teaching Notes

Teachers are often confronted with conflicting opinions about the assessment, placement, and instruction of exceptional ABLE students. Although research has provided compelling support for the continued use of these students' L1 at school and at home (Peña, 2016; Przymus, 2018), teachers, service providers, parents, and even the students themselves often fall back on gut feelings, personal beliefs, and myths that undermine expectations for these children (National Academies of Sciences, Engineering, and Medicine [NASEM], 2017). Although discredited by research, these myths continue to support and strengthen deficit ideologies that influence teachers to push for placements that focus only on the development of these students' English skills (Bird et al., 2016; NASEM, 2017).

Addressing these myths requires recognizing that deficit ideologies are based in both trying to understand bilingualism through a monolingual paradigm and prioritizing expressive language over receptive language. To expose the monolingual paradigm as a root of deficit-based ideologies regarding bilingualism and disability, we must first understand the processes of bilingualism. Work in social semiotics has shown that the process of language production involves both *combination* (syntagmatic axis) and *selection* (paradigmatic axis) (Lodge, 2015). *Combination* is the stringing together of words and phrases in a grammatically correct order to produce a sentence. *Selection*, then, describes humans' creative ability to substitute an alternative word for any one of the words in the sentence. This process is seen as typical and not questioned in monolinguals. Take for example sentence (1) and sentence (2):

(1) Learning a new named language is very hard.

This sentence is modified in (2) by saying:

(2) *Developing* an *additional national* language is very *difficult*.

Learning a new named language is very hard.

Sentences (1) and (2) demonstrate both *combination* and *selection*. Sentence (3) demonstrates the same sentence modified by a bilingual student drawing on their full linguistic repertoire (which includes both named languages, Spanish and English).

(3) ***Aprender*** an additional named language ***es muy difícil***.

Learning a new named language is very hard.

Once the monolingual sentence becomes a bilingual sentence, some, even bilingual educators, will view sentence (3) as abnormal, broken, faulty speech. However, if we analyze sentence (3) from this social semiotics perspective, all of the words combine correctly to form a grammatical sentence that expresses the same meaning as the monolingual sentences. Without this holistic understanding, educators may talk about bilingual speech as being "strong" in one language and "weak" in another—and they may fail to see the bilingual speaker's successful engagement of combination and selection. We see this in Graciela's statement, "Gael can't even spit out a complete sentence in Spanish." This "strengths and weaknesses" rhetoric (common in the language of special education evaluations) runs the risk of ignoring what the student can do holistically with language.

Otheguy et al.'s (2015) distinction between the "external" and the "internal" perspectives of bilingualism is helpful for understanding why so many of us fall into the trap of ideologically and pedagogically dividing ABLE students by language (p. 289). The external perspective represents how listeners hear a bi/multilingual person use more than one named language (Spanish, English, etc.). Otheguy et al. (2015) contrast this with the internal perspective, which represents the unique linguistic ability of each speaker, which in a bi/multilingual person includes linguistic features from multiple named languages that are part of one internal language system.

Thus, rather than seeing a bilingual speaker as alternating/switching between two languages, we can see them as engaging *combination* across their full (bilingual) internal language system. An educator who understands this holistic "internal" perspective on bilingualism and views sentence (3) as the successful engagement of selection and combination will see through myths such as "exposure to *more than one* language will confuse ABLE children" or that "*code-switching* is evidence of this confusion" and will instead embrace the idea that "exposure to *additional language features* will support ABLE children's continued development" and that "*translanguaging* is evidence that they are developing the skills to process and produce language."

Taking into consideration the prevalence of these myths and their influence on decision making, Broughton (2019; see also Broughton et al., 2022) developed the critical consciousness decision-making (CCDM) model that leads educators through a process of critical reflection in steps 1–3 and critical practice/action in steps 4–6 (see Figure 20.1).

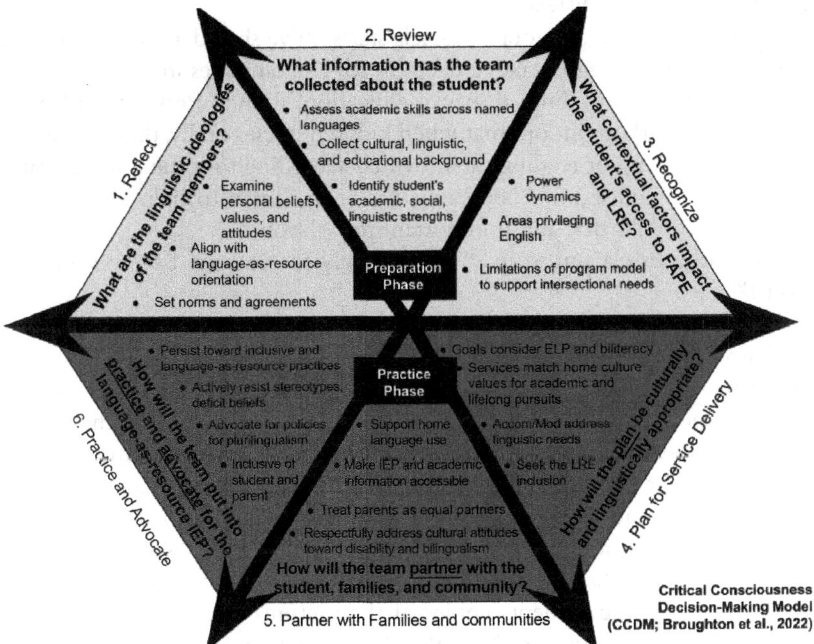

Figure 20.1 Critical Consciousness Decision-Making (CCDM)

Steps 1–3 are designed for educators to reflect on and examine their own beliefs, while becoming critically aware of the sociolinguistic profile of a student. These steps encourage *critical listening* and potentially *engaging discomfort* as educators work to ensure that they are viewing ABLE students from a holistic bilingual perspective and honoring the important role of a student's home language and culture in their development. Steps 4–6 guide educators to *interrogate power* as they integrate data on the student to create and enact critical practice that supports a student's holistic linguistic profile.

Teaching Activities

Activity A: Story Retells for Raising Critical Consciousness

Wednesday, November 11, 2020, 3:30 p.m.
Room #823, Graciela Sanchez's 2nd Grade Dual Language Classroom

Returning to the case narrative, the teachers meet to explore how to develop a content-based story retell activity that might support Gael and other students in his classroom as they continue to develop bilingualism and biliteracy. This time Sandra is greeted by Graciela, Amy, and two other DLE teachers, Oscar and Estela.

"Thanks for coming, Sandra," Graciela starts. "I've shared a little about your story retell idea." Sandra takes a deep breath and launches in.

"Yes, researchers in bilingual special education, such as Przymus and Alvarado's 2019 work, point out that when kids tell stories orally, they mirror the process of writing or reading them, which according to some research, such as Miller and colleagues' 2006 study, has been shown to help kids develop the narrative skills that are so important for school."

Excitedly, Estela jumps in, "This is really interesting. So, how do you do it?"

"Well," answers Sandra, "last year, I helped Patty do this for a social studies lesson for her fourth graders. We developed a content-based story retell about the free enterprise system. Patty's students were tasked with finding pictures about buying and selling goods and also pictures that they could relate to. Students found pictures of characters, such as a mom and son, that resembled their own Mexican American identities, and also images of typical places where someone might buy and sell items, such as a *tienda de abarrotes*.[2]"

Continuing, Sandra described, "On the first day of the lesson, Patty made up a story, using the pictures, and included details related to the content. Then, she gave the students copies of the pictures and had students retell the story, in their own words, with whatever language or combination of languages they needed. Students were excited to share their experiences shopping at a *tienda de abarrotes*, and it turned out some words and phrases seemed more appropriate or comfortable in Spanish and some were better in English. The students' stories were naturally bilingual. Patty allowed time each day for students to pull out the pictures and practice their stories by adding to them or changing them. In order to document the language and content growth of her ABLE students, Patty used her phone to record those students' individual retells at the beginning of the unit and again at the end. She discovered at the end of the unit that this extra engagement with the content, connecting it to a story, and the freedom to translanguage enabled all students to use more language about the content and that they learned the content better, compared to previous years, with other students."

"What I love about this," chimes in Oscar, "is that we can continue to teach the content, but weave in themes that are important to our students' lives."

Graciela lights up and asks the group, "So . . . it's okay that we aren't expected to adhere to language separation in our DLE program? That's so liberating! Maybe it could help not just Gael but all my students to get a chance to show off their bilingualism by telling stories . . . AND it's meeting content objectives!"

"Right," agrees Estela. "I can also see how through telling stories, we might start engaging in uncomfortable, but important conversations that are meaningful for our students and their families, building solidarity with families."

Nodding in agreement, Sandra states, "You are so right! One of the first discomforts could be our personal beliefs and gut feelings about disability and language. If it's okay, I'm going to email you the research I talked about and also some studies about how exceptional ABLE students do not experience any additional language learning challenges than monolinguals with the same disabilities and finally on how exceptional ABLE students in dual language programs exit ESL services in less time than those in English-only settings."

Thanking Sandra for her time, Graciela says, "That would be great Sandra! I'm glad we can work together to give Gael what he needs and deserves. I expect my whole class will benefit."

Discussion Questions

1. What opinions around bilingualism and disability have you previously held or heard others express?
2. What might a culturally and linguistically relevant content-based story retell look like in your classroom?
3. What themes or stories could you use with your students that might get them critically thinking about and questioning beliefs about bilingualism and disability?

Activity B: Practice Tough Conversations

Roleplay a conversation with another dual language teacher who believes that a dually identified student should be removed from the DLBE. Use what you have learned in this chapter, including the use of the critical consciousness decision-making model (Figure 20.1), to advocate for the student's continued placement in DLBE.

Activity C: Using the CCDM Model

With a team of DLBE teachers, work through the CCDM model, with a specific dually identified student in mind and evaluate this process in terms of

1. how well the team engaged the critically conscious decision-making model and
2. what changes the team might need to make to the decision-making process regarding the student or ultimately to the student's IEP, based on this model.

Notes

1. Special Education Admission, Review, and Dismissal (ARD) team.
2. Small Mexican store that sells groceries and other household supplies.

References

Bird, E. K. R., Genesee, F., & Verhoeven, L. (2016). Bilingualism in children with developmental disorders: A narrative review. *Journal of Communication Disorders, 63*, 1–14. https://doi.org/10.1016/j.jcomdis.2016.07.003

Broughton, A. J. (2019). *Cultivating educators' critical consciousness of learning and language needs in emergent bilinguals* [Doctoral Dissertation]. University of South Florida.

Broughton, A. J., Przymus, S. D., Ortiz, A. A., & Suarez, B. (2022). Bilingual/multilingual students with disabilities: Language as a resource in educational planning and instruction. *Teaching Exceptional Children*. May 18, 2022.

Lodge, D. (2015). *The modes of modern writing: Metaphor, metonymy, and the typology of modern literature*. Bloomsbury Publishing.

Mayer, M. (1969). *Frog, where are you?* Dial Press.

Miller, J. F., Heilmann, J., Nockerts, A., Iglesias, A., Fabiano, L., & Francis, D. J. (2006). Oral language and reading in bilingual children. *Learning Disabilities Research & Practice, 21*(1), 30–43. https://doi.org/10.1111/j.1540-5826.2006.00205.x

National Academies of Sciences, Engineering, and Medicine (NASEM). (2017). *Promoting the educational success of children and youth learning English: Promising futures*. The National Academies Press.

Otheguy, R., García, O., & Reid, W. (2015). Clarifying translanguaging and deconstructing named languages: A perspective from linguistics. *Applied Linguistics Review, 6*(3), 281–307. https://doi.org/10.1515/applirev-2015-0014

Palmer, D. K., Cervantes-Soon, C., Dorner, L., & Heiman, D. (2019). Bilingualism, biliteracy, biculturalism, and critical consciousness for all: Proposing a fourth fundamental goal for two-way dual language education. *Theory into Practice, 58*(2), 121–133.

Peña, E. D. (2016). Supporting the home language of bilingual children with developmental disabilities: From knowing to doing. *Journal of Communication Disorders, 63*, 85–92. https://doi.org/10.1016/j.jcomdis.2016.08.001

Przymus, S. D. (2018). Appropriate assessment e instrucción de los emergent bilinguals con disabilities. In J. B. Jimerson & S. Quebec Fuentes (Eds.), *Instructional leadership in the content areas: Case studies for curriculum and instruction* (pp. 321–333). Routledge.

Przymus, S. D., & Alvarado, M. (2019). Advancing bilingual special education: Translanguaging in content-based story retells for distinguishing language difference from disability. *Multiple Voices for Ethnically Diverse Exceptional Learners, 19*(1), 23–43. https://doi.org/10.5555/2158-396X.19.1.23

Przymus, S. D., Faggella-Luby, M., & Silva, C. (2022). It's only a matter of meaning: From English learners (ELs) and emergent bilinguals (EBs) to active bilingual learners/users of English (ABLE). *I-LanD Journal: Identity, Language and Diversity*, 30–50. doi:10.26379/IL2020002_003

21 Professional Development Through Critical Conversation and *Testimonio* at Simón Bolívar Elementary

Caroline Hesse, Jillian La Serna, and Emily Zoeller

Context

Simón Bolívar Elementary (pseudonym, based on a collective case study) is a Spanish-English Title 1 DLBE elementary school in a small university town in the southeastern US. It houses kindergarten through fifth grade and loosely follows the 90–10 model. Approximately half of the students can be described as dominant English speakers, and half can be described as dominant Spanish speakers. Staff members hail from an array of Latin American countries, Spain, and various states in the US. In recent years, staff members at Simón Bolívar have engaged in professional development (PD) that prompted examinations of privilege, power, achievement, and their intersections with race.

For years, PD has been conducted similarly in schools across the country. Often driven by district-determined accountability measures, sessions frequently stem from "packaged" PD coming from outside sources. Accountability measures and standardized testing maintain the focus on quantity instead of quality, strait-jacketing education professionals with required checklists, goals, and forms.

Conditions and structures surrounding PD sessions affect staff readiness for learning and exacerbate the problem. Staff are often tired and thirsty, crammed into uncomfortably small rooms, or obliged to leave the session to attend to personal-life needs. Furthermore, PD sessions are often scheduled monthly or quarterly, such that memories fade, materials are misplaced, and momentum is lost. And so precious time passes without the hoped-for actions, despite many good intentions and genuine efforts.

Key to CC is the notion that critical reflection should be followed by action. Reflection alone does not align to the spirit of CC. Unfortunately, the issues outlined earlier have historically frustrated efforts to offer PD that fosters CC in Simón Bolívar. And such PD is urgently needed. Traditional PD, as it has been conducted in the past, is neither effective nor sufficient in the face of the persistent and pervasive equity problems DLBE programs face (Palmer, 2010; Valdés, 1997). The power imbalance between

DOI: 10.4324/9781003240594-26

majority, privileged families and minoritized, marginalized families is one such problem, and arguably the root of others. A focus on CC can improve matters, but in order to advance CC work, schools such as Simón Bolívar and its staff must teach themselves and learn from each other. The historically designated spaces for PD do not need to be the only spaces for learning; impromptu moments and critical conversations in unnamed spaces are necessary for authentic teaching and learning, and especially developing CC in educators.

So how can educational leaders engage DLBE staff in PD that fosters the development and application of CC? A reimagined type of PD for DLBE educators can prompt development through a Freirean cycle of learning, critical reflection, and action by centering *testimonios* that challenge status quo. *Testimonios* can serve as resources that shift PD from a factory-banking model toward a Freirean model that simultaneously reflects and enhances CC. The definition of "PD leaders" can also be reimagined to focus on individuals' actions and results instead of on their titles. DLBE educators and students can foster CC in each other through day-to-day, informal, impromptu interactions and undefined moments in which critical conversations emerge.

Case Narrative

Directora Lane (principal), Maestra Eleanor (instructional coach), and Maestra Danielle (classroom teacher) leave another typical Simón Bolívar staff PD session feeling disheartened. Despite having scheduled multiple PDs this year on the topic of equity, Directora Lane is concerned. She doesn't see regular critical conversations in staff meetings, hallways, or classroom interactions with students. Eleanor is also frustrated. She observed a few teachers with exceptional skills in leading CC-raising conversations with their students. Yet, these examples go unmentioned in PDs and Eleanor fears that those key teachers and practices will continue to go unnoticed as models for other staff members. Danielle is feeling anxious. She, like many DLBE educators, works desperately to improve academic outcomes for marginalized and minoritized students. She knows there is a lot she doesn't know, and she wants to learn it so she can do her job better. Yet she leaves her umpteenth PD of the year with more questions and busywork than actionable plans or inspiration.

Fortunately, the three educators run into each other as they leave school, and a spontaneous, fruitful, and critical hallway conversation occurs. After they make small talk and commiserate about the underwhelming PD they just experienced, Eleanor sighs and says, "I would have liked to highlight what recently happened with two other staff members."

Danielle replies, "Hmm, say more." And so, as they stand in the doorway, Eleanor recounts to her attentive audience of two what happened a few weeks earlier:

> A classroom teacher, Maestro Galeano, had approached Eleanor in the book room one day, wanting her advice. He said he had concerns about

some classroom language practices of his co-teacher Maestra Alcala, a new colleague from a Spanish-speaking country. Maestro Galeano felt that Maestra Alcala was not always honoring the hybrid language practices of students in the class, especially among simultaneous bilinguals. For example, during a morning meeting conversation about recess activities, one student had offered, "*Voy a jugar* smashball *con mis* friends." Rather than honoring the student's contribution, Maestra Alcala had pointed her finger and replied sternly, "*ESPAÑOL*." Maestro Galeano noticed the student's apparent shame and was troubled by what he observed, but didn't know what to do, and did not intervene. Reflecting back, he asked Eleanor, "What do you think?"

Eleanor said, "I'm glad you talked to me, and I'd like to think about all this—how about we meet tomorrow?" Then, she returned to her office and declined the upcoming district Zoom for instructional coaches in 20 minutes. "I'll read the notes later," she said to herself. "This is most important now." So she sat and thought about both teachers. She thought about what she knew of their ethnolinguistic and socioeconomic backgrounds, their certifications, and teacher training. She re-read some key articles on critical pedagogy and conversation. She considered ways to facilitate honest, critical, and transformative conversation between colleagues that might fruitfully address the issue at hand. Then, she generated a list of questions and statements (see Teacher Notes) to give Maestro Galeano for a potential conversation with Maestra Alcala.

When they met to follow up, Eleanor began by asking Maestro Galeano, "Why does this issue resonate so much with you?" He told her about growing up as a dynamic bilingual speaker, including experiences in which his language practices were sometimes "not allowed."

"Those experiences fostered insecurities about my language and identity that I still struggle with sometimes," he said. Eleanor thought about what he said.

"I see a link between your lived experiences and the language environment you seek to provide students in the school," she observed. Next, she asked him to consider his colleague's prior knowledge and experiences. "Why do you think she said what she said? What training and experiences do you think she had, and how are they different from yours?" Upon reflection, Maestro Galeano realized Maestra Alcala's well-intentioned efforts may match her language ideology and former context.

"I imagine that she was not prepared for this specific context, and she has not yet developed cultural competence for working with US bilinguals and the pedagogy that aligns with it," he reflected. Then he continued, "But, now what? I mean, I'd like to help her learn, for the sake of our students, but how?"

Eleanor replied, "Let's try out some critical conversation strategies and role play to give you ideas for how to open an honest and productive conversation with her." Eleanor showed him the list of prompts she had developed (see Teacher Notes), remarking, "This conversation helped us make sense of what occurred and how we can respond—Maestra Alcala deserves to have a similar conversation." She added, "It's important to talk this out, emails don't work well for issues like this." Maestro Galeano nodded. They spent another half hour trying out the strategies, roleplaying until Maestro Galeano felt prepared for a critical conversation with Maestra Alcala.

When he saw Maestra Alcala during prep period the next day, Maestro Galeano asked if she would be open to chatting when it would be convenient to her. "Sure, in 15 minutes after I make these copies," she replied. When the two sat down, Maestro Galeano used the wording and the practice Eleanor had provided to engage Maestra Alcala in a critical conversation.

First, he anchored the conversation in student observations, saying, "I noticed that some students are contributing less frequently than last month." She replied that she, too, has noticed the trend. Then, when they brainstormed contributing factors, he suggested that student participation might be influenced by how student language behaviors are handled. "Some students might not feel comfortable expressing themselves authentically because they see correction as judgment," he said.

Maestra Alcala's brow knitted, and she replied, "I set high expectations for students and I try to help them develop competency in formal Spanish . . . you're saying I should do something differently?" Maestro Galeano recounted his own story about growing up bilingual (his *testimonio*), as he had with Eleanor. With example after example, he illustrated for Maestra Alcala how his own language practices, though not standard, were part of who he was, and these practices were either honored or rejected by those around him. As she listened, Maestra Alcala's expression grew thoughtful. After he finished, she said, "This is all very new to me, the unique experiences of US bilinguals, and I'm thinking about what that means for the role of language in my classroom."

Maestro Galeano asked, "Would you be open to thinking about instructional practices that honor our students' bilingualism?" She nodded, and they began by discussing the notions of language separation and revisiting practices they now agreed were outdated and hurtful.

As Eleanor finishes telling this story, Directora Lane says, "Maestro Galeano's story reminds me of what I've read recently on *testimonio*." Seeing her colleagues' questioning looks, she explains that *testimonio* can be described as testifying to lived experiences, especially those that have been ignored, undervalued, or untold. She adds that *testimonio* can challenge and disrupt historical power imbalances as well as "raise consciousness" and empower people of historically marginalized groups to "reclaim their humanity" (Valenzuela et al., 2021). Directora Lane recalls from a recent article that *testimonio* "disrupts silence, invites connection, and entices collectivity—it is social justice scholarship in education" (Delgado Bernal et al., 2012, p. 370). Directora Lane says, "I see Maestro Galeano's story as a *testimonio*." Still in the doorway, Directora Lane, Eleanor, and Danielle come to the conclusion that using *testimonio* in K–12 education and in PD for K–12 educators can create critical transformative opportunities. But, they wonder aloud, "Now what should we *do*?"

That evening, Danielle thinks about the conversation further. Feeling inspired, she sends a text message to Directora Lane and Eleanor that she would like to pilot utilizing *testimonios* in her classroom with her fifth grade students. Directora Lane replies "u have my blessing!!" and Eleanor replies "yesss!!! work session, you, me, Monday early release?" Working with Eleanor, Danielle reworks her upcoming unit to integrate *testimonios* to cultivate critical conversations with her students. She kicks off this new endeavor by changing the way the class is learning about migration and immigration. Instead of studying the push-pull factors from the textbook, her students work with community members, family members, and friends to gather *testimonios* about their immigration experiences.

Continuing with these efforts for several weeks, Danielle begins to notice that organic, student-driven, critically conscious conversations are occurring. For example, following a community leader's *testimonio* about growing up in the 1960s when their school district and community were segregated, a student comments, "I am so glad that our neighborhoods are not segregated anymore." Another student replies, "I don't know if that is completely true." Instead of jumping in immediately with a teaching point, Danielle encouraged continued student dialogue, giving time and space for critical conversation to unfold. "What do you all think based on your experiences?" Danielle prompts the class. Another student responds, "Well, we have lots of different kids in our school, but how many neighbors on our street come from different backgrounds?" Students and teacher pause to think, and critical conversation was extended.

Excited about what is happening through critical practices used by Maestras Eleanor and Danielle, Directora Lane asks them to share their experiences and research with the school's social justice committee. (She also asked Maestro Galeano and Maestra Alcala, but they preferred to keep their conversation private.) This committee had formed several years before, to focus on addressing inequities in the school. After sharing their stories with the committee, the group discusses PD structures that have been used at the school. The team comes to the conclusion that fostering CC cannot be relegated to monthly PD sessions. Instead, a school climate needs to be cultivated such that authentic PD can happen through critical conversations between staff members and students on a regular basis. Such conversations must be explicitly recognized and celebrated as critical PD for all staff to understand their importance and truly engage in the reimagined PD efforts.

The critical conversations that occur at Simón Bolívar shift mindset and practice. Danielle is historicizing with her students, helping them make connections between the past and present in order to build a more just future. Mr. Galeano and Eleanor leaned into discomfort to help their colleague critically listen in order to support a more inclusive classroom for all their languaging. The leadership team is working to engage everyone in a constant process of interrogating power to create a more equitable school community. These small shifts in practice lead to shifts replicated across the school, reflecting CC development among staff that is widespread, impactful, and sustainable.

Teaching Notes

Teachers are transformative intellectuals whose efforts can bring about the conditions of a truly democratic society (Giroux, 2018). Simón Bolívar, in this case, found that CC-raising conversations and work flourished when familiar methods of PD were set aside. This is important in any school, but especially in a DLBE setting. Educators at Simón Bolívar had the courage to let go of their ideas of what constitutes "PD" and embrace the uncertainty and ambiguity of a reimagined way of learning and growing, one that centers teachers as problem-solvers and validates critical conversations that confront equity issues both within and beyond the classroom. This case illustrates how replacing traditional PD with a homegrown and reimagined approach engaged teachers in transformation to address inequity, and thus honored the spirit of CC.

We argue that we can and should de-construct the assumptions that undergird current systems. Critical bilingual educators have a unique opportunity to combat inequities, and well-intended but traditional PD is not enough to help them do so. Working meaningfully in DLBE must go hand in hand with CC: with it, we can hijack hidden and harmful curriculum that continues to marginalize students. Recognizing, fostering, and validating critical conversations and CC through reimagined PD is one way to achieve this.

Making space for CC to take hold demands an alternate PD approach. First, we must recognize that our assumptions and approaches regarding schooling and PD are actually detrimental. We must recognize our positionality in oppressive systems before we can hope to operationalize CC. Second, we must recognize that DLBE educators can authentically learn and grow by managing their own Freirean cycle of learning, critical reflection, and action. This is not a once-a-month, agenda-driven, whole-group PD session set on repeat in Google Calendar and facilitated by an administrator. Rather, educators drive their own development as they engage in critical conversations on topics of their choosing, driven by their observations and reflections. It takes place in settings and at times of their choosing and that fit their needs. Third, DLBE educators and students can foster CC in each other, even through day-to-day, informal, and impromptu interactions. For example, staff can study multilingual educators' and students' written and/or recorded *testimonios*; these may serve as concrete models that shift PD from a factory-banking model toward a Freirean model that centers the oppressed. But unexpected hallway conversations that prompt critical learning count, too. Longstanding equity issues will be addressed only through an innovative approach that breaks habits of thought, including the well-established approaches found in outdated, traditional PD.

Discussion Questions/Teaching Activities

1. How does the case study in this chapter compare with your own experience with PD?
2. Reflect on your own context. What conditions support the type of reimagined PD described in this chapter? What barriers exist? What might be an action step to foster your own growth or the growth of others?
3. Maestra Eleanor and Maestro Galeano used guiding questions to prepare for a crucial conversation. Decide on an inequity that could be addressed through a critical conversation with a colleague. Use the following guiding questions to prepare your conversation. After you have answered the guiding questions, roleplay the critical conversation with a thought partner.

    a. What is the inequity you wish to address and with whom would you like to address it? (Choose an issue within scope; you and the participant should have a foundation of trust.)
    b. How does the policy or practice lead to inequities for students or families? What are the effects of *not* addressing this inequity?
    c. Why might this inequity be occurring? Does the participant have an awareness of the issue? Does the participant have a gap in knowledge, skill, or cultural competence? What supports will the participant need in order to remedy the inequity?
    d. Plan out the critical conversation you'd like to take place.

        i. Begin with noticing
        ii. Brainstorm contributing factors
        iii. Engage in joint meaning-making
        iv. Invite further inquiry or follow-up

4. Discuss how you can engage *testimonios* in the following ways:

    a. Formal professional development sessions/school meetings
    b. Informal conversations with staff
    c. Classroom curriculum
    d. Your personal life

References

Delgado Bernal, D., Burciaga, R., & Flores Carmona, J. (2012). Chicana/Latina testimonios: Mapping the methodological, pedagogical, and political. *Equity & Excellence in Education, 45*(3), 363–372. https://doi.org/10.1080/10665684.2012.698149

Giroux, H. A. (2018). Teachers as transformative intellectuals. In *Thinking about schools* (pp. 183–189). Routledge.

Palmer, D. (2010). Race, power, and equity in a multiethnic urban elementary school with a dual-language "strand" program. *Anthropology & Education Quarterly, 41*(1), 94–114. https://doi.org/10.1111/j.1548-1492.2010.01069.x

Valdés, G. (1997). Dual-language immersion programs: A cautionary note concerning the education of language-minority students. *Harvard Educational Review, 67*(3), 391–430. https://doi.org/10.17763/haer.67.3.n5q175qp86120948

Valenzuela, A., Epstein, E., & Unda, M. D. C. (2021). From testimony to testimonio. In E. G. Murillo, D. Delgado Bernal, S. Morales, L. Urrieta, E. Ruiz Bybee, J. Sánchez Muñoz, V. B. Saenez, D. Villanueva, M. Machado-Casas, & K. Espinoza (Eds.), *Handbook of latinos and education: Theory, research, and practice.* Routledge.

22 Bridging Testimonio Pedagogy with Dual Language Bilingual Education in a K/1 Classroom

One Teacher's Journey to Critical Consciousness Through a Master's Course

Juan A. Freire and Judith Flores Carmona

Context

In today's demographic imperative, the need to diversify the teaching population continues in dual language bilingual education (DLBE). However, diversifying teacher participants will not result in substantial and needed changes unless these teachers have developed critical/sociopolitical consciousness, understanding it as the ability to read the world and engage in a messy and radical process of transformation and activism (Freire, 1970). Support for racialized pre-service and in-service teachers' critical consciousness deserves more attention. Many racialized teachers in bilingual and dual language bilingual education programs have been affected by traditions of colonization and internalized oppression (Ek et al., 2013; Rubio et al., 2021). Focusing on teachers is a first step toward supporting children's critical consciousness in DLBE. Teachers and children can benefit from four actions toward critical consciousness development as framed by Palmer et al. (2019): continuously interrogating power, historicizing schools, critical listening, and engaging with discomfort. These are similar actions that take place in testimonio pedagogy. Testimonio is an effective pedagogical tool in revealing how different forms of inequity affect the lives of individuals (Delgado Bernal et al., 2012). In this chapter we introduce testimonio pedagogy as a method for promoting critical consciousness for teachers and students in DLBE classrooms, including a composite testimonio by one of the students. We close this chapter with teaching activities that can be adjusted to pre-service and in-service teachers, which we recommend should be implemented in order to support readers' development of their own critical consciousness.

Testimonio as Methodology and Pedagogy

Testimonio has a long tradition in Latin America. Testimonios are discourses or writings from the margins/from the subaltern and are overtly political

DOI: 10.4324/9781003240594-27

and urgent to divulge. Testimonio differs from life history due to its intent to denounce and its political purpose. While the details and specific context are unique, testimonios encompass struggle, survival, and call for solidarity. Beverly (1992) asserted, "Testimonio represents an affirmation of the individual subject, even of individual growth and transformation, but in connection with group or class situation marked by marginalization, oppression, and struggle" (p. 103).

We are well aware of the power of testimonio in DLBE. Judith collaborated in a university-school-community partnership at a school with a DLBE program. She has extensively written about testimonio, and as a bilingual *Mexicana académica* she has documented her personal testimonio (Flores Carmona, 2017). Juan is a Spaniard/Ecuadorian who has been a Spanish DLBE teacher at an urban school in Utah and became familiar with his students' testimonios. As a teacher educator, he uses testimonio literature with his students. As critical pedagogues in higher education, we draw out deeper meanings and theories from personal experience and insight. Testimonio pedagogy merges the classroom content with sociopolitical realities. By teaching, sharing, and writing testimonios, we seek to enable our students and the readers to understand their individual experiences in relation to larger structures and in so doing become part of a collective that denounces oppressive conditions. In this chapter we share (a) how Señora García (pseudonym) developed her own critical consciousness, (b) Señora García's design of her unit plan based on a Spanish-English children's book, and (c) her implementation of testimonio pedagogy in her DLBE classroom toward her students' critical consciousness as part of a university course taught by Judith.

University Course Context

At a southwestern university located near the US-Mexico border region, Judith taught EDUC 516, Curriculum and Pedagogy, to expose current educators to historical, philosophical, socio-cultural, psychological, and theoretical foundations of these disciplines. The course also supported students in applying principles to teaching and learning settings that were culturally and linguistically diverse. The class engaged with a critical foundational knowledge of the philosophy of curriculum and instruction while examining current classroom practices. Students in the university class learned that curriculum is wrought with teachers' ideologies, informed by their epistemologies, and inseparable from their positionality.

Course objectives in Judith's class included (1) exploring holistic approaches affirming that no standard exists for knowledge, teaching-learning styles, or worldviews; (2) acknowledging the difference between having diversity and being inclusive, and (3) engaging with sociopolitical issues related to the context of master's students' teaching practice. The goal for these objectives was to critique the standardization and biases of curricula through the lenses of social justice, critical pedagogy, holistic education, and other progressive and radical models of curriculum and pedagogy.

Guided by these objectives, students in the class developed their own critical multicultural curriculum. To inform their curriculum, they read material such as *Teachers as Cultural Workers: Letters to Those Who Dare Teach* (Freire, 2005), *Sentipensante (Sensing/Thinking) Pedagogy: Educating for Wholeness, Social Justice and Liberation* (Rendón, 2009), *Growing Critically Conscious Teachers: A Social Justice Curriculum for Educators of Latino/a Youth* (Valenzuela, 2016), and *Un-standardizing Curriculum: Multicultural Teaching in the Standards-Based Classroom* (Sleeter & Flores Carmona, 2017), along with multiple articles by social justice scholars and critical pedagogues.

These master's students, some of them practicing DLBE teachers, faced the challenge of drawing from the pedagogies present in the homes, families, and communities of their predominantly working-class student populations in the US-Mexico borderland. This was especially important because the curriculum content should be relevant to the learners, their lives, and their environment. All stakeholders in the DLBE community, especially educators, need to pay urgent attention to the complex ways institutional issues affect the school community and how the curriculum standardization is connected to the structure of schooling and to curricular and pedagogical processes.

Case Narrative

School Context and Señora García's Classroom

Señora García's testimonio was based on her immigration experience and language learning process. She had moved to the United States as an adult and learned English as her second language. She was a Mexicana DLBE educator who at the time of this study was teaching a combined kindergarten/1st-grade class at a Title 1 school located in the US Southwest borderlands region. Consistent with the school demographics, her class was composed mainly of Mexican and Mexican American students. At the time of the study, approximately 300 students were enrolled in the school; 97% of them were labeled as "Hispanic" and 100% were receiving free lunch. The school had a Spanish-English one-way developmental/maintenance DLBE program. The language allocation was 50:50 according to the Gómez and Gómez model. The program had a two-teacher model; Senora García was the Spanish teacher.

In her work in the master's level course at the university, Señora García indicated that developing her critical consciousness helped her define her positionality as a teacher. For the first six weeks of Judith's class on Curriculum and Pedagogy, all students delved into learning about their intersecting identities, power, privilege, and oppression and then wrote their teaching philosophy. In addition to positioning herself as a Spanish-speaking immigrant who spoke English as her second language, she also positioned herself as a prayerful Bible-reading Christian who drew on contemplative practice, citing Rendón (2009). The reflective exercise of positionality helped her provide better quality education to her students, understand how her teacher positionality impacted instruction, and realize the purpose of the curriculum from a critical perspective.

Her experience in the master's program developed her critical consciousness as she moved toward interrogating power and historicizing schools by learning about systemic inequities. For example, in EDUC 516 she learned about injustice in systems including institutional racism in the prison industrial complex and the poor investment in public education. She also read literature that helped her better understand and name inequities. In one of her course assignments, she credited the course materials for helping her develop critical consciousness, including the documentary films *Our Spirits Don't Speak English* and *Precious Knowledge*. She also commented on how *Waiting for Superman* was a big eye-opener about the deficit mindset of the US educational system. She mentioned that her university coursework was transformative:

> Part of my philosophy has changed. I can see myself detaching from the systematic form forced upon us by politicians. . . . We are detouring from our main goal: guiding children to be inquisitive critical thinkers and problem solvers through transformative intellectual knowledge.

As she developed her critical consciousness, Señora García remarked that her job included deciding what knowledge would be most worth teaching and learning, and what relationship should exist between the students in the classroom and the knowledge selection process. She remarked that now she intended to un-standardize the curriculum (Sleeter & Flores Carmona, 2017) in various ways, including through the incorporation of more multicultural children's literature relevant to her students' lives and toward their development of critical consciousness.

Señora García's study of her positionality, recognition of societal and systemic inequities, and commitment to transforming her teaching were foundational in her development of critical consciousness. These efforts materialized in one of her course assignments, part of a unit of study in Spanish using the concept of developing curriculum around a central idea.

Unit Plan

Señora García's unit plan drew on Sleeter's (2005) suggestion of beginning "curriculum planning . . . by identifying the key concepts, or big ideas, around which a unit, lesson, or course of study will be built" (p. 44). Señora García was inspired by Fein and Horn's (2011) work narrating how a second-grade teacher read aloud Gloria Anzaldúa's (1993)

Spanish-English book *Friends from the Other Side/Amigos del Otro Lado*, which Señora García used for her four-week unit of study. This bilingual children's book, loosely based on Anzaldúa's early life in south Texas, tells of a young Chicana girl, Prietita, who lived near the US-Mexican border, befriending and helping a young Mexican boy, Joaquín, who had recently immigrated to the US with his mother. The book included issues related to im/migration, including the various roles of police and authority. In Señora García's unit plan, the purpose of reading this book was to analyze critical issues and support the students in understanding their own culture, including where their family had come from. Most of her students related to this story because they were immigrants themselves or first-generation Americans. The stories of the main characters, Prietita and Joaquín, were similar to those the kindergarteners and first graders had heard from their parents and grandparents. Señora García valued her students' background knowledge and as discussed by Fein and Horn (2011), she was committed to engaging her students in deep discussions to facilitate critical consciousness.

Lessons

Señora García planned and implemented various lessons and activities based on the reading and discussion of the book *Friends from the Other Side/Amigos del Otro Lado*. Each day for four weeks Señora García presented new vocabulary words and discussed the meaning of terms relevant to critical consciousness supported by her and her students' testimonios. She also read texts aloud and asked the students comprehension questions designed to reinforce traditional academic vocabulary. Señora García built background knowledge by conducting a picture walk and asking questions related to the students' own lives and experiences. Another of her lesson plans was having students create their own family tree based on their family's genealogical knowledge. Students talked with a partner about what they had known and had recently learned about their family background.

Señora García and her students talked about the similarities and differences between Prietita and Joaquín. They also discussed what happened in the story and filled out a graphic organizer to discuss the title, characters, and setting. Rich conversations emerged from reading and discussing the book relevant to the concepts of *migra* [immigration officials], *mojado* [undocumented], and *deportado* [deported], as they interrogated power. One of the students knew about *deportado* because her dad had been deported. Following her comments, as students engaged in critical listening, some of them began sharing their own testimonios, including what they had heard from their parents. A student shared,

> My mom was deported when I was three months. I don't remember her but my older siblings do and they are always very sad. Their teachers

> don't understand. I am glad we can talk about these things and pray that this country will stop destroying families and will treat people better.

These types of discussions facilitate critical consciousness in students because in the sharing of their testimonios teacher and students were all uncovering oppression. Together, they spoke back to the immigration system, injustice, and family separation. This is an example of a testimonio pedagogy that built bridges with students' wealth of knowledge, validated students' personal experiences, and developed critical consciousness for students.

Teaching Notes

We have bridged testimonios with DLBE by focusing on how a Mexicana teacher implemented a testimonio pedagogy by integrating a unit plan with her students' im/migrant sociopolitical realities and by helping them engage in meaningful/critical discussions. This pedagogical method supported students' sharing of testimonios and critical consciousness. We interpret students' sharing/recording of testimonios as (a) an activity that reveals their critical consciousness and (b) a process of supporting their bilingualism and biliteracy in a DLBE program. Students learning a language gradually move from the process of understanding the language, through the receptive domains of listening and reading, to the productive domains of speaking and writing. Similarly, students can transition from understanding inequities and injustice to speaking and writing their own testimonios.

While testimonios can occur in all education programs, we see DLBE as an ideal place for enabling students to express their lived realities in the partner language, in English, by translanguaging, or supported by other vernacular language practices, which can be particularly meaningful and empowering toward their development of critical consciousness and activism in DLBE (Freire & Feinauer, 2022). This principle can be applicable to various language programs in DLBE and to the different types of DLBE.

To begin effective use of testimonios, DLBE educators must develop their own critical consciousness and their commitment to social justice (Freire, 2021). These convictions and dispositions provide contexts where the testimonios of marginalized and oppressed students can emerge. To uncover oppression and promote healing and transformation, testimonio pedagogy requires understanding students' realities and challenges in order to implement activities relevant to their life experiences. Señora García identified im/migration as a relevant topic due to the school's close proximity to the US-Mexico border.

Enabling and sharing students' testimonios can involve various strategies. Children's books can support equity efforts in the classroom, can encourage sharing these testimonios, and can facilitate the development of critical consciousness. Having children take home social justice books can also promote testimonios at home and critical consciousness growth.

Developing critical consciousness is a dynamic and lifelong process. In this chapter we have featured how a DLBE educator formally engaged in the development of critical consciousness and how she bridged testimonio pedagogy to support her students' development of critical consciousness. In reality, this needs to be a multi-bridge process supported by different stakeholders beyond teacher educators and pedagogues in higher education. DLBE needs to be a safe place where parents, community members, administrators, and staff members can bridge their testimonios to support students' development of critical consciousness. As educators and other stakeholders share their own testimonios, students may benefit from a safe space for healing, inspiration, and strength—all while teaching and learning together.

Teaching Activities

1. Readings

We recommend the four books listed at the end of the second paragraph of the section titled "The University Course Context."

1. Complement this chapter with chapters in those books and reflect on your learning, testimonio, and critical consciousness.
2. List questions, prompts, and/or videos that are relevant to the themes covered in the books, and be prepared for small- and large-group discussions.

2. Backward Curriculum Planning

Using backward curriculum planning and the framework designed by Christine Sleeter (2005; see Figure 22.1), you may begin with what we call "identity work": designating your own social positioning, including how your identity as an educator impacts your pedagogical approach. This identity work, which enables you to begin understanding your beliefs and your ideology, is part of the framework (Figure 22.1), enabling you to situate your big concepts and ideas in conversations with the other sections of this curriculum planning. Recalling what Señora García did for her university course, write a lesson plan using this backward curriculum planning supported by your identity work and your testimonio with the goal of supporting students in sharing their testimonios.

3. Teaching Philosophy

- What is your positionality (race, class, language, etc.)?
- How does the teacher's positionality affect the curriculum and how it is delivered?
- What purposes should the curriculum serve?

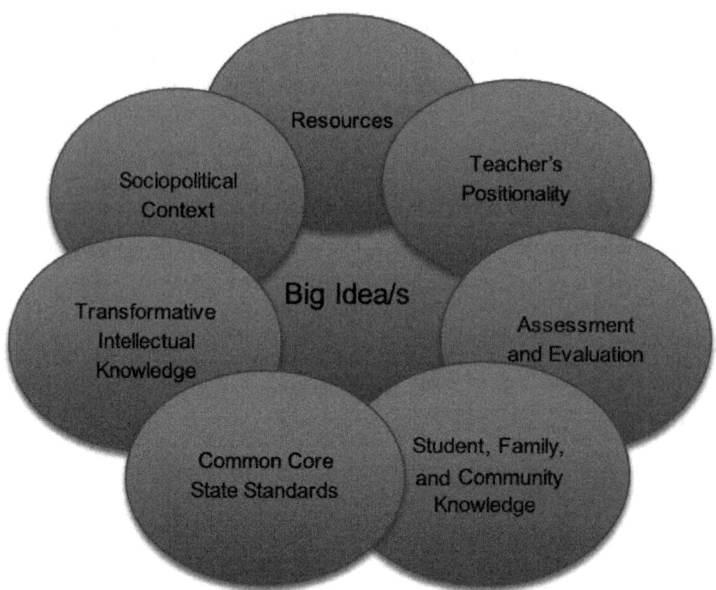

Figure 22.1 Adapted from Sleeter and Flores Carmona (2017, p. 24)

- How should knowledge be selected? Who decides what knowledge is most worth teaching and learning, and what is the relationship between the students in the class and the knowledge selection process?
- How would you describe the nature of students and the learning process? How do these characteristics suggest ways that learning experiences and relationships should be organized?
- How should curriculum be designed and evaluated?
- How should learning be evaluated?
- Was your curriculum culturally relevant? In what ways?

(Adapted from Sleeter & Flores Carmona, 2017, pp. 26–27)

References

Anzaldúa. G. E. (1993). *Friends from the Other Side/Amigos del Otro Lado*. Children's Book Press.

Beverly, J. (1992). The margin at the center. In S. Smith & J. Watson (Eds.), *De/colonizing the subject: The politics of gender in women's autobiography* (pp. 91–114). University of Minnesota Press.

Delgado Bernal, D., Burciago, R., & Carmona, J. (2012). Chicana/Latina *testimonios*: Mapping the methodological, pedagogical, and political. *Equity & Excellence in Education, 45*(3), 363–372. https://doi.org/10.1080/10665684.2012.698149

Ek, L. D., Sánchez, P., & Quijada Cerecer, P. D. (2013). Linguistic violence, insecurity, and work: Language ideologies of Latina/o bilingual teacher candidates in Texas. *International Multilingual Research Journal*, 7, 197–219.

Fein, J. G., & Horn, R. (2011). Valuing home language to support young bilingual children's talks about books. In R. J. Meyer & K. F. Whitmore (Eds.), *Reclaiming reading: Teachers, students, and researchers regaining spaces for thinking and action* (pp. 209–218). Routledge.

Flores Carmona, J. (2017). Pedagogical border crossings: Testimonio y reflexiones de una mexicana académica. *Journal of Latinos and Education*, *17*(1), 92–97.

Freire, J. A. (2021). Conscientization calls: A white dual language educator's development of sociopolitical consciousness and commitment to social justice. *Education and Urban Society*, *53*(2), 231–248.

Freire, J. A., & Feinauer, E. (2022). Vernacular Spanish as a promoter of critical consciousness in dual language bilingual education classrooms. *International Journal of Bilingual Education and Bilingualism*, *25*(4), 1516–1529.

Freire, P. (1970). *Pedagogy of the oppressed*. Continuum.

Freire, P. (2005). *Teachers as cultural workers: Letters to those who dare to teach*. Westview Press.

Palmer, D. K., Cervantes-Soon, C., Dorner, L., & Heiman, D. (2019). Bilingualism, biliteracy, biculturalism, and critical consciousness for all: Proposing a fourth fundamental goal for two-way dual language education. *Theory into Practice*, *58*(2), 121–133.

Rendón, L. I. (2009). *Sentipensante (sensing/thinking) pedagogy: Education for wholeness, social justice, and liberation*. Stylus Publishing.

Rubio, B., Palmer, D. K., & Martinez, M. (2021). Si no estás defendiendo a tus alumnos, ¿qué estás haciendo en el salón? A Mexican immigrant teacher's journey to critical consciousness. *Journal of Language, Identity & Education*, *20*(1), 45–57.

Sleeter, C. E. (2005). *Un-standardizing curriculum: Multicultural teaching in the standards-based classroom*. Teachers College Press.

Sleeter, C. E., & Flores Carmona, J. (2017). *Un-standardizing curriculum: Multicultural teaching in the standards-based classroom*. Teachers College Press.

Valenzuela, A. (2016). *Growing critically conscious teachers: A social justice curriculum for educators of Latino/a youth*. Teachers College Press.

23 A Sense of Belonging

Biliteracy Instruction That Loves and Centers Latinx Emergent Bilingual Students and Their Families

Carmela Valdez and Rosalyn Harvey-Torres

Context

In the writer's workshop (Calkins, 1986; Graves, 1983) students choose their writing topics, write every day for authentic audiences, explore different genres through mentor texts, and confer with their teacher and peers. Research has shown the promise of the writer's workshop for multilingual students (Zapata & Laman, 2016) and has called for writing instruction that attends to the unique strengths and experiences of students of color who are multilingual (Reyes, 1992) and multidialectal (Delpit, 1988). Important work explores the writing and languaging of emergent bilingual students in writer's workshop and workshop like settings (Durán, 2017; Gort, 2012), as well as reimagining writing instruction to center the knowledge and experience of Latinx bilingual students, in and out of school spaces (de los Ríos, 2017; Flores, 2021). However, little research explores the traditional writer's workshop model as a pedagogical approach in bilingual classrooms, where students and the teacher read, write, speak, and sense-make across at least two languages daily.

To explore a bilingual writer's workshop, Carmela and Rosalyn conducted a study in Carmela's first grade Spanish/English bilingual classroom in a Title I school in a large urban city in Central Texas. Carmela identifies as Latina; she is the child of Mexican American educators and grew up in south and central Texas. Carmela grew up speaking and listening to English and Spanish at home, and some at school, but became more fluent in Spanish upon deciding to become a bilingual educator; she explains, "Relearning Spanish was like finding a missing piece of myself." Rosalyn is a White university researcher and sequential English/Spanish bilingual. She was a bilingual paraprofessional in her rural hometown's summer program for the children of migrant farm workers, and later became a bilingual elementary school teacher in Texas. Her interest in multilingual students and equity come from her experiences of language loss of her heritage language, Romanian, as well as attending rural schools in K–12. Puente Elementary (pseudonym), the school site, had a two-way dual language model in grades

DOI: 10.4324/9781003240594-28

K–5. Carmela and her English partner teacher shared two homerooms of first graders under a 50/50 dual language model. Puente has been committed to dual language with the goal of hiring and retaining teachers and administrators dedicated to maintaining and growing the language and cultures of the predominantly Latinx working-class students in the school.

There were 40 students across two homeroom classes. Roughly 90% of these students identified as "Hispanic/Latino"; these Latinx students had a wide variety of home and community experiences with Spanish and English and learned in both languages at school.

Case Narrative

Now entering her fifteenth year of teaching, Carmela reflects on four years prior, when she knew she needed a change:

> I was ready to leave the classroom. I felt the heavy weight of not feel ing like I fit in as a teacher. The things I valued were not valued by the system. Then I received a call to action. A new president had been elected and he was very anti-immigrant and anti-Mexican. My class was full of immigrants and kids with families from Mexico. They asked me a question I wasn't sure first graders were capable of knowing or asking. "Ms. Valdez, why does the president [Trump] hate Mexicans?" I was floored! I didn't know what to say. I think I just said, "That is a good question. I don't know."
>
> I realized that the next four years would be very difficult for them and not just because of policies but because they felt like they didn't belong in the country where they lived. It might not have started out as their home but it was their home now and they felt like there was a target on their back. There was. They shuddered whenever their parents were a few minutes late to pick them up because they thought they got picked up by ICE and deported. I realized that not only did they feel scared but powerless to change. They were not wanted, and their parents and families felt the same. I searched for something. I didn't know what I was looking for until I found it and then it was like I fell in love with teaching.

The "something" that Carmela was searching for took shape in a collaborative community of writers and teachers. This community is the Heart of Texas Writing Project (HTWP), a month-long intensive summer institute that is part of the National Writing Project. These educators sought to learn how to teach writing as a craft, and to deepen their own writing lives in the process. This group's mission centers on honoring students as storytellers and agentive people capable of deciding what and how they will write. HTWP's mission aligns with many aspects of critical consciousness, namely interrogating power through positioning student writers as experts, historicizing communities by recruiting teachers from schools serving historically resource-withheld communities, engaging with discomfort of "normalizing the struggle" of living a writerly life, critically listening to the ideas of the classroom community, and collectively engaging in the messiness of adopting a teaching approach that changes in response to students' desires, interests, and needs. Engaging students in a writer's workshop meant guiding students in exploration of mentor texts and offering them experience with the entire writing cycle, including following students' own writing agendas instead of implementing more scripted and discrete literacy practices (for example, banking education approaches such as using basal readers or primarily phonics drill-focused literacy instruction).

Because no bilingual writer's workshop practitioner texts existed during our time in HTWP, Carmela and Rosalyn brainstormed what a bilingual writer's workshop may look like, and Carmela re-envisioned the writer's workshop for her Latinx emergent bilingual students. Carmela expressed an awareness that this was unique, and she interrogated the power relations present in dual language throughout its complicated history. As she explains,

> Old school dual language was born out of the rich people wanting their kids to have access to the minority language. Dual language in Texas is the underprivileged trying to acquire the majority language, but from a place of weakness. As teachers, we were told how to implement, don't switch languages because we want to make sure students have good language models. Administrators told us, some of our "*pobrecitos*" are not dominant in any language, they are confused. We are there to model for them. Top down all the way. Our directives were to stay in the target language. Students were encouraged to speak in the target language and [we] were to model for them if they said something that was perhaps translanguaging or not correct grammar.

Carmela highlights an important tension in dual language wherein teachers often feel pressure to create strict separations between languages, and how the dynamism of multilingual students' full linguistic repertoires (García & Wei, 2014) is often unnoticed, or even prohibited in dual language classrooms.

In response to Carmela's critically conscious writer's workshop pedagogy, students explored different genres of writing and choose the topic, language, and modality of their writing. For instance, some students primarily wrote in Spanish, some mostly in English, others translanguaged throughout their stories, and still others composed mostly through illustration and talk. All of these options were seen as authorly choices, and students' stories and ideas were both welcomed and celebrated in the classroom community. As Carmela explains,

> Once again, my students taught me who I really was. They wrote about their passions and their obsessions but from their perspective. They

> hadn't yet been made to feel ashamed of their language complexities but had used them. They wrote about Pokémon in English and Spanish. They embraced mainstream culture and their own and turned their writing into something that was a beautiful mix of both. I marvel at them daily. For the first time in my teaching career I really enjoyed my students. I didn't have to judge them and see the flaws. I saw the gems in their work and they were not hidden.

Carmela's assertion that her students actually taught *her* who *she was* through their writing and dynamic languaging is a profound inversion of the power relations often present in school; it is an example of how engaging with critical consciousness can make space for students to make decisions about their learning and step into the role of expert. For Carmela's class, publication was the culmination of weeks of working diligently, and editing and revising their work with a specific audience in mind. For the first publication event of the year, Carmela invited all first grade classes and their parents to a publishing party held in the evening in the school cafeteria. Parents brought food ranging from tamales, atole, and tacos to pizza and fresh fruit. While families ate and younger siblings played, Carmela emceed the event, making each announcement in Spanish and then English, and reminding the adults and older siblings to look at students' stories and see the beauty in them, not just the spelling errors or missing pieces. In setting this expectation, she invited parents to view the "hidden gems" (Bomer, 2010) in students' writing, affirming students' identities as authors. Each class's published writing was laid out on tables for guests to read and provide feedback on with sticky notes. Parents, administrators, teachers, classmates, and older siblings circulated, reading students' personal narratives and often responding with words or illustrations on sticky notes. Carmela described one mom's actions at the publishing party with particular appreciation.

> All the students had written a memoir of their six-year-old lives. I told families to remember that it was first grade writing and that it might not look perfect but it was perfect to us. We had worked hard and were excited to share so please celebrate the brilliance that was on the page. I walked around, talked to families, and then noticed that families were heading home. Then I looked at the tables where the students' writing was displayed. Alicia's mom was still writing notes. She was the last parent there making sure that every student had a positive word about their work. She knew! She knew that these writers deserved positive feedback. She gave my students affirmation and encouragement like she was writing words to Sandra Cisneros for her next book. I realized in that moment that she was an ally in a deeper way than just, "let me know what you need." She was a heart partner in this work. Knowing that this work had meaning today and would carry them through tomorrow.

Alicia's mom's actions illuminate how making space for families to feel comfortable, agentive, and knowledgeable in school spaces (such as this publishing party) are an example of interrogating power relations that often devalue the knowledge and skills of parents, especially immigrant parents. Carmela's realization that parents were allies in the work of a critically conscious writer's workshop stemmed from critical listening and reflection on her part, and as a result she focused on building spaces of *acompañamiento* (Heiman & Nuñez-Janes, 2021) where the teacher convened with students and families in ways that centered their cultures, knowledge, and experiences.

Carmela describes how the time spent in their first grade bilingual workshop has stayed with students as they transition into upper elementary.

> In the hallway I saw two former students. I said good morning to Juan and Celia, and Juan said, "Good morning, I'm still writing."
>
> "Good mijo, tell all the stories in your heart!" I responded. Then quietly rejoiced in my heart.
>
> Celia had drawn a lot during writing time. One day I noticed that her writing didn't have any color in the illustration. I asked why, and she said that it was a story from a long time ago and that is why it was black and white. Amazing! "Writers do that all the time, they tell stories with the details in their illustrations too!" She shared her work all the time after that. Kids process the world in ways that we couldn't even teach if we wanted to, and all we have to do is pay attention.
>
> Celia told her third grade teacher, "Of course I'm a writer, I wrote like six books in Carmela's class!" Her identity as a writer carried her to tomorrow and beyond. She takes pride in it and knows that her voice has value. She knows that in school, she doesn't only have to respond to the standards that have been chosen for us by rich White men—she can take the first turn and tell her own story.

This "taking the first turn" is a recognition of the agency of both teachers and students to contest White-centric curriculum, working against a banking education to advocate for meaningful learning that follows students' interests and desires.

Teaching Notes

Carmela's classroom shows that for critically conscious teachers who seek to center their emergent bilingual students, a version of the writer's workshop can upset phonics heavy banking approaches to literacy by positioning students as experts with ideas, interest, and lived experiences worth exploring in school. By interrogating the power imbalance inherent in the use of prompts to direct student writing, Carmela's writer's workshop facilitated students "taking the first turn," choosing what topics, languages, and modalities they wrote in. If the teacher simply assigns writing topics via prompts (for example "Write about a time you felt surprised"), students' voice would be heavily constrained. Banking writing instruction purports to teach children to write without offering students the latitude and exploration necessary to live a writerly life. When the teacher is making all creative decisions for students, neither the teacher nor the students can live in the messiness that is a critically conscious DLBE writer's workshop. Carmela continues to engage in the messiness of this struggle. As she explains, "If workshop is to give rich kids a voice to continue their privilege, I'm not down. But if it is for my students to find their voice, to read books with the lens of writers, books with Brown people in them, then I'm all in. How will we have authors of color if they don't start in my classroom in kindergarten and first grade?"

This workshop went beyond the walls of the classroom, engaging with parents as important members of the writing community. By historicizing the experiences of marginalization and exclusion many immigrant families' have experienced in US schools, Carmela worked to create spaces, such as the publishing party, that welcomed parents and families as allies and fellow teachers. This *acompañamiento* is evidenced by Carmela's realization that Alicia's mom was a "heart partner in this work" illustrates the importance of interrogating power relationships, critically listening to community members, and making space for parents and students to share their knowledge and skills. Carmela's praxis-cycle involved critical reflection about her pedagogy, the ways students and parents changed her thinking, and, in turn, her teaching. Carmela's critically conscious actions, informed by critically listening to students and families and reflecting on her own pedagogy, worked towards her goal of building a community in which all members have access to agency, love, and belonging.

Teaching Activities

A. Mini Workshop Lesson with Parents

Carmela does a lesson at Back to School Night so that parents can experience the writer's workshop by engaging them in a mini lesson. Parents are encouraged to value and share their writing voice by writing about their own experiences and identifying the writerly moves already present in how they see the world.

Mini lesson:

> Parents are invited to write about a topic of their choice. If they want a starting point, one strategy we try is to choose an object in the classroom and simply allow that object to lead our writing (for example, one mom chose the map of the world, and wrote about her own specific

experiences with traveling). After parents write and share about their experiences, pose some reflection questions, for example:

1. We are bilingual people and that means our brains think in two languages and two cultures. We navigate the world in a different way. How does this impact our writing?
2. How did your writing go today? What was difficult/interesting? Why?

B. Writing About What Matters to Us

These first days of workshop include lessons that help students choose their own agendas and find their identities as writers, and these are writing topics they can always revisit when they don't know what to write about.

Point of the Mini Lesson: Writers write about what they love/like:

Connection:
I've noticed in your writing that . . . you all are writing about all kinds of things. I love reading your writing but I noticed some of you have a blank page. I wondered if sometimes you don't know what to write about.

Teaching point:
Today I'm going to teach you . . . a strategy to use when you don't know what to write about. Writers write about what they love. When I don't know what to write, I think about what I love. I have a heart that I drew that has all the things I love so that I can write about them if I don't have any other ideas.

Demonstration:
Watch me while I . . . draw my heart and fill it with the things I love so I can pick something off of my heart if I don't know what to write.

Active engagement:
Right now, I'd like you to . . . think about what you want to put in your heart. Do you want to put people to write about like I have in my heart? Do you want to put something you love to do in the heart? What else do you love?

Link:
So, today and every day . . . you can think about the things that you love, make a heart, and fill it with them. You can use those things to write about if you don't know what to write.

Follow-up:
See if kids are trying this out during work time. Remind them of the strategy if they are still having trouble getting started.

References

Bomer, K. (2010). *Hidden Gems: Naming and teaching from the brilliance in every student's writing*. Heinemann.

Calkins, L. (1986). *The art of teaching writing*. Heinemann.

de los Ríos, C. V. (2017). Toward a corridista consciousness: Learning from one transnational youth's critical reading, writing, and performance of Mexican corridos. *Reading Research Quarterly*, *45*, 118.

Delpit, L. (1988). The silenced dialogue: Power and pedagogy in educating other people's children. *Harvard Educational Review*, *58*, 280–298.

Durán, L. (2017). Audience and young bilingual writers: Building on strengths. *Journal of Literacy Research*, *49*(1), 92–114.

Flores, T. T. (2021). Somos Escritoras/We Are Writers: Latina mothers and daughters writing and sharing "En Convivencia." *Urban Education*. doi:10.1177/00420859211003920

García, O., & Wei, L. (2014). *Translanguaging: Language, bilingualism and education*. Palgrave Macmillan.

Gort, M. (2012). Code-switching patterns in the writing-related talk of young emergent 19 bilinguals. *Journal of Literacy Research*, *44*(1), 45–75.

Graves, D. (1983). *Writing: Teachers and children at work*. Heinemann.

Heiman, D., & Nuñez-Janes, M. (2021). "Research shows that I am here for them": Acompañamiento as language policy activism in times of TWBE gentrification. *Language Policy*, *20*(3), 491–515.

Reyes, M. D. L. (1992). Challenging venerable assumptions: Literacy instruction for linguistically different students. *Harvard Educational Review*, *62*(4), 427.

Zapata, A., & Laman, T. T. (2016). "I write to show how beautiful my languages are": Translingual writing instruction in English-dominant classrooms. *Language Arts*, *93*(5), 366–378.

24 Growing Critical Bilingual Literacies

Counter-narratives and Social Justice in Bilingual Education

Luz Yadira Herrera and Carla España

Context

Crystal is in her fifth year of teaching as a third grade dual language bilingual education (DLBE) teacher. She teaches in a Latinx (im)migrant community in California where she grew up. It is a mid-size city with a population of just over half a million surrounded by agricultural farmland and smaller rural towns from which students and families often commute. The town's largest employers include the agricultural industry, several healthcare facilities, a large comprehensive university, junior colleges, and the meat processing industry.

The city's population is predominantly Latinx at 50%, followed by 27% white, 14% Asian, 7.4% Black, 4.2% from two or more races, and 1.2% American Indian and Alaskan Native (US Census, 2019). What's more, 43.4% of the city's households speak a language other than English, the median household income is $50,432, and a quarter of the population (25.2%) lives in poverty given the US Census Bureau's definition of the poverty threshold of $31,275 (US Census, 2019).

Unlike the larger cities across the state that usually lean toward more progressive politics, this region is split along conservative and progressive party lines. This political divide is apparent both racially and geographically. The Latinx population is concentrated in the southwest part of the city and makes up a significant percentage of the surrounding rural communities, reflecting the largely Latinx (im)migrant labor force on which the agricultural sector heavily depends.

Pacific Unified School District (a pseudonym) where Crystal teaches includes many comprehensive high schools, middle schools, and elementary schools to accommodate 77,000 students, with approximately 53,000 of these students identifying as Latinx—about 70% of the student population district-wide. Crystal teaches at Océano Elementary, one of the few elementary schools that is a fully dual immersion bilingual school. Other schools in the district offer a strand model of dual language bilingual education (DLBE), meaning that only one or a few classes per grade offer a bilingual curriculum. Océano is a small school with 359 students in grades K–5, with

DOI: 10.4324/9781003240594-29

about 90% of students identifying as Latinx and about a quarter (24.1%) classified as "English language learners" (Ed-Data, 2020). It is little wonder that students question the ways their families' (im)migration narratives are distorted given the polarized political climate in the region—a microcosm of the harmful rhetoric reverberating across the nation, especially given the contentious 2020 election and the preceding four years.

Case Narrative

As a Mexican American born and raised in this region of California, Crystal is no stranger to the political divide here. She regularly saw lawn signs and big flags carried in large pickup trucks supporting the 2020 incumbent presidential candidate who led a political campaign immersed in anti-immigrant rhetoric. This made Crystal feel uneasy as a daughter of immigrants from Michoacán and as a teacher in an almost entirely Latinx school. Many of the students' families are immigrants. Some are in mixed-status families—an added source of stress to Crystal in an uncertain socio-political landscape.

During one Tuesday morning in class shortly before the 2020 election, Crystal noticed that Máximo seemed particularly distracted. She set up the class for small group work time and pulled Máximo aside to ask what was on his mind. Max's dad, Carlos, is a project manager at a construction company. Carlos started out as a construction worker alongside his dad working for cash payment since he and his father are undocumented. He is married with two US-born children, including Max. Carlos now holds much responsibility in managing construction crews and overseeing various construction projects across the city.

Crystal learned that Max overheard his dad telling his mom about an incident during one of his visits to a construction site where there was a group of protesters outside holding up signs, blocking entry to workers and construction vehicles, while yelling at the mostly Latinx construction crew to go back to Mexico and to stop stealing American jobs. They chanted slurs and threatened to call Immigration and Customs Enforcement (ICE). Carlos was upset as he recounted the events to his wife and expressed the fear and anxiety he felt by the threat of both the protesters and ICE. As Máximo overheard this story, he became scared and wanted to know more. His parents explained to him what happened and reassured him that everything would be okay. But as Crystal heard Max tell what was on his mind, it was evident that he still felt worried about the safety of his dad and the other workers. What's more, this was not an isolated incident in Crystal's class.

Another student in Crystal's class, Samantha, had also recently shared feeling upset after watching a news report about a person being yelled at for speaking Spanish in a convenience store, and being told that they were in America and should be speaking English. Samantha asked Crystal why they were learning Spanish in class if people can get upset with Spanish being spoken in the US. Crystal reminded Samantha of the importance of embracing Spanish not only for herself and her family, but also for her community.

Between learning about Max's anxiety involving his father's workplace threats and Samantha's questioning her use of her community's language practices, Crystal knew that it was time to come together as a classroom community to address the harmful effects of an anti-immigrant narrative both locally and across the country, one that was deeply impacting her students' socio-emotional well-being.

Crystal sought out the recommendations from her school librarian, public librarian, third grade colleagues, and teacher education program instructor to curate a list of books that would serve as her co-teachers in this process. She approached the reading of children's literature that featured stories of immigration, migration, and home, with a critical lens, interrogating power in the (im)migration journeys. In planning her read-alouds, Crystal knew that it wouldn't be enough to focus on the reading strategies that were part of her literacy unit: tracking character change by noticing how they respond to challenges, identifying how the setting impacts the character and how the character responds to changes in their setting, and paying attention to how relationships between primary and secondary characters are developed in the story through dialogue and action details. All of this was important to support the readers in her class, but Crystal knew that this was an opportunity to also address intentional text selection and facilitate the processing of a difficult reality in children's lives. Therefore, Crystal merged character analysis reading objectives with a critical reading.

Crystal's *Dreamers* read-aloud included opportunities for students to discuss the challenges faced by author Yuyi Morales and her son when they arrived in San Francisco from Mexico. Crystal strategically selected excerpts to reread together as a class, emphasizing the changes and challenges as well as the illustrations to pause and discuss how Yuyi and her son faced those challenges. Crystal created a space for critical listening throughout the experience of engaging with *Dreamers*. Students listened to the author's experience as told through words and illustrations and had the support to hear from one another in discussions. When reading *My Papi Has a Motorcycle*, Crystal made side-by-side charts with words in English and in Spanish that they found in the text, noticing when the author, Isabel Quintero, included words in each of the languages, and adding an additional comment column where students added their ideas on what they wanted to try in their narrative writing. In reading Quintero's book and pausing at the illustrations by Zeke Peña, Crystal had students practice the dialogue between a parent and a child going through their beloved neighborhood and noticing the changes. Crystal wanted students to have ample opportunities to practice their reading and performance through these "scripts" made up of the content from the book and see the different ways we can talk about how and why communities change. This merge of reading strategies, writing applications, and critical reading, created spaces for children to learn about community change. Crystal's teaching moves were centered on children bearing witness to their realities and feeling empowered with the tools of analysis to understand the written word and their experiences.

Teaching Notes

Schools across the nation continue to see children and youth that bring with them their varied cultures, identities, literacies, and language practices. As the case study shows, it is crucial that schools respond to the dynamic lives of the kids in their classrooms by being aware of the community's socio-cultural and political landscape. Teachers must develop critical bilingual literacies (España & Herrera, 2020) that can position them to not only be responsive to children's lives but also grow a community of teaching and learning that values students' entire ways of being. A critical bilingual literacies approach is defined by four guiding principles—the first principle asks educators to engage in ongoing self-reflection of their language ideologies. The second principle calls for an unlearning of racialized and hierarchical language structures. The third urges educators to engage in an analysis of the ways that language, literacies, and power intersect. Finally, the fourth principle is to celebrate children and youth's dynamic language practices, including translanguaging—that is, creating intentional spaces to bring our entire linguistic repertoire for meaning-making (García, 2009).

A critical bilingual literacies framework is rooted in critical consciousness. For Freire (1970), critical consciousness means interrogating societal structures that maintain the status quo while affirming our role in disrupting hierarchies of power that reproduce oppression. In calling for ongoing self-reflection, we urge educators to grow their understanding of their ideas about language and literacy practices and how these impact their pedagogical approaches. In unlearning racialized language hierarchies, we call for an undoing of harmful narratives around students' community language practices that position "standard" English as the only acceptable way to communicate in learning spaces. In calling for educators to engage in an analysis of the relationship between language, literacies, and power, we recognize the importance of seeing our language and literacy practices through the lens of power and understanding how power can limit our ability to show up as our full selves in learning spaces. Lastly, celebrating students' translanguaging disrupts the linguistic borders (García & Solorza, 2021) that are often imposed in education; it encourages students to express themselves using all their linguistic repertoire, thereby normalizing children's dynamic language practices.

Scholars argue that critical consciousness must be foundational in a dual language bilingual education program (Cervantes-Soon et al., 2017; Palmer et al., 2019), and we argue here that in enacting a critical bilingual literacies framework, educators can grow their critical consciousness. For Crystal, this meant that she had to plan her teaching with a temas, textos, and translanguaging approach that is grounded on the CBL framework (España & Herrera, 2020). Temas are themes or topics that are culturally and linguistically sustaining (Paris & Alim, 2017) to the children and youth in our particular schooling contexts. Textos are multimodal texts that aid in teaching meaningful topics and affirm students' experiences, cultural, and language practices and support students in engaging with their own histories of struggle and community. Educators must also create intentional spaces for translanguaging pedagogy that engages students' entire linguistic repertoire and normalizes multilingual learning experiences—making room for students to develop as critical listeners to their own and their peers' experiences. The CBL approach to teaching can enable educators to be responsive to their students' particular socio-political and bilingual contexts, and create a powerful space for processing important issues while bringing with them their whole experiences, cultural ways of being, and language practices.

Teaching Activities

It was necessary for Crystal to respond by constructing a counter narrative to the harmful anti-immigrant rhetoric echoing outside the classroom walls by creating a unit of study that forged a space for meaningful learning about the topics of community (particularly centering immigrant experiences) and exploring the meaning of home. Crystal planned the unit with the three Ts in mind, thinking about topics that were central to the community context, and texts that would support the learning of those topics and affirm students' sense of belonging—their right to stay (see Table 24.1). Moreover, it was also important for students to bring in their entire selves by creating intentional spaces for translanguaging. That is, students were encouraged to use their entire linguistic repertoires in the reading of *Dreamers*, for example, when the author Yuyi Morales shares her immigration journey and how books became the safe space that sparked her sense of belonging in a new

Table 24.1 Planning with a Topic, Texts, and Translanguaging Approach

Topic: Community; the meaning of home

Texts:

- *Mi Papi Has a Motorcycle* by Isabel Quintero (2019), illustrated by Zeke Peña
- *¿De dónde eres?* and *Where Are You From?* by Yamile Saied Méndez (2019), illustrated by Jaime Kim
- *Soñadores: Dreamers* by Yuyi Morales (2018)
- *Alejandria Fights Back!/¡La lucha de Alejandria!* by Leticia Hernández-Linares and The Rise-Home Stories Project (2021), illustrated by Robert Liu-Trujillo

Translanguaging:

- Discuss and annotate using our entire language repertoire
- Play with language use in our own stories
- Perform scenes paying attention to translanguaging in texts
- Return to mentor texts to study word choice

country. Students used language fluidly, drawing from features of English and Spanish to share Yuyi's journey. Students were able to similarly use their entire linguistic resources to discuss how Yuyi navigates her new home. They shared about the spaces, people, and experiences that made them feel like they belonged.

Discussion Questions

1. Consider the issues that your school community is grappling with. Discuss with your learning community or thought partners the topics you may want to explore in the classroom to create space for children to process these issues.
2. What are the texts that can support the learning of the topics that you have identified? Discuss some possible text sets with your thought partners. We encourage you to see the resources on the Learning for Justice, Social Justice Books, and En Comunidad Collective websites.
3. What are the language practices of your students? How can you support students' translanguaging to ensure your students can bring their whole selves into the classroom community and into their learning?

Since Crystal's administration is expecting her to examine literary moves, she weaves in a language study across the different literacy units and pairs texts to provide students the space to analyze author's craft—particularly the ways authors engage with translanguaging in their writing—and uses those as mentor texts for showing students to use their entire linguistic repertoire in their own writing. This can help normalize the use of features from different languages alongside English in published work, thereby affirming students' own dynamic language practices. A language study can also give students an opportunity to critically explore ways authors use language by creating spaces for discussing notions about language hierarchies—specifically providing opportunities to disrupt harmful ideas about which language practices hold more value. When reading *Octopus Stew* by Eric Velasquez (2019) during a lesson on intergenerational connections, students in Crystal's class put into practice how they might use all their available linguistic features in their writing while also speculating the reasons for an author's specific language choices (see Table 24.2).

Discussion Questions

1. Consider the language demands of your curriculum. What are some ways you can use culturally and linguistically sustaining children's literature to support students in developing language for different purposes?
2. What are some ways that you can support the development students' writers' identities (that includes their fluid language use)?
3. How else can you incorporate mentor texts in your teaching? Discuss with your thought partners.

Table 24.2 Language Study Chart

Book Excerpts from Octopus Stew by Eric Velasquez (2019)	*Observations of Language Use*	*How can I try this as a writer?*
"Grandma snapped at me, 'I've been making pulpo guisado since your dad era un niño, since he was a boy.' I didn't want to upset her, so I didn't ask any more questions." (p. 2)	The author uses Spanish in this dialogue between Ramsey and his grandma. The author translates the words in Spanish in the same sentence.	This shows that I can also use all my languages when writing dialogue in my narrative writing to convey an authentic interaction between characters.
"The octopus got so big, it blew the lid off the top. '¡Wela, tenga cuidado!'" (p. 15)	Ramsey uses the word "*wela*" for grandmother, which is a variation of "*abuela*."	I can consider the language variations that exist in my community and include these in my writing; I can also include in my writing the different terms of endearment I use to refer to my family members and other loved ones.

Through her teaching, Crystal created a space for students to process and resist harmful narratives about their communities. Specifically, she was able to disrupt notions of language hierarchies, one of the guiding principles of CBL, by planning meaningful learning experiences with culturally and linguistically sustaining children's literature, which not only helped children process their ideas on immigration and belonging, but also provided opportunities for children to use all of their linguistic repertoire to discuss, annotate, and express their own ideas on belonging, implementing another CBL principle of valuing students' translanguaging. In applying a critical bilingual literacies framework in her planning and teaching, Crystal's critical consciousness grew as she recognized the power and possibility of impacting her students' lives.

References

Cervantes-Soon, C. G., Dorner, L., Palmer, D., Heiman, D., Schwerdtfeger, R., & Choi, J. (2017). Combating inequalities in two-way language immersion programs: Toward critical consciousness in bilingual education spaces. *Review of Research in Education, 41*(1), 403–427. https://doi.org/10.3102/0091732X17690120

Ed-Data. (2020). District summary. *California Department of Education*. www.ed-data.org/district/Fresno/Fresno-Unified

España, C., & Herrera, L. Y. (2020). *En comunidad: Lessons for centering the voices and experiences of bilingual Latinx students*. Heinemann.

Freire, P. (1970). *Pedagogy of the oppressed*. Continuum.

García, O. (2009). *Bilingual education in the 21st century: A global perspective.* Wiley-Blackwell.

García, O., & Solorza, C. R. (2021). Academic language and the minoritization of U.S. bilingual Latinx students. *Language and Education, 35*(6), 505–521. https://doi.org/10.1080/09500782.2020.1825476

Hernández-Linares, L., & The Rise-Home Stories Project. (2021). *Alejandria fights back! ¡La lucha de Alejandria!* The Feminist Press. https://www.feministpress.org/books-a-m/alejandria-fights-back-la-lucha-de-alejandria

Méndez, Y. S. (2019). *Where are you from?* HarperCollins.

Morales, Y. (2018). *Dreamers.* Neil Porter Books.

Palmer, D. K., Cervantes-Soon, C., Dorner, L., & Heiman, D. (2019). Bilingualism, biliteracy, biculturalism, and critical consciousness for all: Proposing a fourth fundamental goal for two-way dual language education. *Theory into Practice, 58*(2), 121–133. https://doi.org/10.1080/00405841.2019.1569376

Paris, D., & Alim, S. H. (2017). *Culturally sustaining pedagogy: Teaching and learning for justice in a changing world.* Teachers College Press.

Quintero, I. (2019). *My papi has a motorcycle.* Kokila.

US Census. (2019). *Quick facts.* www.census.gov/quickfacts/fact/table/fresnocitycalifornia,fresnocountycalifornia/PST045219

Velasquez, E. (2019). *Octopus stew.* Holiday House.

25 Building on Emotion

Experiencing, Confronting, and Reflecting on Patterns of Language Use in a TWI DL Classroom

Brenda Santiago González and Rachel Snyder Bhansari

Context

Two-way immersion (TWI) dual language education is relatively new in Washington state, and rapidly expanding. In 2019, 75 schools offered TWI DL, and in 2020, the Washington Office of Superintendent of Public Instruction released its goal of offering all students access to DL education by 2030 (Washington OSPI, 2022). This case study takes place in Dual Language Elementary School (DLES, pseudonym), which is one of the four dual language pathway elementary schools in Bellevue School District (BSD). DLES is a Title 1 DL school and its classroom teachers, 57.1% of whom were white, served 364 students during the 2020–21 school year. Its DL program follows a 90:10 English-Spanish TWI model, with one self-contained classroom per grade level.

DLES's student racial distribution is categorized as 35.7% "Hispanic" or Latino, 26.9% White, 21.2% Asian, 9.3% Black or African American, 6% two or more races, and 0.8% Native Hawaiian/Other Pacific Islander. In the 2019–2020 school year, Maestra Brenda's fourth grade classroom included 16 students. DLES follows a 50/50 quota model for student population (50% "native speakers" of Spanish, 50% "native speakers" of English). Brenda's fourth grade class included seven bilingual Latinx students, one multiracial student whose dominant language was English, and eight White students who spoke English at home. The class was majority female, with 12 students identifying as female and 4 as male.

Author Testimonio*: Brenda*

Born in Mexico City, Mexico, I was raised as an undocumented immigrant in the affluent and red-leaning Orange County in Southern California. My K–12 education took place during the era of Proposition 227, a 1998 law that made it significantly difficult for school districts in California to offer bilingual education to its students, allowing it only to be offered to students whose parents "opted in" to dual language classes. As a child to parents

DOI: 10.4324/9781003240594-30

who neither spoke English nor felt that schools were a place of service to the Latinx community, my parents were not privileged enough to be made aware of the option to opt in, and thus I received my K–12 education in English only, learning to understand, speak, read, and write Spanish at home, as a heritage Spanish speaker. My K–12 educational journey and my acquisition of Spanish language through my mother's commitment to my learning to love and appreciate the language of our Mexican culture was the bittersweet driving force that led me to pursue a master's in teaching, with a focus in bilingual education.

During one of my graduate courses, one professor asked us, "How do you feel knowing that you have to pay thousands and thousands of dollars in order for others to finally learn about you, your language, and your culture? How do you feel knowing that *you* have to pay so much to finally learn about *yourself*?" He was speaking to his Latinx students, and it was at that moment that I realized that I had never seen myself represented at school, aside from stereotypes and moments of tokenism. I realized that education in the US is rooted in racism and that it is not meant for my people. I also realized that it does not mean that we cannot work to change this narrative. My name is Brenda, and I identify as a Latina-Mexicana, and I learn and teach *por mi gente*, for my people.

Author Positionality: Rachel

I am a white woman who learned Spanish as an additional language in school. I worked as an elementary level bilingual teacher in Chicago for five years. I began my teaching career with limited awareness of the impacts of my identity, and have gained critical perspectives through relationships, and experiences working in bilingual education. During this case I was a doctoral candidate at the University of Washington and had the opportunity to teach and learn with Brenda.

Case Narrative

When Brenda began teaching in 2019, the majority of her fourth grade students had been classmates since kindergarten. DLES encouraged strict language separation by asking teachers to follow a predetermined schedule of language minutes in Spanish and English. Although the purpose of this policy was to give equitable time and attention to both languages, the culture of the school and existing relationships between students had positioned white students as both English experts and content experts, while Latinx students were frequently marginalized in classroom discourse occurring in either language. Engaged in a collaborative ethnography centered on power and racial inequities in her classroom, Maestra Brenda and I began to observe and discuss this dynamic. A collaborative ethnography is a research project that involves participants in collecting, analyzing, and/or writing about data in ways that are meaningful for all involved (Nagar, 2014). In what follows, we describe the ongoing and messy cycle of dialogue, reflection, and action that built critical consciousness for both of us and Brenda's students over the course of the year (Cervantes-Soon et al., 2017).

During one of our first conversations at the beginning of October, Brenda and I both noted that her white students had a shared culture of speaking to each other in Spanish with a heavy English-speaker "gringo" accent, jokingly, and also frequently used English to respond to classroom discussions in Spanish and/or Latinx peers. Brenda shared that she felt that this was frustrating and responded by telling them, "We (Latinos) don't talk like that," in reference to the students' joking accent. In an ongoing conversation regarding her students' linguistic attitudes with a teacher colleague, Brenda also noted that students preferred "English time":

Teacher Colleague: When I say we're switching to English, my kids are like, "Yayyyy!"

B: I hate that! I feel so disappointed.

Teacher Colleague: I know, me too. Every time, they're always happy . . .

B: Sometimes I get so annoyed, I tell them, "Stop it. I don't like your disrespect, that you're trying to say that you have some kind of relief because you're not speaking *my language* anymore." And it's like a relief for them, they're done with this horrible thing. Speaking Spanish.

As Brenda and her colleague highlighted, this emotional preference for English was painful for them as Latinx teachers. This dialogue and Brenda's reflection on her emotional reactions was significant in raising her critical consciousness of language use, and Brenda felt it was important to push white students to engage with discomfort and produce Spanish during Spanish-medium lessons.

Further, Brenda's emotions and related reflections supported her to notice moments when existent power dynamics in her classroom led to harm. In October, Brenda was leading a reading lesson in English when a Latinx student, Nadia, chose to share. As the student formulated her words, a white student, Sam, turned around and began to make taunting facial expressions. Nadia immediately put her head down on her desk and was unable to continue. Brenda whispered to her to take a break in her "cool-down" area, and later checked in with her, saying, "Does he know you? People will say stuff to us (as women of color) and we need to learn how to know ourselves and believe in ourselves." She also later asked the entire class to consider the impact the interaction had during the lesson; they had the following class conversation:

B: There's a difference between saying sorry to me and understanding the impact. It makes me sad that you're not getting the most out of our time together because this is really about your learning.

Lynn (White student): I think some people are also not being respectful because they're making fun of others when they try to share.

B: Do you think that's a problem?

Jonathan (Latinx student): Yes, because when you try to share and you're being made fun of, you don't want to, you feel sad.

B: What is the false assumption that people are making about you if you don't share?

Multiple Students: That you're not smart.

B: Right and who's the problem there? The person who is not sharing or the person who is making them feel bad and assuming things about them?

Jonathan: The person who is assuming.

In this moment, Brenda drew upon her emotional reaction and related critical consciousness to dialogue with students about assumptions and stereotypes. Brenda taught students a critical lesson regarding impact and acted in solidarity to support the student who had been harmed.

The existence of these power dynamics between white students and Latinx students in her class led Brenda to take action and require Spanish from all students during "Spanish time." Brenda felt it was important that white students experience discomfort and develop humility through acknowledgement of what they did not know. Further, Brenda called out moments when students were using English during Spanish time, explicitly asking white/English-dominant students to produce Spanish. Thus, Brenda used strict language policy during Spanish blocks as she worked to transform existing power dynamics in her classroom.

Centering Latinx Students: The *Leyendas*[1] Unit

Later, Brenda taught a unit she designed on *leyendas*, a set of lessons in Spanish that promoted authentic engagement from her Latinx students and increased Spanish use for all. In late January, Brenda and her students were working on writing their own *leyendas*, and Brenda had planned a lesson on *diálogo* (dialogue). At the end of the lesson, Jessica, a Latinx student who typically did not raise her hand in class, asked Maestra Brenda to share her *diálogo* because she was so proud of her work. Maestra Brenda waited until the whole class was seated and read the student's dialogue aloud, offering the student positive feedback based on her use of emotion. The student was visibly proud of herself and her work—a winning moment for the student and the Spanish language.

Two weeks later, after working on their *leyendas*, Brenda's students orally shared stories in Spanish in front of the class. This project and students' engagement shifted the established discourse patterns. Not only did White students who often avoided Spanish, such as Sam, read their stories aloud in Spanish, but they also offered feedback to peers in Spanish and dynamic mixtures of Spanish and English. Additionally, all students highlighted their academic smartness, and Brenda supported all students to share. Brenda stood with Nadia and Jessica, who had been afraid to speak in front of classmates previously. They read their *leyendas* and received praise from peers such as "*Me gustó que estabas diciendo a la maestra que no lo querías hacer pero lo hiciste.*" (I liked that you were saying to the teacher that you did not want to do it, but you did it.) Brenda later told me, "I wanted my students, particularly my Latina students, to know that their voices matter. That they are as important as anyone else."

Through these efforts, Brenda was able to raise the status of Spanish in her classroom and support the participation of her Latinx students. She also began to critically question the strict language policy of "Spanish-only" she had been using in Spanish blocks. Engaging in further dialogue, Brenda and I criticized the idea of language separation embedded in district language policy. In what follows, Brenda shares this reflection as a key part of her ongoing learning as a teacher.

Brenda's Reflection

My teaching graduate school program centered greatly on social justice in education. During this academic journey, I moved beyond the raw experience of racist education ideologies that oppressed me to a more removed academic examination of them; I was able to name and validate my experiences through critical thought and analysis. I felt very privileged for the opportunity to learn about ways through which we, as educators, can work towards disrupting and dismantling the systems in education that oppress certain student communities, and so I left my graduate school program with a newfound conviction that it was my duty to do just that. And it is, but perhaps not in the way I initially thought.

When I left my program, I was still deeply hurt. All of the trauma and sadness I experienced and endured as a bilingual student of color was unresolved, and I believed that the only way I could make justice for education's silencing of my language and my Latinx culture was to overcompensate through the safeguarding of them. I felt my language and my culture had become fragile crystals that I had to keep safe, and that I could empower them through the rigid adherence of my school district's 50/50 "Spanish minutes and English minutes," creating boxes for languages, as though that would help students see them as equals. In fact, during my first year, if a student came to me during "Spanish time" and asked me a question in English, I would insist that they use their Spanish. If the student told me they did not know the words, I would ask them to use our classroom's resources to try to find the words and then come back. I did this a few times and, each time, I felt in my heart that I was doing something wrong, yet I had convinced myself that I needed to do this lest I let the crystals I was guarding be shattered.

Thankfully, the love and beauty that shone so greatly in each of my students let me see that though what I wanted—equity in bilingual education—was right, the way I was approaching it was not. I realized I was striving to be better but was falling short. Through a lot of self-reflection, readings on equity in education, and the feedback of my students, I decided to change my perspective: I decided to be my authentic self; the one who is both from here *and* there, the one who uses Spanglish at home, the one who uses code-switching as a language all on its own, the one who sometimes prefers Spanish because "it's just not funny in English," and who sometimes prefers English because "I forgot how to say it in Spanish."[2] Both of these languages, and the experiences I learned them from, make me who I am, and I see this repeated in my students.

To be dedicated to equity means, I believe, to be responsive to our student communities, and if code-switching or Spanglish is part of or their preferred language repertoire, who am I to oppress it? Language should be taught and learned with love and, as educators, we need to remember that we are both teachers and students of our students. To laugh in Spanish, cry in English, both, or the other way around—it can happen all at the same time, in a beautiful complexity and naturalness that make us, bilingual speakers, who we are. The celebration of Spanish time being over in my classroom, by some students, signaled an imbalance not just of power, but of love for the languages. By creating a classroom with more fluid language changes, students felt more free to be their authentic selves. This was important not just for White students, but perhaps more to Latinx students, since my district does not account for the extra English they receive during specials and everywhere else in the school—they don't account for that hardship. So, if they want to speak more than 50% of Spanish in our class, why not?

Teaching Notes

This case study has considered the complex process of building critical consciousness regarding language use in TWI DL. Although teaching is emotional work, teachers are often expected to manage emotions in the midst of busy classroom days. For teachers of color, emotions are linked to personal histories and experiences, particularly the impacts of racism and linguicism in dominant society (Pacheco & Hamilton, 2020). Therefore, emotions can indicate knowledge of racial and linguistic inequity in the classroom (Sandoval, 2000). Also, emotions can support teachers to take action to shift these inequities and reflect on outcomes. Brenda's strong emotional reactions to existing discourse patterns helped her to take action and supported her to reflect and connect authentically with students through translanguaging. When did you last acknowledge your emotions or discuss these emotions with a colleague or mentor? We suggest that acknowledging emotions is an important part of the process of building and enacting critical consciousness.

One of the goals of an anti-racist bilingual education program should be students' achievement of biculturalism, or the development of positive cross-cultural attitudes, in order to become an aware and empathetic global citizen. To cultivate biculturalism in our classroom, we need to understand that every lesson planned either dismantles or maintains systems of oppression. And to dismantle oppression, we need to move beyond academics and connect with the organic beauty of our Spanish language and Latinx culture.

Discussion Questions

1. How is language used in your classroom space? How is that use related to power?
    1. Which students use English and the partner language and when? What status does English and/or the partner language hold in the classroom?
    2. How do students feel about using English and the partner language? How do students connect language to their identities? How can you support students to experience discomfort as part of language learning?
    3. To what extent do you model and invite translanguaging in your classroom? How do you use translanguaging in your life outside school?
    4. How could you potentially share your observations with students or bring them into a discussion regarding language use? How could you involve parents or community members?
2. What emotions are you experiencing in your daily work? How are these emotions related to your positionality?
    1. When you notice an intense emotion, where is it coming from? How might it relate to your awareness of power in your classroom?
    2. What do those emotions tell you about inequities in your classroom reality?

Recommended Resources

As educators, we are in a position of power and thus are able to create either liberating or dehumanizing experiences for our students. To delve deeper into this idea as well as to read about tools for justice in bilingual education, we recommend reading Drs. Carla España and Luz Yadira Herrera's book *En Comunidad: Lessons for Centering the Voices and Experiences of Bilingual Latinx Students*. We also recommend the PBS documentary *New World Rising*.

Notes

1. *Leyendas* can translate to legends or myths in English.
2. We consider code-switching and Spanglish to be a part of the broader language repertoire of multilingual communities, and treat them as practices included within translanguaging or dynamic language use (García, 2009).

References

Cervantes-Soon, C. G., Dorner, L., Palmer, D., Heiman, D., Schwerdtfeger, R., & Choi, J. (2017). Combating inequalities in two-way language immersion programs: Toward critical consciousness in bilingual education spaces. *Review of Research in Education, 41*(1), 403–427. https://doi.org/10.3102/0091732X17690120

García, O. (2009). *Bilingual education in the 21st century: A global perspective*. Wiley-Blackwell.

Nagar, R. (2014). *Muddying the waters: Co-authoring feminisms across scholarship and activism*. University of Illinois Press.

Pacheco, M., & Hamilton, C. (2020). Bilanguaging love: Latina/o/x bilingual students' subjectivities and sensitivities in dual language immersion contexts. *TESOL Quarterly, 54*(3), 548–571. https://doi.org/10.1002/tesq.585

Sandoval, C. (2000). *Methodology of the oppressed*. University of Minnesota Press.

Contributors Biographies

Stacie Aldana, MA, is a bilingual educator at a dual-language elementary school in Gilbert, AZ. She is a graduate of the Principal-Educational Leadership program at Northern Arizona University. She is endorsed in Bilingual Education and Structured English Immersion. Stacie is passionate about multilingualism and the benefits it creates for students developing their love for language.

Esmeralda Alday is the Executive Director of the Dual Language, ESL, and Migrant department in the San Antonio Independent School District (SAISD). Ms. Alday brings ten years of educational leadership experience to her role in SAISD in addition to seven years as a classroom teacher. She began her career working as a sheltered instruction middle school teacher in Houston ISD. Ms. Alday has her master's degree in curriculum and instruction from the University of Texas at Arlington and is currently pursuing a PhD in Educational Leadership and Policy at the University of Texas at San Antonio.

Cristina Alfaro, PhD, is the Associate Vice-President of International and Transborder Affairs at San Diego State University where she also served as Provost Chair of Diversity, Equity, and Inclusion. Dr. Alfaro is a Multilingual and Global Education Professor and Past Chair of the Dual Language and English Learner Education Department in the College of Education where she championed and led the largest bilingual teacher education program in the state of California. As a researcher she has examined and published on the role of educator critical ideological consciousness and pedagogical practices that situate access and equity at the core of Dual Language Bilingual Education.

Michael Bacon is Principal of Rose City Elementary School, Portland Public Schools. He worked in Portland Public Schools (PPS) as the Director of the Department of Dual Language for the past five years overseeing program, professional, and curriculum development for 16 dual language immersion (DLI) programs in Spanish, Japanese, Mandarin, Russian, and Vietnamese across 26 schools K–12. As a teacher he taught English in Japan for three years in a junior high school and then Japanese as a world language at middle and high school in Portland. He then taught Japanese and Social Studies for eight years in immersion designing, planning, and implementing innovative practices and curricula that continue today. This fall Michael made the decision to step back into the heart of the education school system as the interim principal of Rose City Park Elementary, home of a Vietnamese DLI program.

Luis "Tony" Báez, PhD, Urban Education, University of Wisconsin, Milwaukee. Retired. He is the Former Vice-President of the Board of the Milwaukee Public Schools; former member of the Executive Committee of the Wisconsin Association of School Board Members; former Chair of the National Latino Educational Research and Policy (NLERAP); former Provost and Chief Academic Officer of the Milwaukee Area Technical College (MATC); former Provost of Hostos Community College at the City University of New York in the Bronx; and Coordinator of the National Origin Desegregation Assistance Center at the University of Wisconsin, Milwaukee. He has been the recipient of many awards for racial and social justice including the Martin Luther King Heritage Award for Social Justice. In his name, the Wisconsin Association for Bilingual Education annually awards the Tony Báez Leadership and Advocacy Award. In 2020, he was the recipient of the prestigious international OHTLI Award given by Mexico to an advocate for the civil and educational rights of Latinos in the US.

Rachel Snyder Bhansari, PhD, is an Assistant Professor of Education at Portland State University, working in the Bilingual Teacher Pathway (BTP) program. She began her career as a third grade bilingual teacher in Chicago Public Schools, and taught in both transitional bilingual and dual language bilingual education programs. Her research focuses on teacher education for bilingual educators and racial equity in dual language classrooms.

Rhonda J. Broussard is Founder and CEO of Beloved Community, based on native Bulbancha land also known as New Orleans, Louisiana, which works at the nexus of Equity in Schools, Equity at Work, and Equity at Home. Previously, she founded a network of language immersion and International Baccalaureate world authorized schools, was a National Board-Certified Teacher and taught in public schools in drop-out recovery, college access, working-class, immigrant, and affluent school communities. Rhonda has earned a Bachelor of Arts in French and Secondary Education from Washington University in St. Louis, a Master of Arts in French Studies from The Institute of French Studies at New York University, and has studied in Cameroon, Martinique, Finland, New Zealand, and metropolitan France. Rhonda is the author of *One Good Question: How Countries Prepare Youth to Lead.*

Cory Buckband, MEd, is a Doctoral Student and Research Assistant Studying Educational Policy and Evaluation at Arizona State University, Mary Lou Fulton Teachers College. His areas of inquiry utilize anthropological perspectives of language and education to study the coloniality of language policy, dual language bilingual education and bilingualism, critical consciousness, and family engagement. Before joining the doctoral program, Cory was an educator in Phoenix, Arizona, teaching a range of secondary history and social science courses to culturally and linguistically diverse students.

Judith Flores Carmona, PhD, is Associate Professor in the Honors College and Interim Director of Chicano Programs at New Mexico State University (NMSU). Her academic and community work is guided by a sense of responsibility and commitment to social justice. Her research interests include critical pedagogy, critical race feminism, critical multicultural education, and *testimonio* methodology and pedagogy.

Claudia G. Cervantes-Soon, PhD, is Associate Professor of Bilingual Education at Arizona State University and a former K–12 bilingual educator. Her research draws on ethnographic approaches, critical pedagogies, and Chicana/Latina feminisms to examine sociocultural, pedagogical, and policy factors affecting the teaching and learning experiences of children, youth, and families from historically marginalized communities, particularly in bilingual, bicultural, and borderlands communities. She is the author of the award-winning book *Juárez Girls Rising: Transformative Education in Times of Dystopia*, and the recipient of many awards including a 2017 Spencer Postdoctoral Fellowship, the 2019 AERA Bilingual Education SIG Early Career Award, and the 2019 Doug Foley Early Career Award from the Council of Anthropology and Education.

Ayanna Cooper, EdD, is a Consultant, US Department of State English Language Specialist alumna, and current TESOL Board Member. She is the author of several publications including *And Justice for Els: A Leader's Guide to Creating and Sustaining Equitable Schools*, and serves as *Language Magazine's* "Pass the Mic" series editor.

Emily R. Crawford, PhD, is an Associate Professor at the University of Missouri in the Educational Leadership and Policy Analysis department. Her research examines the intersections among immigration policy, educational policy, K–12 leadership, and ethics. Her projects seek to understand the ways Pre-K–12 educators—particularly school leaders—perceive and provide educational and schooling access for immigrant students and families of mixed legal status.

M. Garrett Delavan, PhD, is an Assistant Professor of World, Dual, and ESOL Language Education at Georgia State University. He studies whether language education planning creates equitable access to program types, effective teaching practices, and curriculum content (especially regarding ecojustice).

David DeMatthews, PhD, is an Associate Professor in the Department of Educational Leadership and Policy at the University of Texas at Austin. David has worked with urban districts as a high school teacher, middle school administrator, and district administrator. He studies issues related to school leadership, bilingual and special education, and social justice.

Lisa M. Dorner, PhD, is an Associate Professor in the Department of Educational Leadership and Policy Analysis at the University of Missouri, Columbia, a teacher, researcher, life-long learner, and a lover of language, intercultural connection, and the idea of *educación*. Her work falls into three main areas: the politics/planning of bilingual education, educational policy implementation, and immigrant family integration in "new" spaces (like rural Missouri), including the work children do as language brokers. She is especially interested in developing community-engaged studies of educational policy enactment with local organizations, educators, immigrant families, and youth. Her website is *lisamdorner.com*.

Caitlín Dougherty, MA, is a Doctoral Candidate in the Equity, Bilingualism and Biliteracy program at the University of Colorado, Boulder. A former Language Arts and Social Studies teacher at a DLBE middle school in Baltimore, her research uses critical theory to investigate how teachers implement language policies in multilingual classrooms with a focus on the interactions between ideology and identity.

Carla España, PhD, is an Assistant Professor of Bilingual Education and Puerto Rican/Latinx and Latin American Studies at Brooklyn College, City University of New York. She is a middle-grade teacher, researcher, author, and co-founder of the En Comunidad Collective. She is the co-author of *En Comunidad: Lessons for Centering the Voices and Experiences of Bilingual Latinx Students* with Dr. Luz Yadira Herrera.

Nelson Flores, PhD, is an Associate Professor in educational linguistics at the University of Pennsylvania Graduate School of Education. His research examines how language and race intersect in bilingual education policies and practices in ways that are harmful to racialized bilingual students. He is the recipient of many awards including the 2017 AERA Bilingual Education SIG Early Career Award, a 2017 Spencer Postdoctoral Fellowship, and the 2019 James Alatis Prize for Research on Language Planning and Policy in Educational Contexts.

Juan A. Freire, PhD, is an Associate Professor in the Department of Teacher Education at Brigham Young University in Provo, Utah. He worked for several years as an elementary school teacher in Spain and a Spanish-English dual language bilingual education (DLBE) program in

Utah. His research focuses on equity in DLBE in the areas of multicultural/bilingual teacher research and the analysis of policy, planning, and programming.

Belinda Bustos Flores, PhD, is an Associate Dean of Professional Preparation and Partnerships, and Professor in the Department of Bicultural-Bilingual Studies in the College of Education and Human Development at the University of Texas at San Antonio. Dr. Flores has been recognized for her work by various organizations including the San Antonio Women's Hall of Fame and Texas Association for Bilingual Education, and has received the 2015 AERA Hispanic Research Issues SIG Elementary, Secondary, and Postsecondary Award and the 2019 AERA Bilingual Research SIG Lifetime Achievement Award.

Brittany L. Frieson, PhD, is an Assistant Professor of Literacy and Antiracist Education at the University of North Texas. Her research interests include critical perspectives of bilingual education, Black languages, and literacies in dual language bilingual education, anti-racist and critical pedagogical practices in literacy, and bilingual education. Her research has appeared in multiple academic outlets including *Race Ethnicity and Education*, *Annual Review of Applied Linguistics*, *Bilingual Research Journal*, *Teaching and Teacher Education*, and *Literacy Research: Theory, Method, and Practice*, among many others.

Mary Gilreath, MAT, has been teaching first grade in a dual immersion program in Boulder, CO for 22 years. She received her Masters in Teaching Linguistically Diverse Students from the School for International Training in Vermont. Despite being a veteran teacher, Mary pushes herself to challenge the pedagogical practices in her classroom and school every year. She loves to collaborate with the University of Colorado School of Education and believes that being a lifelong learner is essential to being an effective educator.

Rosalyn Harvey-Torres, PhD, is an Assistant Professor of Reading and Biliteracy in the Department of Early Childhood and Elementary Education at Georgia State University. Before becoming a professor, she was a bilingual paraprofessional and elementary school teacher in Michigan, Texas, and Mexico. Rosalyn's work focuses on student and teacher agency, biliteracy, and writing pedagogy.

Dan Heiman, PhD, is an Assistant Professor of Bilingual/Biliteracy Education in the Department of Teacher Education at the University of Texas at El Paso. A former bilingual teacher in El Paso, Texas, and teacher educator at the University of Veracruz, México, his critical ethnographic research examines critical pedagogies, social justice, and *acompañamiento* in dual language bilingual education (DLBE) and bilingual teacher preparation contexts. He teaches and publishes in both English and Spanish and his work has appeared in *Anthropology & Education Quarterly*, *The Journal of Language, Identity, and Education*, *Language Policy*, and *La Revista Bilingüe*.

Kathryn I. Henderson, PhD, is an Associate Professor in the Department of Bicultural-Bilingual Studies in the College of Education and Human Development at the University of Texas at San Antonio. She completed her PhD (2015) at the University of Texas at Austin in the Bilingual/Bicultural Program in the Department of Curriculum and Instruction. After completing her BA (2004) at Washington University in St. Louis, she taught elementary school for five years abroad in Guadalajara, Mexico, during which time she earned her M.A. (2009) in education. Her education interests include language ideologies, language policy, and dual language bilingual education programs.

Olivia Hernández, EdD, is a Southwest Region Consultant Partner at The New Teacher Project. Throughout her 37-year career in bilingual education, she has served as a bilingual teacher, assistant principal, principal of a dual language campus, bilingual director in Austin ISD, and as the Assistant Superintendent for Learning, Language, and Literacy in San Antonio ISD. Dr. Hernández holds an EdD in educational leadership from the University of Texas, Rio Grande Valley. She is also the 2022 Texas Association for Bilingual Education president and recently founded the nonprofit organization Dual Language de Tejas. She strives every day to establish dual language education as the norm nationwide.

Luz Yadira Herrera, PhD, is an Assistant Professor of bilingual education in the School of Education at California State University, Channel Islands. She is the co-author of *En Comunidad: Lessons for Centering the Voices and Experiences of Bilingual Latinx Students* with Dr. Carla España.

Caroline Hesse, EdD, is a (Dual Language) Bilingual Teacher who has taught for 18 years in a variety of bilingual and monolingual K–21 settings, from high school and middle school to college and elementary levels. She holds a BS from Beloit College, an M.A. from Viterbo University and the Universidad de Salamanca, and completed her doctorate in curriculum and instruction with a focus on bilingual education at the University of Texas, Rio Grande Valley. Her research interests lie at the intersections of curriculum, multilingualism, identity, dual language bilingual education, and social justice.

Andrew H. Hurie, PhD, is an Assistant Professor of Bilingual/Biliteracy Education at Texas State University. A former bilingual teacher and school administrator in Milwaukee, he earned a PhD in curriculum and instruction from the University of Texas at Austin. His research uses qualitative methods and critical theories to examine education policies and practices, with specific attention to educational justice for language minoritized students and communities.

Elena Izquierdo, PhD, is a Professor of Bilingual/Biliteracy/Dual Language at the University of Texas at El Paso. She is a linguist by training, holding a PhD in Applied Linguistics and Bilingual Education from Georgetown University in Washington, DC, and an educator in practice with 13 years as an administrator in Washington, DC Public Schools where she served as the principal of one of the first dual language bilingual education (DLBE) models in this country: the Oyster Bilingual School. Her research, interests, and expertise are in the areas of leadership in dual language bilingual education and biliteracy.

Faith R. Kares, PhD, is the Senior Director of Research and Impact at Beloved Community and professor at the University of Illinois at Chicago. She has nearly twenty years of experience conducting mixed-methods research in various contexts, including but not limited to evaluating the efficacy of California's juvenile justice system, studying the impact of STEM out-of-school time programming on the science and career identities of historically excluded youth in Chicago, conducting ethnographic research among working poor families in Metro Manila advocating for affordable housing, and evaluating the operations and practices of the Chicago Police Department as part of the city's police reform efforts. Dr. Kares's work raises questions of power, (in)equity, in/exclusion, and justice, through an enduring commitment to innovative research design and participatory methodologies. She holds a PhD in cultural anthropology from Northwestern University.

Yalda M. Kaveh, PhD, is Assistant Professor of Bilingual Education at the Mary Lou Fulton Teachers College at Arizona State University. Her research focuses on the intersections of language practices in immigrant families and communities, educational policy, and the connections between educational and family language policies. For the past three years, Yalda has led a research partnership with a dual language program in a Title I urban public school in Arizona.

Tatyana Kleyn, EdD, is Associate Professor in the Bilingual Education and TESOL Programs at the City College of New York. She is Principal Investigator for the City University of New York—Initiative on Immigration and Education (CUNY—IIE). Tatyana has written about and produced and directed videos in the areas of migration, language, and education. Her latest book is titled *Living, Learning and Languaging Across Borders: Students Between the US and Mexico*. For more information see *TatyanaKleyn.com*.

Jillian La Serna, PhD, is an Assistant Professor of Educational Leadership at the University of North Carolina at Charlotte. She received her BA from California State University, Sacramento. She earned her MSA and EdD in Educational Leadership from the University of North Carolina at Chapel Hill. Jillian has worked in education for over twenty years of K–12 experience having worked as an instructional assistant, classroom teacher, assistant principal, dual language reading specialist, and dual language principal. Her research centers on race, culture, social justice, and leadership in K–12 schools, with an emphasis on dual language bilingual education.

Sandra Leu Bonanno, PhD, is an Educational Researcher at WestEd, whose work examines Multilingual and Multicultural Education and Leadership, with particular attention to culturally and linguistically sustaining education. Dr. Leu Bonanno's current work engages multiple invested partners across state, district, and school educational contexts to implement equitable policy for multilingual learners.

Dina López, EdD, is Associate Professor in the Bilingual Education and TESOL Programs at the City College of New York. Her research is located at the intersection of sociocultural approaches to language and literacy, the anthropology of education, and immigration and education. She has written extensively about bilingual education, immigration, and adolescent literacy both in Latin America and the United States. Most recently, her work has examined translanguaging as both a language practice and pedagogical tool in elementary bilingual education classrooms.

Christopher Milk Bonilla, PhD, is a Professor of Teacher Education at Texas State University at San Marcos. He has published articles on bilingual teacher and community leadership development around critical issues in Latinx education. He has led workshops on how to integrate the community into educational programs, improve home-school relationships and community educational leadership development. He combines his knowledge of community organizing and instructional theory and practice to promote more inclusive Latinx community-based educational leadership.

Leyla Olano, BA, is an Elementary School Administrator in Central Texas. She is a graduate of the Texas Principal Leadership Academy at the University of Texas at Austin. Leyla studies issues related to dual language education, restorative practice, and instructional coaching.

María de los Ángeles Osorio de la Rosa, PhD, is Program Director at University of Colorado, Boulder, School of Education, working to advance equitable partnerships between families and educators in the Denver metro area. Her work is informed by community organizing theories that guide her research in family and community engagement and participation in educational matters of CLD students.

Deborah Palmer, PhD, is Professor of Equity, Bilingualism, and Biliteracy in the School of Education at the University of Colorado, Boulder, and affiliate faculty in the Department of Ethnic Studies and the Culture, Language and Social Practice (CLASP) program. A former dual language bilingual teacher in California, she is a qualitative researcher who conducts critical ethnography and discourse analysis in bilingual and multilingual classrooms. Her research focus is on supporting equity and justice in dual language bilingual contexts and supporting all teachers to effectively teach bilingual students.

Jennifer Phuong, PhD, is a Visiting Assistant Professor of Educational Studies at Swarthmore College. She holds a PhD in educational linguistics from the University of Pennsylvania, where she studied teacher collaboration and the social construction of categories of learners considering the intersection of race, language, and disability. Prior to academia, Jennifer was a special education high school teacher in Brooklyn, New York, where she worked primarily with multilingual students of color labeled as disabled. These professional experiences, in conjunction with her personal experiences as a multiply marginalized woman, have mediated her commitment to educational justice in research and teaching.

Vivian E. Presiado, MS, is Assistant Professor of Bilingual and Bicultural Education in the School of Teaching and Learning at Illinois State University. She is a former early childhood bilingual education teacher who is deeply passionate about the language and literacy practices of young linguistically diverse children and their families participating in bilingual programs. Her research has appeared in various academic outlets including *Literacy Research: Theory, Method, and Practice* and *Journal of Literacy Research*.

Steve Daniel Przymus, PhD, is an Associate Professor of Educational Linguistics at Texas Christian University (TCU). Steve earned a doctorate in Second Language Acquisition and Teaching (SLAT) from the University of Arizona in 2016 and has lived in the Dominican Republic as a Peace Corps volunteer (2003–2005) and in Mexico as a Fulbright Distinguished Awardee in Teaching (Chiapas, 2010). He teaches courses in Bilingual Education, Bilingual Special Education, and Sociolinguistics. His research focuses on conceptual metonymy and metaphor in school-scapes and translanguaging in instruction, in assessment for distinguishing language difference from disability, in online gaming/spaces for language and identity development, and in community-based biliteracy development.

Nicole Caridad Ralston, PhD, is the Director of Education and Programming at Beloved Community where she supports the team in strategy, processes, and visioning as it relates to Beloved's content, curriculum, and facilitation services, and is an adjunct professor at the University of New Orleans. In her previous career in higher education, she developed retention and community engagement initiatives, built social justice education programs, taught courses on the White savior complex, and led the undocumented student support committee. She is devoted to creating spaces where those who have been pushed to the margins can be centered, seen, and heard. Dr. Ralston's doctoral research focused on how women of color in higher education navigated their identities in their leadership roles.

Brenda Santiago González, MAT, is a first-generation Latina college graduate. She received her Master's in Teaching from the University of Washington and is currently a fourth grade dual language teacher. Brenda loves learning about race and equity and its impact in the public education system, especially on Latinx students.

Maria Patrizia Santos is a social epidemiologist who specializes in race/ethnicity, social and economic disparities, and belongingness. Santos has more than three years of experience conducting mixed-methods research in various contexts, including but not limited to exploring the social and structural factors affecting micronutrient powder adherence and childhood anemia, social inequities in the double burden of malnutrition, and practices promoting equity and belongingness in schools and at work. Maria Patrizia holds a Master's of Science in Public Health from Tulane University and is a current PhD student in Epidemiology at Tulane.

Jody Slavick, PhD, is Research Associate for the BUENO Center at the University of Colorado, Boulder, where she directs professional development for the Literacy Squared® project. Her research interests include the design and implementation of bilingual/dual language programs, strategies to promote biliteracy, and preparing teachers to work with emerging bilingual students.

Wenyang Sun, PhD, is Assistant Professor of multilingual/multicultural education in the Department of Education, Culture, and Society at the University of Utah. Her research interests include bilingual education, immigrant families, and Asian American studies. Her current inquiries focus on the language ideologies and the social context of language education for language minoritized communities.

Vân Truong, EdD, came to the United States as a refugee from Vietnam when she was a high school student. Dr. Truong has over thirty years of experience increasing student achievement and closing opportunity gaps through students, educators, and families/partners. She was most recently Portland Public Schools' (PPS) Interim Assistant Superintendent of Teaching and Learning where she led district curriculum departments, including Dual Language programs. She started the Vietnamese Dual Language (VDL) program in PPS eight years ago; when it was the second VDL program in the United States. Dr. Truong is fluent in French, Vietnamese, and English.

Carmela Valdez, MEd, is an early childhood dual language teacher in Austin, Texas. She has an undergraduate degree from the University of

Texas and a Master's in education from Texas State University. Carmela has been a teacher for 15 years and loves to walk alongside young writers as they discover their voice.

Verónica E. Valdez, PhD, is Professor in the Department of Education, Culture, and Society at the University of Utah. Her research focuses on critical language policy and planning, dual language bilingual education, preparation of teachers serving culturally and linguistically diverse students, and the language education efforts in families, schools, and communities of linguistically diverse students.

Angela Valenzuela, PhD, is Professor in both the Cultural Studies in Education Program within the Department of Curriculum and Instruction and in the Educational Policy and Planning Program within the Department of Education Leadership and Policy at the University of Texas at Austin where she also serves as the director of the Texas Center for Education Policy. She is the author of *Subtractive Schooling: U.S. Mexican Youth and the Politics of Caring* (1999), *Leaving Children Behind: How "Texas-style" Accountability Fails Latino Youth* (2005) and *Growing Critically Conscious Teachers: A Social Justice Curriculum for Educators of Latino/a Youth* (2016). Valenzuela's research and teaching interests are in the sociology of education, minority youth in schools, educational policy, urban education reform, culturally relevant curriculum, ethnic studies, and indigenous education, as well as policy studies and analysis.

Karla Venegas, MSEd, is a doctoral candidate in the Educational Linguistics department at the University of Pennsylvania Graduate School of Education. Her research focuses on interrogating the construction of leadership as it relates to the experience of racialized school leaders in bilingual educational settings. Karla is an educator who leads with joy and works to sustain and affirm the excellence and genius of children of color. She holds a certification in school leadership from the University of Pennsylvania, an MSEd in Early Childhood Education from Hunter College, and a BA from the University of Pennsylvania.

Emily Zoeller, EdD, is Assistant Professor at Edgewood College in Madison, Wisconsin, where she coordinates the Language and Literacy program for teacher preparation in Reading, ESL, and Bilingual Education. Emily holds a BA from the University of Notre Dame and an MA from the University of San Diego. She earned an EdD in Educational Leadership from Edgewood College, where she researched teacher leadership in two-way dual language education. Emily has over 15 years of experience serving in K–12 public schools as a bilingual teacher, an instructional coach, and a bilingual reading specialist; these experiences fuel her research interests in bilingual teacher preparation and biliteracy development. Emily is passionate about leading anti-racist work among teachers of multilingual youth.

Index

Note: Page numbers in *italics* indicate a figure and page numbers in **bold** indicate a table on the corresponding page. Page numbers followed by "n" refer to notes.

Academia Cuauhtli (AC) 10–11, 168, 169–173; *cariño* 172–173; *convivios* 169–170, 171, 172, 173; critical examination of indigenous knowledges 172–173; *curanderas* (women healers) 170–171; *plantas medicinales* (medicinal plants) 169–171; *pláticas* 169, 170, 171, 172, 173
acompañamiento 4, 12, 41–42, 43, 44, 150, 151, 226, 227
activist burn-out 143
African Americans 8, 11, 95, 114, 179–185; Black English 106, 179, 180, 181, 183, 184; of Haitian descent 30–38; leadership 104–111; mindsets pertaining to Black students 106–107, 109
Aldana, S. 188, 189–192, 194n3
Alday, E. 5, 40
Alfaro, C. 8–9
anti-racism 8, 33, 48, 104–111, 107
anti-racist practices 8, 108, 109
Anzaldúa, G. 12, 216–217
authentic caring 172

backward curriculum planning 219
Bacon, M. 8
Báez, L. T. 10, 162–163
Baker-Bell, A. 184
Bellevue School District (BSD) 238
Beverly, J. 214
Bhansari, R. S. 13, 239
bilingual-bicultural education (BBE) 158–159, 162
Bilingual Education Act 108, 158, 159
bilingual education program: 50:50 model 98, 133, 223, 238; 80:20 model 133; 90:10 model 98, 205; 1.5-way bilingual education 55–65; one-way developmental bilingual education 5, 7, 10–11, 14, 21–28, 39–46, 196–203, 213–220, 230–236; one-way foreign language immersion 14, 104–111, 112–119, 139–147; two-way immersion 2, 14, 30–38, 47–53, 55–56, 67–74, 77–84, 85–93, 95–102, 131–138, 149–155, 179–185, 187–194, 205–211, 222–228, 238–244
bilingual redesign committee (BRC) 85–93; meeting agendas, planning **91–93**; objectives 90–91
biliteracy 25, 37, 108, 117, 179, 222–228, 230–236
Boston Public Schools (BPS) 30–38
Brackenridge High School (BHS) 39–40, 41; recruitment of students 40–41; selection and training of teachers 41–42; structuring DL program 41; teacher *testimonios* 42–45
Brochin, C. 191
Broughton, A. J. 200
Broussard, R. J. 8
Buckband, C. 10

calpulli 169
Carmona, J. F. 12, 214, 215, *220*
Cervantes-Soon, C. G. 192
charter schools 8, 55–65, 104–111, 159, 162
children's literature 232

Chinese 9, 96–97, 98, 131–138
Cioè-Peña, M. 70
City-Wide Bilingual Bicultural Advisory Committee (CWBBAC) 158, 159, 163, 164
Civil Rights Act 144, 158–159
Collier, V. P. 70, 112
commodification of language 112, 115, 117–118
community(ies): of color 36, 82–83, 163, 179; engagement 9–10, 32–33, 36, 37, 50, 125, 136, 144, 155, 158–162, 163, 164; of solidarity 139, 143, 144–145, 146, 147
community learning exchanges (CLE) 90
conscientization calls 68, 69, 70, 72
constructive feedback 107
content-based story retells 12, 198–199, 201–203
contextual distrust 145
convivios 169–170, 171, 172, 173
Cooper, A. 5
counter-narratives 230–236
COVID-19 pandemic 10, 149–155
Crenshaw, K. 13
critical consciousness 2–4, 23–26, **28**, 78, 104, 144, 149–150, 153–154, 233; *acompañamiento* 4, 12, 41–42, 43, 44, 150, 151, 226, 227; affirming identities 3, 12, 42–45, 90, 225; critical listening 3, 23, 40–41, 51–52, 57, 58, 70, 71, 72, 73, 88, 90, 118, 122, 132–133, 135, 136, 137, 150, 152, 184, 191, 201, 210, 217, 224, 226, 227, 232; embracing discomfort 3, 23, 25–26, 40–41, 57, 60–61, 70, 71–72, 73, 88–89, 90, 118, 122, 189, 191, 201, 210, 224, 241; historicizing 3, 23, 24, 26, 35, 51, 70, 73, 81, 87, 100, 118, 124, 126, 136, 165, 170, 173, 210, 216, 224, 227; interrogating power 3, 9, 24, 41, 51, 52, 73, 86, 100, 118, 124, 126, 133–135, 136, 170, 173, 184, 201, 210, 216, 217, 223–224, 226, 227, 240, 241; translanguaging 4, 13, 44, 45, 60, 72, 79–80, 190, 200, 233, 234–235, 236, 243
critical consciousness decision-making (CCDM) model 200–201, *201*, 203
critical conversations 24, 26, 183, 206, 207–208, 209–210
critical ethnography 150
critical pedagogy 47–53, 124, 149, 150, 154, 155
critical policy analysis 67–74
culturally and linguistically sustaining school leadership (CLSL) 82–83
curanderas (women healers) 10, 170–171
curriculum 25, 98, 169–171, 172, 182, 214–216; backward curriculum planning 219; bilingual-bicultural education 163; Haitian Creole two-way immersion 32–33; Spanish two-way immersion 48–50, 51; Vietnamese two-way immersion 116
Curry, M. 172

Danticat, E. 48
Dantley, M. E. 81
Delavan, M. G. 6
DeMatthews, D. 7
Diemer, M. A. 82
disability rights 196–203
discomfort, embracing 3, 23, 25–26, 40–41, 52, 57, 60–61, 70, 71–72, 73, 88–89, 90, 118, 122, 189, 191, 201, 210, 224, 241
distrust 145
DLBE communities, research methods: counter-narratives 230–236; critical policy analysis 67–74; ethnography 55–61, 64–65, 150, 239–240; *pláticas* 7, 88–89, 90, 169, 170, 171, 172, 173; *testimonios* 12, 42–45, 85, 206, 208–209, 211, 213–220
DLBE programs, types of 179–185; 50:50 model 98, 133, 223, 238; 80:20 model 133; 90:10 model 98, 205; developmental bilingual education 14, 21–28, 39–46, 196–203, 213–220, 230–236; one-way foreign language, one-way world language 14, 104–111, 139–147; transitional bilingual education 23, 26, 85, 89, 108, 164; two-way immersion 2, 14, 30–38, 47–53, 55–56, 67–74, 77–84, 85–93, 95–102, 112–119, 131–138, 149–155, 187–194, 205–211, 222–228, 238–244
Dorner, L. M. 50, 101
Dougherty, C. 12, 190
Dreamers (Morales) 232, 234–235

Elementary and Secondary Education Act 144
Equal Protection Clause 101
equity 89, 136, 210, 218, 243; dual language bilingual education 1–2,

6, 36, 51, 67–74, 79, 205; family engagement 154–155; linguistic 115; racial 8, 113–114, 117
Escuela Bilingüe Foster 10
España, C. 13
ethnography 55–61, 64–65, 150, 239–240
Every Student Succeeds Act (ESSA) 144
external perspective of bilingualism 200

family engagement 9–10, 102, 136, 139–146, 144, 149–155, 169–174, 181, 225–226
feedback 107, 108
Fein, J. G. 216, 217
Ferrón, M. 40
Fleurissaint, Rev. D. J. 35
Flores, N. 6, 59
Freire, J. A. 6, 12, 214
Freire, P. 104, 125–126, 127, 143, 233
French 8, 32, 96–97, 104–111
Friends from the Other Side/Amigos del Otro Lado (Anzaldúa) 217
Frieson, B. L. 11
Fujianese 132

Gamere, J. 35
García, O. 13
gender/gender identity 12, 187–194
gentrification 47, 50, 51, 67, 69, 70, 71, 72, 95, 97, 99
Germain, D. 33
Gilreath, M, 188–189, 190–192, 194n3
Gramsci, A. 123
Green, T. L. 165

Haitian Creole 5, 30–38
Harvey-Torres, R. 13, 222, 224
Heart of Texas Writing Project (HTWP) 223–224
Henderson, K. I. 5, 7
Henderson, W. 35
heritage/indigenous language revitalization 14
Hernández, O. 5, 7, 85, 86–87, 88
Herrera, L. Y. 13
Hesse, C. 12
historicizing 3, 23, 24, 26, 35, 51, 70, 73, 81, 87, 100, 118, 124, 126, 136, 165, 170, 173, 210, 216, 224, 227
Hogu, L. 33, 37
hopelessness 143
Horn, R. 216, 217
Howards, A. 7, 77–81, 83
Hurie, A. H. 10

identity 81–82, 219; affirming 3, 12, 42–45, 90, 225; African American 105–106; awareness of 78; gender 187–194; indigenous 173; and language 105, 106; and leadership 107
ideological clarity 122, 123, 126–127, 163
ideological consciousness 122, 123, 125, 126
ideology(ies): definition of 123; raciolinguistic 55–61; and teaching 125–126
internal perspective of bilingualism 200
intersectionality 191–192
Ishimaru, A. M. 145
Izquierdo, E. 5

Kares, F. R. 8
Kaveh, Y. M. 10
Kettering Foundation 124
Kleyn, T. 5

language: production process 199–200; separation policy 72, 239, 242
language immersion: one-way foreign language immersion 14, 104–111, 112–119, 139–147; two-way immersion 2, 14, 30–38, 47–53, 55–56, 67–74, 77–84, 85–93, 95–102, 131–138, 149–155, 179–185, 187–194, 205–211, 222–228, 238–244
languagelessness 56, 59, 61
languages taught in DLBE programs: Chinese 9, 96–97, 98, 131–138; French 8, 96–97, 104–111; Haitian Creole 30–38, 55; Spanish 5, 7, 10–11, 21–28, 39–46, 47–53, 55–65, 67–74, 77–84, 85–93, 95–102, 112, 139–147, 179–185, 187–194, 196–203, 205–211, 213–220, 222–228, 230–236, 238–244; Vietnamese 8, 112–119
La Serna, J. 12
Latino Network 112
Latinx 6, 7, 11, 27, 41, 47, 68–74, 114, 183, 230–236, 238–244; Academia Cuauhtli 168, 169–173; culturally sustaining school leadership 77–84; Nuestro Grupo 168; parents 139–143, 158–164; raciolinguistic ideologies

55–61; school leadership 95–102; social movements 158; writer's workshop 222–228
Lau Remedies 158–159
Leu Bonanno, S. 7
LGBTQ+ students 12, 187–194
López, D. 5
L'Ouverture, T. 31

Mama's Nightingale: A Story of Immigration and Separation (Danticat) 48–50, 51–52
Mandarin 131–138
Mattahunt Elementary School 31, 32
Mayer, M. 198
Mendez, E. 162–163
Milk, C. 10
Milwaukee Public Schools (MPS) 158–160, 161, 164
Moore, S. C. K. 70
Morales, Y. 232, 234–235
Mountain View Elementary (MVE) 187–194
Muhammad, G. 184
Murillo, L. A. 185
My Papi Has a Motorcycle (Quintero) 232

neoliberalism 118, 146, 159, 164
No Child Left Behind 144
Noddings, N. 172
Nuestro Grupo 168

Ochoa, A. 124
Octopus Stew (Velasquez) 235, **236**
Office for Civil Rights (OCR) 139
Okun, T. 108
Olana, L. 7
one-way developmental bilingual education 14, 21–28, 39–46, 196–203, 213–220, 230–236
one-way foreign language immersion 14; French 104–111; Spanish 139–147
Osorio de la Rosa, M. A. 9
Otheguy, R. 200
Ozuna, E. 40

Pacific Education Group (PEG) 113, 114
Palmer, D. K. 12, 51, 68, 100, 187, 188, 213
parent committee 160–162, 163
parent/family activism 10, 143, 158–165
parent teacher association (PTA) 96–97, 99
pedagogy: Academia Cuauhtli 169–173; anti-racist 180–185; critical 47–53, 124, 149, 150, 154, 155; culturally and linguistically sustaining 83; gender-inclusive 187–194; and ideological consciousness 122; *testimonio* 12, 213–220; writer's workshop 222–228
Peña, Z. 232
Pfarr-San Juan-Alamo ISD (PSJA) 39, 42
Phuong, J. 6, 58
Plancher, I. 31–32
plantas medicinales (medicinal plants) 10, 169–171
pláticas (dialogues) 7, 88–89, 90, 169, 170, 171, 172, 173
Plyler v. Doe 101
policy(ies) 5–6, 23–24, 50, 61, 87, 122; anti-immigrant 48; critical policy analysis 67–74; development, and leadership 27–28; enactment 5, 50, 52; implementation 23–24, 27, 50; language 125, 139, 141, 241, 242; language separation policy 72, 239, 242; teachers as policymakers 50–51
Portland Public Schools (PPS) 112–119
power 51, 98, 190, 192, 205–206, 208, 225, 233; and background of parents 101; and distrust 145; and family engagement 154–155; interrogating 3, 9, 24, 41, 51, 52, 73, 86, 100, 118, 124, 126, 133–135, 136, 170, 173, 184, 201, 210, 216, 217, 223–224, 226, 227, 240, 241
Presiado, V. E. 11
professional development 25, 27, 39, 42, 79, 99, 168, 205–211
professional learning 33–34
professional learning communities (PLCs) 68, 69–74
Proposition 58 125
Proposition 227 123, 238
Przymus, S. 12

qualifications of teachers 71–72
Queer Endeavor, A (AQE) 187
Quintero, I. 232

race 8, 79; and language 59; and power 184; racial equity 113–114, 117; racial justice 104–111, 112–119, 179–185, 216; and school leadership 104–111; segregation 95, 163, 164; *see also* African Americans
Racial Education Equity Policy (Portland Public Schools) 113–114, 115
raciolinguistic perspective 55–61

racism 89, 106, 113, 114, 136, 216, 239, 243
Ralston, N. C. 8
Rands, K. E. 194n1
redesign, program 7, 85–93
relational distrust 145
Rendón, L. I. 216

San Antonio's Independent School District (SAISD) 39, 40, 45
Sánchez, M. 13
San Diego State University (SDSU) 123, 124–125
Santiago González, B. 13, 238–243
Santos, M. P. 8
school districts: Austin Independent School District 168; Bellevue School District 238; bilingual redesign committee 85–93; Boston Public Schools 30–38; Milwaukee Public Schools 158–160, 161, 164; Portland Public Schools 112–119; San Antonio's Independent School District 39, 40, 45
school leadership 6–9, 56–61; African Americans 104–111; culturally sustaining 77–84; identities of 81–82; and identity 107; Latinx 95–103; and policy development 27–28; practices for fostering critical consciousness 78–81; Vietnamese 112–119
schools: administration 26, 39–40, 41, 56–57, 59, 67, 77–82, 83, 95–99, 104–111, 115, 160, 161; charter schools 8, 55–65, 104–111, 159, 162; climate 79, 80, 83, 209; district public school 21–28, 85–93, 112–119; elementary (K-5) 30–38, 47–53, 55–65, 67–74, 77–84, 95–102, 131–138, 139–147, 149–155, 158–165, 168–174, 179–185, 187–194, 196–203, 205–211, 213–220, 222–228, 230–236, 238–244; magnet program 112; preschool 36, 196–203; private 159; secondary (6–12) 39–46, 55–65
Schultz, K. 145
segregation 95, 115, 163, 164
Sepúlveda, E. 4
Sexton, J. 184
Sheltered English Immersion Endorsement 33–34
Singleton, G. 113, 114
Slavick, J. 9
Sleeter, C. 216, 218, *220*
social semiotics 199–200
Spanish 5, 7, 10–11, 21–28, 39–46, 47–53, 55–65, 67–74, 77–84, 85–93, 95–102, 112, 117, 139–147, 179–185, 187–194, 196–203, 205–211, 213–220, 222–228, 230–236, 238–244
State of Texas Assessment of Academic Readiness (STAAR) exam 41, 45
structural distrust 145
Sun, W. 9

Tarpley, N. A. 181
teacher preparation program 121–127, 185
teacher unions 143
temas (topics) 233, 234
temazcal 169
testimonios 12, 42–45, 85, 206, 208–209, 211, 213–220
textos (texts) 233, 234
Thomas, W. P. 70, 112
Toussaint L'Ouverture Academy (TLA) 5, 31, 32–37; connecting with culture and community 34–35; curricula development 32–33; professional learning 33–34; student achievement 36; teacher-created alphabet poster *34*; teacher credentials **35**
trans-adaptation 33
transitional bilingual education (TBE) 23, 26, 85, 89, 108, 164
translanguaging 4, 13, 19, 44, 45, 60, 72, 79–80, 200, 233, 234–235, 236, 243
Trump, D. 48
Truong, V. 8
trust 44, 98, 145, 146
two-way immersion (TWI) 2, 14, 55–56, 149–155; Chinese 131–138; Haitian Creole 30–38; Spanish 47–53, 67–74, 77–84, 85–93, 95–102, 179–185, 187–194, 205–211, 222–228, 238–244; Vietnamese 112–119

urban neighborhoods, gentrification of 67

Valderrama, M. 40
Valdés, G. 1–2
Valdez, C. 13, 222, 223, 224–227
Valdez, V. E. 6
Valdiviezo, L. 50
Valenzuela, A. 10, 104, 172
Vela, A. 40
Velasquez, E. 235, **236**

Venegas, K. 6, 59–60, 61
Vietnamese 8, 112–119
virtual education 10, 149–155; centering minoritized families during instruction 152–153; modeling of importance of community 153; parents and caregivers as virtual co-teachers 151–152; viewing families as experts 151
voucher schools 159, 162

Wall, D. J. 36
White mainstream English (WME) 179
whiteness 104–111, 107, 136–137, 163–164, 184–185
white supremacy 8, 52, 106, 108
writer's workshop model 222–228

Zoeller, E. 12

9781032127934